A Theology of
Political Vocation

A Theology of
Political Vocation

Christian Life and Public Office

John E. Senior

BAYLOR UNIVERSITY PRESS

Chapters 1 and 5 draw on my article "Cruciform Pilgrims: Politics between the Penultimate and the Ultimate," published by Georgetown University Press in the *Journal of the Society of Christian Ethics* 32, no. 1 (2012): 115–32.

Cover design by theBookDesigners
Cover art courtesy of Shutterstock/JohnKwan

Library of Congress Cataloging-in-Publication Data

Senior, John E., 1977–
A theology of political vocation : Christian life and public office / John E. Senior.
234 pages cm
Includes bibliographical references and index.
ISBN 978-1-4813-0035-3 (hardback : alk. paper)
1. Vocation—Christianity. 2. Christianity and politics. 3. Christians—Political activity. 4. Political science—Philosophy. I. Title.
BV4740.S45 2015
261.7—dc23

2015001633

Printed in the United States of America on acid-free paper with a minimum of 30% post-consumer waste recycled content.

CONTENTS

ACKNOWLEDGMENTS

This book is the culmination of a long process of reflection that began in my undergraduate work. I studied abroad in Tübingen, Germany, in my junior year of college. In the spring I had the vague notion that I might like to write an honors thesis in the study of religion. I didn't know where to begin. So I called Dr. Eddie Glaude, then associate professor of religion at Bowdoin College, and asked him whether he would consider working with me on an honors project. For reasons still unclear to me (I think in part because I was calling from Germany), Eddie suggested that I might like to explore the work of Jürgen Habermas, and in particular Habermas' response to public theologians who had engaged his discourse ethics. At the time I had no idea who Jürgen Habermas was, what discourse ethics was, and why theologians might care about discourse ethics. I had no idea, therefore, why it might be interesting to write a thesis on that topic. I soon discovered, working with Eddie the next year, that to work on Habermas was to wade very quickly into deep waters of critical, social, and political theory. I thoroughly enjoyed it. That project set me on a path that ultimately led to this book. The first debt of gratitude, then, is owed to Eddie Glaude, for his creativity, energy, and good mentorship.

I cherish the experiences I have had with teachers and friends from whom I learned how to think theologically: Francis Schüssler Fiorenza, Ronald Thiemann, Cornel West, Sarah Coakley, Doug Hicks, Kathryn Tanner, Phillip Clayton, Mark Douglas, and Ted Smith all showed me how challenging and life-giving theological reflection can be. I recognize the influence of all of these teachers, as I often find myself pondering issues from the perspectives they introduced to me.

As I wrote this manuscript, I was often surprised by how deep an impression a certain mantra I internalized in my graduate studies at Emory University made on my habits of thought, a mantra that Alasdair MacIntyre first articulated: "A moral philosophy," he wrote, "characteristically presupposes a sociology."[1] And every sociology, my teachers at Emory added, characteristically presupposes an ethic. Jon Gunnemann and Steve Tipton taught me how to understand the complexity of moral experience in terms of both of these propositions. From Liz Bounds and the late Nancy Eiesland, I learned that ethicists ought to listen to the voices of ordinary people because they speak with rich and theologically resonant insight. From Tim Jackson and Liz Bounds, I learned to situate my own emerging theological voice in relationship to the history of Christian theological and social ethics.

Liz Bounds deserves a special word of thanks. As my doctoral advisor, Liz pushed me to interrogate critically the political sociology that contemporary political theory presupposes. With Liz's guidance, I began to see MacIntyre's insight at work. The kinds of political spaces that liberal political theorists and contemporary theologians imagine in their theories of politics do not capture the complexity of the way people actually experience political life. Dominant theories of politics imagine sociologies, in other words, that ignore the moral complexity of political space. That insight first emerged in my doctoral work and motivates on a fundamental level the arguments developed in this book.

For almost twenty years, I have benefitted from conversations with my friend Seth Jaffe, now a very skillful interpreter of Thucydides. I befriended Seth in college at about the same time I began working on the Habermas project. Seth knows the history of Western political thought and its interpretation inside and out. His responses to my writing, which he has read occasionally since our time together in college, have always been insightful. Our conversations about thinkers and issues that matter to us both, even when they happen only annually or semiannually, are exciting and energizing. As I think back through this project, I realize how much of my thinking has gained both clarity and inspiration in many years of conversation with Seth.

I am grateful for Amy Levad, Matthew Bersagel-Braley, and Katy Shrout, Emory colleagues who read and responded to early drafts of this project. Conversations and collaborations with many other Emory colleagues—Brad Burroughs, Letitia Campbell, Jennifer Ayres, Dan Cantey, and Joe Wiinikka-Lydon, among others—continue to feed my scholarship and teaching. I also offer my gratitude to Andrew Gardner, Lance Henry, and Jon Gaska, who read and responded to chapters of this book as I wrote them at Wake Forest I'd also like to thank Hilary Floyd for assembling the index for this book.

I approached Carey Newman of Baylor University Press very casually at a recent AAR meeting about the possibility of supporting this project. He was enthusiastic about it from the start. Carey is an excellent editor; he has a gift for disabusing junior faculty of unhelpful writing habits inculcated in the doctoral process. He is also a colorful and entertaining writing coach. Carey constantly prodded me to stop "carrying the baggage" of other scholars in my writing, so that the book would feature my voice rather than the voices of others. I often wondered whether I had two hundred and more pages, worth of my own insights to share about political vocation. Carey's insistence that I feature my voice in the book led me to new insights about theoretical ground I've explored for quite some time.

A grant from the Wabash Center for Teaching and Learning in Theology and Religion freed up ten weeks in the summer of 2013 for writing. During that time I completed three chapters of the manuscript, the most productive writing period in the whole project. The grant was connected to a Pre-Tenure Teaching Workshop (2012–2013), a profoundly formative experience in which I learned much about teaching and also built lasting relationships with theological school colleagues. I am deeply grateful for this experience. A grant from Wabash also underwrote a week long writing retreat in Santa Barbara, California, hosted by my friends Amy and Marshall Miller, for whose hospitality and friendship I am most thankful.

The most profound gratitude goes to my family. My parents, Joan and David Senior, never so much as raised an eyebrow as I made choices about my education and career path that often evoked the query: "What are you going to do with *that?*" Thankfully, my parents never asked that question. They insisted that I should do whatever I want, as long as I do it well. As I love my work, I try to honor that counsel every day. I am daily reminded of my parents' commitment to my success, and I appreciate it.

I could not ask for better parents-in-law, David and Diane Dalbo. They love our children, and they spend lots of time with them. That is wonderful for many reasons, not least of which is that David and Diane's commitment to our children made possible many weekend escapes to the office or the basement to get writing done. Were it not for their dedication to our children, I would still be working on this book, and our kids would be a lot less happy for it.

Finally, and most importantly, I thank my spouse, Raegan Dalbo, who shows me every day what it means to be a good partner. Raegan has made many sacrifices so that I can teach and write. She interrupted a teaching career at a school in Atlanta that she very much enjoyed so that our family could move to Winston-Salem. She has worked hard at home to raise our two wonderful children, Ty and Dori, while I spend my days at Wake Forest. Raegan knows that I love to work, and while she supports me in it, she reminds often that working isn't sufficient to live life well. I love Raegan very much; it is a privilege to be her husband.

Introduction

STATECRAFT IN A MACHIAVELLIAN AGE

In a recent interview, political theorist Quentin Skinner remarked, "I think it would be fair to say that we are in a very strongly Machiavellian phase of our political practice at the moment." The current phase to which Skinner was referring is the post–September 11th context in which all nations are aware of the threat of globalized terror. The "liberal state," Skinner continued, "cannot do what it always promised," which is to "guarantee security to its citizens." The state was an effective means of security as long as its opponents were other states. September 11th marked a moment when so-called first-world nations realized that the modern state is neither a necessary condition nor an effective mitigation of political violence. Not unlike globalized capital, political violence in the form of terrorism flows across national borders through decentralized networks of loosely affiliated organizations. Skinner was suggesting that political practice in response to these threats is Machiavellian in the sense that it is preoccupied with generating effective ends, even if dubious means are required to do so. To many, however, such strategies "look very immoral."[1]

For Skinner, the Machiavellian quality of political practice is intensified in the post–September 11th world. Responses to terrorism in particular—in judgments about enemy detention and interrogation, targeted killings, drone warfare, special operations, and the like—surface the morally ambiguous character of political decision making. Underneath these issues, however, lies a more fundamental question about the moral structure of statecraft, or, to use Skinner's term, the "practice of politics." That question needs to be reconsidered in a "strongly Machiavellian" era.

To wrestle with the Machiavellian quality of statecraft is to acknowledge a moral ambiguity that belongs to the practice of politics. Politics, as the term is used here, is the sorting out of "collisions between human purposes."[2] Purposes are what people care about—their values, interests, aspirations, goals, and aims, that which makes life good. Human beings desire that their social arrangements conduce to the purposes they are after. But there are different purposes, many of which work at cross-purposes with others. Unrestrained liberty, for example, cannot coexist with complete equality. "Liberty for the wolves," the political theorist Isaiah Berlin put it, "means death to the lambs."[3] Politics, then, is a struggle to determine, through cooperation or competition, how colliding purposes will be arranged in social life. The practice of politics is morally ambiguous because it entails the sacrifice of someone's good, either in whole or in part, in the course of this struggle.

One can use the term "politics" to describe the struggle to advance purposes in many different settings. There is a sense in which politics is everywhere: in universities, corporations, religious communities, and the like—anywhere cross-purposes need to be sorted out. In this book, however, "politics" is used in a specific sense, to mean those formal and informal settings that constitute what is commonly called "political life." Political life, as the term is used here, refers to the places where the work of ruling is done; it is that collection of institutional spaces that provide structure and direction for all others. Persons who serve in leadership roles in these spaces occupy political offices and are known as political officials. An office is a more or less formal role that reflects and embodies a set of socially sanctioned values and practices, which empower the officeholder to perform particular and "characteristic" actions.[4] A political office, then, is such a role in the context of political life.

The practice of politics is morally ambiguous owing in part to the role political power plays in the struggle over purposes. Power per se is simply the capacity to bring about states of affairs. Political power is the capacity to require, through sanction and incentive, a political community to configure itself in particular ways.[5] The capacity to require particular political configurations is a kind of binding power. One might have said that political power is coercive rather than binding. Indeed, many definitions of political power, the German sociologist Max Weber's prominent among them, emphasize the legitimate exercise of violence that backs up political power, suggesting that political power is ultimately coercive in nature.[6]

But there is a subtle difference between coercive and binding power. The exercise of political power, especially in representative bodies, often has a heteronomous, rather than an autonomous, quality. That is, political power implies the exercise of power by an actor (or group of actors) in ways that constrain or enhance the agency of other actors, rather than the exercise of power by an actor to constrain or enhance his or her own agency. Coercion, however, implies something more: that the exercise of power is not only heteronomous but that it is also unsanctioned, unwelcome, and detrimental. When used properly, the binding exercise of political power limits the freedoms of persons and communities in order to create new freedoms and goods they would not otherwise have enjoyed.[7] Citizens, for example, do not often have much direct input into tax codes that determine the size of their paychecks. Indeed, if they were consulted directly about taxation, citizens might express a preference not to be taxed at all. But taxation (in theory, at least) funds the creation and maintenance of public goods (like public education, defense, social provision, etc.) that empower persons and communities in ways that they would not otherwise enjoy if they were not arranged in political communities. Tax codes are therefore always binding, but they need not be coercive.

Political power is therefore typically *legitimate* binding power, in the sense that the use of political power is sanctioned in the structures and operations of the state. Political officials make, enforce, and interpret laws and policies that impose requirements on citizens. Only on pain of punishment can citizens ignore or reject the duties and obligations the state imposes on them. Part of what makes binding power legitimate in a liberal democratic regime is that its use not only constrains citizens; it thereby creates spaces in which citizens enjoy freedom from constraint, which the state or their neighbors might impose, to pursue the purposes they deem best.

There are important questions, which will be considered in detail below, about whether the modern state, the dominant political configuration in the West since the sixteenth century, continues to be a viable model of political life. Powerful arguments suggest that political power in a globalized economy has devolved into economic power; in this view, politics (and war), to rephrase Carl von Clausewitz, is the extension of economic commerce by other means.[8] In any case, in political life, politics is the struggle among competing purposes in the medium of political power. The medium of political power raises the stakes of the struggle: whoever wins in political struggle, partially or completely, will see their agenda enforced through the structures of the state. Whoever loses, correspondingly, will be subjected to laws and policies that do not reflect their purposes.

SEEING BETWEEN TWO MIRRORS

Skinner's comment, that we live in an age in which a Machiavellian framing of statecraft is prominent, poses an interesting challenge to Christian theology. Such a framing, in a broad sense, emphasizes the ways in which statecraft takes advantage of the morally ambiguous relationships between the struggle over competing purposes and the use of political power. In the fields of political ethics, political theology, and public theology, Christian theologians have dealt with questions about the nature and purpose of secular political life, the best normative aspirations of politics, the position of the church vis-à-vis the secular polity, and the responsibilities of Christian citizens in modern democracies.[9] By and large, however, Christian theology has neglected a theological treatment of statecraft in the modern era. Lacking, then, is a theological treatment of the moral ambiguity of political practice of the sort that the Machiavellian framing of statecraft emphasizes.

Though it has fallen out of fashion, theological reflection on statecraft is not a new endeavor. In medieval and Renaissance periods, theologians made contributions to the body of literature known as "mirrors for princes." Writing at the pinnacle of the Renaissance, for example, Desiderius Erasmus offers a Christian humanist account of political instruction in *The Education of a Christian Prince* (1516). Erasmus writes for a hereditary prince who maintains his realm by cultivating himself as an example of Christian virtue. The Christian prince's highest obligation, Erasmus argues, is to the common good, the "welfare of his people," even if it comes "at the cost of his own life."[10] The Christian prince must always strive to be a "good man," one who manifests the "godlike virtues" of wisdom, goodness, and benevolent power.[11] In all things, the Christian prince observes and models for others the teachings of the Gospel. Rejecting the trappings of wealth, power, and glory that motivate pagan rulers, the Christian prince strives to cultivate "blameless character," which serves as the "sheet-anchor for the ship of state."[12] Erasmus, well known for his pacifism, instructs princes to avoid war at all costs and never to initiate war unless it "cannot by any means be avoided."[13] In short, if one cannot be a good prince and a good man at the same time, then one should give up being the former.[14]

Machiavelli's own mirror in *The Prince* could hardly be more different from the one Erasmus proposed just years later.[15] Unlike Erasmus, Machiavelli is particularly concerned with the statecraft of "new," rather than hereditary, rulers. The prince's fundamental aim is to maintain the state (*mantanere lo stato*), which he understands to mean both the maintenance of the state qua political community and the maintenance of the standing of the ruler qua head of state. While the ruler's fundamental aim is *mantanere lo stato*, his highest aspiration is the achievement of praise and glory in this life and fame everlasting.[16] Praise, glory, and fame can only be achieved through the careful cultivation of *virtú*, the proactive, manly qualities that endear the prince to unpredictable fortune (*Fortúna*). While it is advantageous to appear to be virtuous in the conventional sense (e.g., merciful, faithful, honest), the prince should feel obliged to do whatever it takes to "win and maintain his state." If the prince can do this, "the means" he uses, no matter how dubious, "will be praised by everyone."[17]

For Erasmus, the good prince's highest aspiration is to lead a good Christian life: "It is quite possible to find a good man who would not make a good prince," Erasmus writes, "yet one cannot be a good prince without at the same time being a good man."[18] Machiavelli would affirm exactly the opposite proposition; indeed, in *The Prince*, he famously encourages princes "to learn to be able not to be good," using this skill "according to necessity."[19] In his later work *Discourses on Livy*, Machiavelli argues that the virtues that sustain republican political leadership and those that sustain the Christian life are not only incompatible; they are hostile to one another. The ancient religions of Greek and Roman antiquity located the highest good in the world. Thus, these religions trained persons to develop worldly virtues and esteem worldly goods. The ancient religions, which ground the republican tradition, value "greatness of spirit, strength of body, and all other things capable of making men very strong."

Christian religion, by contrast, teaches persons to despise the world and to strive toward an ultimate good that resides beyond the world. "Our religion," Machiavelli writes, "has glorified humble and contemplative more than active men." Christianity values as the "highest good" virtues like "humility, abjectness, and contempt of things human." For this reason, Machiavelli saw a relationship between the political corruption of his age and the worldly indifference that Christianity teaches: "this mode of life [the Christian mode of life] thus seems to have rendered the world weak and given it in prey to criminal men, who can manage it securely, seeing that the collectivity of men, so as to go to paradise, think more of enduring their beatings than avenging them."[20] Contra Erasmus, Machiavelli says, statecraft cannot be a project in which the prince makes the state over in a Christian image.

Machiavelli embraces the consequentialist quality of political practice: what is good is what maintains the state and secures glory for the prince. As long as the ruler's actions maintain the state and achieve glory, few moral barriers stand in the way of his pursuit of this goal.[21] Machiavelli's consequentialism opens an exploration of what is perhaps the most import-ant political skill, the mastery of timing: responding in the right way at the right time to situations in order to mitigate the adverse effects of chance, luck, and contingency.[22]

Erasmus seems to be aware of, and worries about, the kind of prince Machiavelli would endorse. He understands that politics can be conducted on a consequentialist logic aiming at the prince's fame and fortune. Eras-mus insists that the prince can do the work of politics while resisting the consequentialist temptations of political life. Politics of the Machiavellian sort can exert a corrupting influence on the prince. But a good prince, Eras-mus holds, can transform politics.

There is a simple evaluation of these two figures: Machiavelli is remem-bered as the consummate theorist of statecraft, and Erasmus is not. Machi-avelli is respected for his clear-eyed assessment of political conduct and his willingness to engage the moral ambiguity of political life, even if it entails "dirty hands" from the perspective of conventional morality. He understood better than anyone that good rulers will always need luck, but they also exercise some control over luck by cultivating political virtuosity (*virtù*). To cultivate political virtuosity, rulers need to immerse themselves in the moral logic of politics. Rulers will learn how not to be good and will prefer being feared to being loved when it is necessary. They will at best live in tension with Christian conceptions of virtue; perhaps good politicians will reject the Christian virtues altogether. Many of Machiavelli's concrete recommenda-tions are outrageous, but his fundamental insights into the nature of politi-cal virtuosity still resonate today.

This book develops a theological account of statecraft. It is not a "mir-ror for princes" in the traditional sense. That is, it neither offers insights into how rulers should be educated nor recommends technical advice about how rulers should go about achieving particular political ends. Theology is not equipped to offer political advice in that way. The book resembles a traditional mirror for princes, however, in that it engages the more general question of what makes for good statecraft.[23] It does so with a conviction that, for such a mirror to be meaningful, it must take Machiavellian insights seriously. That is, an adequate mirror will follow Machiavelli into the moral ambiguity of political life, first by diagnosing it and then by responding to it from a theological point of view.

GOOD POLITICAL WORK

More still needs to be said about the kind of question a theological account of statecraft is answering. The impetus for this book comes out of a concern for the state of professional politics in the U.S. context. At the end of 2013, Congress earned a 13 percent approval rating, the lowest since Gallup began tracking congressional approval ratings in 1974.[24] Indeed, Congress had been scoring very low points with Americans for some time. In late 2012, as the 112th Congress debated the "fiscal cliff" situation that threatened to ruin a fragile American economy, a Gallup poll showed that Americans ranked the honesty and ethical standards of members of Congress at the bottom of a list of twenty-two professions. Only car salespeople ranked lower.[25] In a similar poll administered in late 2013, only lobbyists earned a lower honesty rating than members of Congress.[26]

Americans have good reason to distrust their political representatives. In the U.S. context, public policy has in significant measure created the conditions for unprecedented economic inequality.[27] The policy preferences of affluent constituents are more often reflected in policy outcomes than are those of middle-class and lower-income constituents.[28] More troubling, perhaps, is the finding that "elected officials are utterly unresponsive to the policy preferences of millions of low-income citizens."[29] Increasingly, it appears that American politicians serve the wealthy. American democracy, it would seem, is degenerating into an oligarchy.

In many ways, then, the work of democratic politics in the U.S. context, on the federal level and in other settings, is not being done very well. This raises a question about what constitutes good political work, an understanding of which is desperately needed in American political life. The theological mirror for statecraft developed here is concerned, then, with responding to that question.

To do so, this book develops a theology of political vocation. Vocation is a particular way of understanding what constitutes good work, a "calling to" do some kind of work. It begins as a "calling in." That is, vocational work is always located in a particular space. Political vocation, therefore, begins in political space. The idea of vocation takes seriously the location of political work in institutional spaces and structures and considers how it is conditioned by these spaces and structures. Machiavelli's account of statecraft is compelling in part because it takes seriously the moral complexity of political space. Machiavelli is aware that politics requires a particular kind of morality. It will not do, he recognizes, to imagine that political morality can be collapsed into religious morality—that, in other words, the good Christian prince can simply make political life over according to Christian norms, as Erasmus held. Instead, political space has its own kind of normative contours. These need to be delineated and reckoned with.

Vocation, moreover, is a way of understanding work that emphasizes how work forms the worker. In the framing of vocation, work makes the worker into a particular kind of self. A politician, therefore, is made in the doing of political work. To be formed as a politician is to navigate and negotiate the norms and practices that constitute political life, however morally ambiguous they may appear from a Christian theological perspective. By attending to the space in which work is done, vocation acknowledges and assesses the kind of self that is formed in that space.

While vocation recognizes that work begins in space, it also directs work in a particular way; it is a "calling to" in addition to a "calling in." A theological understanding of vocation, the argument below will show, holds that work is good when it participates in God's ongoing project to redeem creation, to repair the brokenness of creation by restoring God's relationship with it. Vocation understands that work is not ultimately of one's own devising; the project of vocation is God's work. God, not the worker, has initiated vocational work and calls human beings to participate in it in a variety of different ways, politics being one of them.

Vocation acknowledges the norms and practices of any vocational setting. In that way it is grounded, with Machiavelli, in political space. But vocation also pulls work in the direction of God's project, an aim to which Erasmus aspired. Vocation seeks to understand good work in any institutional setting in light of the pull of God's redeeming purposes in the world. This book develops a theology of political vocation, first by understanding what political work is and then by showing how political work can be transformed in relationship to God's work. A theology of political vocation both understands God to be *working in and through* the particular norms and practices of political institutions and to be *working toward* a reality that ultimately transcends them, holding in creative tension the worldliness of politics and the beckoning of God's redeeming purposes.

❊ ❊ ❊

A theology of political vocation, then, responds to John Calvin's claim that "civil authority is a calling, not only lawful and holy before God, but also the most sacred and by far the most honorable of all callings in the whole life of mortal men."[30] Two elements of this assertion sound strange to modern ears. First, the notion that politics (civil authority) is a calling is striking because, as James M. Gustafson suggests, the concept of calling itself seems to be "moving rapidly toward obsolescence."[31] A calling connotes something about work that is noble, but it is not clear what that something might be or whether it is possible for work to exhibit such noble qualities in the contemporary moment. It certainly is not clear, second, that there is any-thing at all noble about political work. Calvin's suggestion that the civil authority is "the most sacred and by far the most honorable of all callings in the whole life of mortal men" will strike many as absurd.

Calvin is cited here both because he clearly names a possibility that has provoked the present book-length consideration and also to signal the author's formation in and commitment to the Reformed theological tradi-tion. Calvin is a primary conversation partner, both because his reflections on vocation suggest a theological framing of that concept that has much to offer and because he explicitly considers what it might mean to under-stand politics as a vocation. Max Weber and Dietrich Bonhoeffer also figure prominently in these pages. Weber in many ways names the problems about the moral complexity of political vocation in the modern world that the book addresses, while Bonhoeffer's Christocentric ethics forms the basis of a theological response.

Calvin's remark about the sacredness of the political calling also points to a conviction that this author shares: that God works through a variety of institutional settings (not just the church) to advance God's redemptive purposes in the world. There is wisdom in the sentiment that the institu-tions of political life "during the world" constitute an "ersatz practice," a "way of coping," while the world awaits "the proper form of public life" that unfolds in the eschaton. It is certainly the case that worldly political life is a "mixed blessing."[32] But it is also true that God works to redeem creation both by bringing it to fruition in the ultimate moment and also, paradoxi-cally, by working within its cracks and fissures in the person and presence of Jesus Christ in penultimate time, our time. God redeems creation, in other words, both by utterly transfiguring it in an eschatological moment and, in the person, presence, and ministry of Jesus Christ, by not changing it at all. The mystery of God's character and God's redemptive work emerges in the paradoxical ways in which these two realities hang together.

The emphasis here on the paradoxical quality of God's redemptive agency reflects the author's appreciation for the work of Reinhold Niebuhr. At the heart of Niebuhr's project is his insistence that human experience is both conditioned and unconditioned, that it exists both under the condi-tions of finitude and, in eternal space, without condition at all. The limited capacity for self-transcendence, the capacity to exercise a measure of uncon-ditioned freedom, constitutes the human likeness to the divine Creator. Human beings are not wholly bound to and determined by their experi-ence of the world. Instead, they have some capacity to step outside of them-selves and critically evaluate their own drives, desires, and motivations. This limited capacity for self-transcendence creates the condition for Christlike love for the neighbor, an unconditional love that sets aside self-interest and self-regard. At the same time, human beings remain anchored to the world. Freedom induces an awareness of finitude; freedom is that condition that makes the moral meaning of finitude intelligible to human beings. Human beings are creatures who know that their lives will end. Their experience of freedom is therefore on some level deeply at odds with their destiny as creatures whose lives come inevitably to an end. The tension between the experience of freedom and that of finitude causes anxiety, a tension that goes unresolved in this world.

For Niebuhr, the cross symbolizes the "perfection of Christ" in "transcendent *agape*."[33] The cross, Niebuhr argues, discloses that the ultimate meaning of human experience is perfected in the agapic love of Christ. The cross therefore shows that Christlike love renders human possibility intelligible. At the very same time, however, the cross makes these destinations elusive in the context of history.[34] At the heart of the cross, then, is paradox: the cross shows what it ultimately means to be human, but it also shows that such perfection is impossible under the conditions of history. Thus, Niebuhr writes, the truth of human experience "remains subject to the paradox of grace. We may have it; and yet we do not have it. And we will have it the more purely in fact if we know that we have it only in principle."[35]

Several features of Niebuhr's vision, particularly his institutional theology, require critical response, which the discussions below provide. But his insight about the irreducibly paradoxical quality of human experience gives the argument of this book its basic shape. Finitude and freedom both constitute conditions of human possibility; both, therefore, are theologically relevant. But freedom and finitude work in human experience in paradoxically countervailing ways. In all regions of social life, including politics, human beings strive to reach beyond what is, attempting to realize what could be. And yet the very mechanisms that make such strivings possible—in particular the institutional patterns human beings have developed to organize their life together—limit their capacity to create new worlds of meaning and practice for themselves. To live in the unresolved tension between freedom and finitude is to be human. Were that tension resolved, human beings would no longer recognize themselves in their own experience. Christians hope that, in due time, God does indeed resolve that tension. In the meantime, human beings negotiate the tension between freedom and finitude as best they can. And in the person, work, and continuing presence of Jesus Christ in the world, so does God.

A theology of political vocation attends, then, to the paradoxical sit-uation of political work. To pursue a vocation in politics is to strive for unrealized possibilities of political organization that better provide for the common good. Political strivings are defined, empowered, but, paradoxi-cally, also bound and hampered by political institutions. Political institu-tions offer patterns of action for organizing human relationships in political life. Such patterns are both salutary and problematic: human beings cannot live without institutions, and yet institutions inevitably create the condi-tions of moral ambiguity in social life.

It comes as no surprise that morally thorny terrain runs through polit-ical institutions. Niebuhr complains that contemporary theologies offered "no guidance for a Christian statesman for our day." The "crisis" theology of Karl Barth, he argues, "[fights] the devil if he shows both horns and both cloven feet." It is easy, Niebuhr suggests, to recognize the devil when the devil is someone like Hitler. But more often the devil is concealed in the moral shadows of political life. Theologians like Barth, Niebuhr continues, have failed "to make discriminating judgments about good and evil if the evil shows only one horn or the half of a cloven foot."[36] Political institutions generate valuable norms and practices that maintain order and peace and promote human flourishing. But as human organizations, political institu-tions also inevitably create the conditions of moral ambiguity, obscuring, as it were, the horns and feet of the devil.

Any theology of political vocation must therefore determine the extent to which to affirm or critique the institutional patterns and practices that make political work possible. Thinking theologically about political voca-tion requires a careful description of the ways political institutions condi-tion both work and worker in morally complex and ambiguous ways. That careful description, in turn, invites theological reflection on the nature of institutions as contexts of the moral life. In conversation with Reformed and Catholic sources, therefore, the book develops a theological analysis of political institutions. If paradox constitutes the theological form of the book's argument, then, institutional analysis constitutes the sociological lens in which this paradox is disclosed.

One motivation, then, for writing this book is to make theological sense of good political work. Underlying this motivation is another: to provide a theologically adequate account of the challenges and possibilities of politics. Many theologians are rightly concerned about the relationship of Christian commitments to political power. Some worry that American Christians in recent decades have "politicized" their theological commitments, relying on "the instrumentality of the state . . . to find solutions to public problems."

But the turn to the coercive power of the state to enforce theo-political commitments, in this view, inevitably courts disaster: "Within fallen humanity . . . all power is tainted, infected by the same tendencies of self-aggrandizing domination. The natural disposition of all human power is to its abuse."[37] Others are concerned that stripes of Christian "triumphalism"— uncompromising forms of public witness naïve to their own participation in oppressive social structures and processes—are "especially detrimental" when "coupled with sociopolitical power and affluence."[38] Similarly, others call into question "apocalyptic" public theologies that are overly confident about the shape of the future and overly impressed by the agency they antic-ipate exercising in bringing it about.[39]

All of these views address problems that can arise when Christian con-viction ventures into political space. Such views often imagine selves capable somehow of standing wholly within the boundaries of Christian conviction, Christian tradition, or "the church," and of speaking from these spaces into an oppositional "secular," "public," or "political" space. Such selves are *near* or *in* but somehow not *of* political space. But there are no such selves. An argument this book develops is that persons of faith are always complex selves: they are multiply formed in a variety of institutional settings—in faith communities, polities, families, schools, militaries, marketplaces. We are citizens, customers, soldiers, patients, students, parents and children, and children of God, all at the same time. These multiple identities all entail multiple and distinctive moral formations that, in a fallen world, do not hang together very well. Different moral formations exist in tension with one another; some are even in important respects incompatible with others.

And yet, as God redeems through a variety of institutional settings (not just the church), it is no surprise that we human beings are multiply formed, multiply equipped to participate in God's redemptive work. All persons in well-functioning democratic societies are formed (granted, not always well formed) to participate as citizens in political life, whether they choose to par-ticipate or not. Politics, of course, is, from the perspective of garden-variety Christian commitments, morally ambiguous in many ways. Still, God works through politics; therefore, Christians need to understand what political work looks like when it is done well. This book offers one perspective.

1

WHAT IS A POLITICAL VOCATION?

The word "vocation" is often used to connote some noble dimension of work. Vocational work is supposed to engage a person's sense of purposefulness, their understanding of why they "were put on this earth," to do what one is "meant" to do. Vocational work, therefore, is understood to be intrinsically meaningful: one pursues a vocation even if it does not generate instrumental goods, like wealth or status. Often, the idea of vocation also suggests a commitment to a "greater good." Vocational work contributes to a project that transcends, but also includes, the individual's good. Such a project, one might say, is for the "common good."

Politics, in popular perception, is simply not this kind of work, for the reasons cited above. Politics is, no doubt, morally inhospitable terrain, rendering problematic the very possibility of political vocation. It is helpful, then, to begin by clarifying what it might mean to suggest that work is a vocation and that politics can be understood as vocational work.

VOCATION AS FRAMING

Vocation, from the Latin *vocatio* (calling) and *vocare* (to call) (related also to the Greek *klesis*), is a framing of work.[1] A framing, as used here, is a kind of interpretation. A frame imputes explicit and implicit moral meanings to an interpreted object. Framings often sound like descriptions, as though they are simply providing an objective account of a phenomenon. To call a description of some reality a frame is to signal the way in which descriptions are morally freighted. The meaning of work can be framed in a number of ways. Each frame provides an account of what work is, what makes work meaningful, and the motivations one has for doing work.[2]

To frame one's work as "a job," for example, is to invoke a particular understanding of what work is and why it is meaningful. A job is ordinarily a discrete task, often done with a view to compensation. The word "job" sometimes signals a kind of distancing from work, implying that one's work is not a constitutive element of one's identity. The expression, "It's just a job," likely means that work is toilsome and meaningful only to the extent that it provides a livelihood. Indeed, the money-earning potential of a job may be the most decisive reason for doing it. Of course, people do sometimes use the word "job" in more expansive ways. But never does one hear the expression "It's just a vocation" to capture the money-earning potential of work.

The frame of a career captures a somewhat different nuance. Like a job, a career yields income that sustains a lifestyle. To frame work as a career is to signal that work is caught up in one's identity and sense of purpose in life. In a career, as people often use the term, the center of value is likely one's own experience of fulfillment and purposefulness. A career denotes a diachronic movement: one's working life, perhaps over thirty or more years, produces a significant cumulative achievement, reflecting one's fundamental commitments and sense of value.[3]

The idea of vocation brings yet another set of meanings to work. When persons talk about "being called," they often mean that they feel summoned *to* some kind of work that would be valuable even if they hadn't been called to it.[4] To be called to some work, furthermore, implies that another has initiated a project in which one is being called to participate; it is not work, in other words, of one's own devising. That project, whatever it is, is a center of value that makes work meaningful. The project that is the focus of vocation is a center of value in that it confers a sense of purpose to the lives of persons who dedicate themselves to the work. Thus, if one has a calling to law, presumably that calling is meaningful not only because legal work is lucrative or because one is a skillful lawyer. Law is a vocation because the law itself is a project worthy of a substantial, perhaps lifelong, commitment.

Like a job and a career, a vocation is work that provides for one's own flourishing. Unlike a job, and like a career, however, the work of a vocation is meaningful in ways that transcend the work's potential for livelihood. A career is meaningful ultimately because it provides a person with a sense of purpose. Vocation takes this a step further. Vocational work is meaningful because it includes but also transcends one's sense of purpose, aiming ultimately at an external and more holistic purpose, a common good.

Work in a particular area often permits all three framings. If work in the law, for example, is framed primarily as a job, the focus of the lawyer's concern may be on the material rewards that the work produces. If it is framed as a career, the emphasis may be on one's sense of identity and self-fulfillment in relationship to the law. If, however, this work is framed as a vocation, the lawyer is likely to understand her work primarily as dedication to an external source of meaning and value, such as, for example, the ideals of justice and fairness that the law is supposed to uphold. Those goods—justice and fairness—give the lawyer's work a center of value outside of her experience of the work. At the same time, one's lifelong dedication to the goods of justice and fairness contributes to one's own sense of identity and thus the pleasure that comes with doing the work.[5] A framing of work, then, is never simply attached to work. Instead, a person must actively assert the meaningfulness of work in a particular framing. A person must, in other words, claim that her work is a vocation. To do so is to express a particular motivation for doing work, that it contributes in some sense to a common good.

The above discussion turns on wordplay, which should not be confused for rigorous analysis. But wordplay does begin to excavate traditions of meaning associated with different framings of work. Wordplay suggests four claims associated with the idea of vocation: (1) as a "calling," there is a calling party, a caller; (2) the calling party initiates a project; and (3) invites others, the called, to participate in the work of the project; and finally, (4) the project constitutes a locus of meaning, value, and purpose for all working participants and even for others who are not actively working on the project.

This chapter develops a theological frame in which to explore these four claims. Vocation is work on a project, initiated by another, conferring meaning and purpose on both work and worker. The theological frame developed here borrows heavily from John Calvin's understanding of vocation. Calvin emphasizes the relationship between vocational work and the project that is its focus. His approach also underscores the struggle involved in becoming the kind of self capable of doing vocational work. Both of these insights enrich contemporary understandings of political work.

Vocation as Pilgrimage

Following classical philosophical patterns, Catholic traditions subordinated matter to spirit, body to soul, the *via activa* to the *via contemplativa*. Medieval religious orders stratified these distinctions socially. Vocational work was reserved for monks and other religious, who, through a life of prayer, study, and work, expanded the soul's capacity to know God. All other work that created and sustained the material conditions of existence fell outside the scope of vocational work.[6]

The Protestant Reformation radically reoriented vocation.[7] In Martin Luther's theology of grace, persons are genuinely free only because God, in God's grace, has chosen to redeem them. No work of any kind can achieve redemption.[8] Thus, the hierarchy of *via activa* over *via contemplativa* does not hold. Monasticism, Luther argues, falsely elevated monastic work to "supererogation or perfection which has no like or equal."[9] Instead, all Christians are free to live sanctified lives in whatever context in which they are called to work.[10] All persons can be called to vocational work.

Calvin shared Luther's understanding that all are called to work in ways that participate in God's redemptive purposes. Calvin situated vocation in the journey of sanctification. Through the movement of the Holy Spirit, the image of God is gradually regenerated in persons as they make a pilgrim's journey through a treacherous and inhospitable world. For Calvin, the ultimate call—the redemption of creation—constitutes the context of earthly vocation.

In Calvin's account, the moral life is a long and arduous journey with Christ toward final communion with God.[11] The journey begins with an awakening to God's redeeming work from within, when human beings are joined with Christ by way of the Holy Spirit, "the bond by which Christ effectually unites us to himself."[12] The journey continues with regeneration in Christ. It includes encounters with suffering and toil that mark existence in this world and mirrors Christ's own journey through it. And the journey ends with the resurrection of the body, for which Christ's resurrection on the last day is the "prototype."[13]

Earthly existence has an indispensable role in the greater movement toward salvation. With Augustine, Calvin views earthly existence as a penultimate stage, a pilgrimage, that finally gives way to the culmination of creation in the life to come.[14] In comparison with the "life to come," the "present life," Calvin writes, must be "utterly despised." The earth is but a "place of exile."[15] However comparatively loathsome earthly exile is, Calvin is careful to say, earthly life ought still to be considered a gift from God.[16] Thus, the stages of a pilgrim's progress toward final reconciliation with God are not equally valuable in an absolute sense. Earthly exile is an impermanent condition that ultimately gives way to the fulfillment of creaturely being in the final resurrection. But each stage of the pilgrimage discloses, by way of "lesser proofs," the shape of creation ultimately fulfilled, "the inheritance of eternal glory."[17] This point is crucial for understanding the status of the earthly pilgrimage as an intermediate movement that is also necessary and valuable in its own way.

The moral life unfolds in the time between the awakening in the Holy Spirit and the resurrection of the body on the last day. It amounts to the gradual restoration of the image of God in which human beings are made and which has been obscured by sin. Calvin calls this process "regeneration."[18] He suggests that regenerate life must "correspond with the righteousness of God"—it has to be a life, that is, marked by obedience to God's will. As such, the regenerated life is a life of repentance, an ongoing process of turning away from the self and turning toward God, both "in the soul itself" and also in "outward works."[19]

The pilgrimage of regeneration is arduous, requiring that persons be conformed to the cross-carrying Christ. Under the weight of the cross, life is "hard, toilsome, and unquiet," Calvin remarks. It is "crammed with very many and various kinds of evil."[20] Bearing the cross is a discipline of hardship that disabuses persons of overweening self-love and arrogance in order to teach obedience and attention to God's grace. More fundamentally, the earthly pilgrimage is a "condition" that moves the saints toward "the end that they be conformed to Christ." As Christ "passed through a labyrinth of all evils into heavenly glory," so too must his disciples, conformed to him, "be led through various tribulations to the same glory."[21]

The discipline of bearing the cross teaches the elect that existence in this world is only a penultimate stage, which, "by continual proof of its miseries," bears witness to "the future life."[22] However miserable the world is, Calvin insists that worldly goods are gifts from God that assist progress in the moral life and are to be appreciated in appropriate ways.[23] Among these gifts is vocation, the particular station in life to which a Christian is called to attend.

Calvin argues that human beings, left to their own devices, are inclined to wander aimlessly through life, getting themselves into trouble along the way. God brings order out of disorder by way of the calling:

> For [God] knows what great restlessness human nature flames, with what fickleness it is borne hither and thither. Therefore, lest through our stupidity and rashness everything be turned topsy-turvy, he has appointed duties for every man in his particular way of life. And that no one may thoughtlessly transgress his limits, he has named these various kinds of living "callings."[24]

The demands of the moral life become concrete by virtue of the stations where people are positioned "as a sort of sentry post"—a place of work over which persons have ownership, defined "duties," and by virtue of duties, "limits." Limits alleviate the overwhelming weight of absolute moral obligation. Vocation marks out an ordered sphere of responsibility so that persons are not required to attend to every moral problem. Everyone bears a cross, just as Christ bore the cross in the world. But the burden looks different in different vocational contexts. A calling, by structuring the moral life, gives it intelligibility.

Vocational work is meaningful because it has a place in God's greater purposes. "The Lord's calling," Calvin writes, "is in everything the beginning and foundation of well-doing." By adhering to their calling, persons can be assured that their life will be "best ordered" when it is "directed toward this goal."[25] Ultimately, work, because it is oriented to the "Lord's calling," is situated in the common destiny in which all of creation participates. Work is often arduous and tedious, but persons should be content to work conscientiously because they know that work belongs to a larger project. The purpose of vocational work, then, is to glorify God as God works to redeem creation. Vocational work is intelligible because it participates in God's work for the ultimate common good. Work should therefore also contribute to the common good of human communities. Calvin writes, "Scripture . . . warns that whatever benefits we obtain from the Lord have been entrusted to us on this condition: that they be applied to the common good of the church. And therefore the lawful use of all benefits consists in a liberal and kindly sharing of them with others."[26] God's work transforms and transfigures a broken world in the direction of wholeness and restoration. Similarly, human work, though subject to the corrupting effects of sin, should contribute to the ongoing reform of social structures so that they more completely align with God's purposes.[27]

Calvin's conception of vocation, because it is rooted in his doctrine of election, removes success as a necessary condition of good work. No amount of good work will earn a person eternal life. People are free, Calvin argues, to pursue their vocations courageously, just as brave soldiers charge into a battle without regard for their prospects of winning.[28] Vocation therefore invites spirited, intimate, and transformative engagement with the world.[29]

For Calvin, vocation participates in God's project of redemption by creating space in which pilgrims are re-formed even as creation itself is remade. Vocation ties the eschatological destiny of creation to a cruciform ontology. Standing fast in their vocational work, pilgrims negotiate, always imperfectly, the demands of sanctification in worlds fallen around and within them. That negotiation is itself transfigured into the cross-bearing likeness of Christ as cruciform pilgrims are conformed to Christ in their journey with him through the world.

There is much in Calvin's understanding of sanctification in general and of vocation in particular that merits critique. Calvin's contention that God intentionally inflicts hardship in the process of sanctification lends itself to all manner of abuse, particularly in justifying patterns of injustice that uphold the interests of the strong and dominant over the weak and marginalized. His assertion that persons should adhere to the work of their calling no matter how tedious it is threatens to validate exploitative forms of work.

Three insights in Calvin's discussion of vocation, however, are worth preserving, even if they need to be considerably revised. First, work is not simply a task but an occasion for self-transformation and a contribution to a greater purpose initiated by God. A person becomes a certain kind of self in the process of doing vocational work. Vocation, then, is more like a pilgrimage than a station. Second, vocational work, in whatever context it is done, is to be done well. Grace frees the pilgrim to do the best she can without the anxiety that expectations of success impose. Third, the meaning of vocational work is related to a larger context, a project in which it is situated, which for Calvin is God's work to redeem creation. Calvin has a particular understanding of what this larger context is. One may think of it more generally as a conception of the common good, in the context of which all created things flourish.

Vocation relates, then, to agents (the formation of selves who do vocational work), actions (the form vocational work takes), and the ends of action (the goal in reference to which vocational work is done). These three features are interrelated. God's redemptive project (the end of action) takes form in part in the ongoing transformation of selves who participate in it (agents). Agents craft their identity in relationship to the fundamental moral commitments that the project represents.[30] The project (end of action) makes each person's calling intelligible—it gives each person's work a particular shape—and it also empowers persons to do their work well (action). The work (action) contributes in its own way to the unfolding of the project (end of action), and it is also an occasion of the ongoing transformation of persons who participate in it (agents). Vocation, then, is a framing of work that accounts for workers and work in relationship to the broader context in which both the work and the worker acquire meaning and purpose.

Vocation as Public Argument

The understanding of vocation outlined above is teleological (goal oriented) in two respects. It holds, first, that there is an ultimate condition, a common good, in the context of which work is meaningful. That ultimate condition is God's work for the redemption of creation. This project of God's redeeming work constitutes the ultimate end of all vocational work, so that all vocational work aims at it. The second respect in which vocation is a teleological concept has to do with human purposefulness. In the context of vocational work, persons are understood to flourish and their lives to take on meaning and purpose in the ways God ordains. In participating in vocational work, persons and communities not only do work; they engage at the same time in a process of personal, moral, and spiritual formation in which they become the persons God intends them to be.

Authors have examined a host of modern social, political, and cultural conditions that complicate the very possibility of vocation as it has been understood in Christian theological traditions.[31] Both teleological dimensions of vocation have challenges associated with them related to the structure of modern societies. To render these challenges intelligible, a brief account of modernity and its more recent successor, postmodernity, must be provided. There are many interrelated ways to tell this story. One could, for example, focus on the development of secularism as a distinctive marker of social life in the modern and postmodern milieus.[32] Alternatively, one could emphasize moral anthropology, the selves that emerge in modern and postmodern moments. The account offered here is sociological; its focus is on the development of institutions in modern societies and the ways institutional structures bear directly on the meaning of work and workers. The view of modernity and postmodernity from the perspective of institutional life illumines vocation as a response.

Institutions are, on a basic level, patterns of cooperative meaning making and coordinated action that organize social life.[33] They provide more and less formal, more and less explicit, frameworks that structure cooperative endeavors. Institutions exist in formal laws, policies, and procedures; in customs, mores, and practices; in understandings of value and acceptable behaviors in relationship to values; and in the concepts and categories human beings use to make meaning of their experience. Institutions, sociologist Robert Bellah argues, can be as simple and informal as a handshake or as complex and formal as a tax code.[34]

Institutional patterns distinguish political spaces from other institutional spaces in modern societies. In legislative bodies, for example, politicians propose laws and policies, debate the merits of such proposals, and, at some point, vote to approve, defeat, or table them. Legislative bodies operate on the basis of complex parliamentary procedures, some of which are inscrutable to outsiders and insiders alike. Politicians engage in various forms of competition, cooperation, and compromise, often behind the scenes, to advance their purposes. Legislators not only govern; they also campaign to secure their hold on power. The campaign trail has its own distinctive norms and practices that render the work of campaigning intelligible.[35]

Any institutional setting has a central logic, an organizing principle that orients meaning making, practice, and understandings of identity.[36] Actors rely on institutional logics to know what work they are to do in an institutional setting, how they are to go about doing it, and why the work is meaningful. The institutional logics of politics empower actors to make decisions about the distribution and use of limited resources amid competing claims on them. Compromise is one political logic, enabling politicians to make decisions about when and to what extent they will forgo some of what they want in order to get some of what they want in return. The logic of compromise is at home in political institutions, but it may not be relevant in the same way in other institutional settings. In faith communities, for example, persons are not seen fundamentally as actors making competing claims on limited resources. Compromise is not therefore taken to be a primary expression of the institutional logic in these spaces (though it may be relevant at times).[37]

Institutions, moreover, occasion formative processes for those who inhabit them. Persons become a certain kind of self through their participation in institutional life. On a basic level, institutions define belonging; they create spaces in which some participate and others do not. The boundaries of institutional space therefore confer identity by defining sameness.[38] Through rehearsing institutional logics and practices, institutions shape habits of mind and heart, cognitive capacities and affective responses to the world.[39] Institutions, in other words, induce processes of moral formation.

Moral formation, as the term is used here, refers to a process whereby a person becomes a particular kind of moral agent by inhabiting and working in institutional settings. Moral agency is the power to do work that is morally relevant in some way. It consists of the capacities, practices, and skill sets efficacious in particular institutional settings in which persons engage in work. Moral agents are, in the context of this discussion, persons or communities capable of exercising moral agency.

Moral formation involves a deeper formative process than simply technical learning. Formation is not simply a matter of learning how to perform certain kinds of tasks in particular institutional settings—though technical learning is certainly a component of moral formation. More deeply, moral formation describes the process of becoming an agent whose identity, worldview, sense of purpose, and technical skills are all shaped by their participation in institutional settings. In legislative bodies, legislators must learn

the relevant practices and skills required to do legislative work. More fundamentally, they must learn how to think and act like a legislator, in whatever
ways institutional patterns determine are appropriate. An ordinary citizen
elected to legislative office, therefore, *becomes* a legislator not simply by virtue of election but through a process of moral formation.

Like all institutions, political institutions are normatively laden spaces
that give shape to the work done in them and to workers as well. Institutional patterns in political life determine what counts as good political work,
what it means to do political work well, and what kind of self is required to
do the work. The moral weight of institutional life, moreover, cannot simply
be circumvented or ignored. Candidates often campaign on the conceit that
they are not "political insiders"; that is, they have not been corrupted by
the pernicious workings of "Washington," or whatever the relevant setting
is. Therefore, the conceit goes, they will somehow be able to do political
work in ways that align more authentically with the candidates' own commitments and those of their constituents. Of course, no one waltzes into
Congress, or any other legislative body, and gets to do things her own way.
Any politician must contend with the patterns of meaning and practice that
constitute political institutions.

Modern societies have multiple institutional centers—the family, the
marketplace, the polity, faith communities, militaries, health-care systems,
educational systems, prison systems, and the like. Each of these has particular schemes of moral meaning, practice, and authority.[40] Persons inhabit different (though not always radically different) and morally relevant roles in
each of these institutional settings. In a family, a person is a parent or child;
in the marketplace, a consumer; in the military, a soldier; in a hospital, a
patient; in a faith community, a child of God. Each of these roles imposes
different expectations about what it means to make moral meaning of experience and what it means to do morally relevant work. Customers use an
instrumental logic to fulfill as many of their needs and wants as they can
with limited means. Patients passively await the advice and ministrations of
expert health-care providers who know what is best for them. Congregants
of a Christian church love their neighbors unconditionally and seek to provide for the least in society. Prisoners, stripped of many of their civil rights,
await punishment and reform. Soldiers obey commands from superiors and
seek to develop the virtues of courage and patriotic service to God, country,
and unit.

To the extent that different institutional roles and identities require
different moral commitments, virtues, and skills to do work well, persons
are formed as moral agents differently in relationship to them. Lawyers

are trained to argue and persuade in order to make cases about the necessity of punishment or compensation. Licensed clinical social workers are trained to offer counsel and support in order to help persons be restored in community with others. For the former, justice might primarily mean retribution for wrongs done or compensation for loss; for the latter, justice might primarily be a matter of restoration and healing. These two professionals require different moral training and therefore represent, in significant ways, different moral agents. Additionally, the different identities and life experiences persons bring with them inform how they understand and perform work.

The moral schemes that characterize differentiated institutional settings are not always radically different from one another, but they are often considerably different. Their differences generate morally resonant tensions. The duties of a soldier, therefore, might conflict with Christian understandings of neighborly love. The utilitarian calculus persons use to value goods in the marketplace might orient, for better or for worse, their valuation of goods in social, political, and religious life.[41] Navigating modern social systems presents moral challenges related to the pluralism that is a fundamental condition of modern social life.

Moral pluralism has emerged not only as an institutional condition but also as a primary framework in which human experience is valued and interpreted. Human persons and communities in different times and places have different experiences of the good life. The Western Enlightenment and its legacy have embraced the toleration of multiple accounts of truth, beauty, and goodness in social, political, moral, and religious life. As the modern world has opened up to a postmodern one, the mere toleration of difference gives way to the possibility that difference can be celebrated and actively engaged.[42] Rather than alleviating tensions that might exist between multiple accounts of human experience, postmodern worldviews encourage the exploration of these tensions with the hope of fostering constructive relationships and mutual transformation among persons who inhabit different ways of viewing and experiencing their worlds.[43]

These developments are mostly positive, but they do pose a problem for both of the teleological dimensions of vocation. In the postmodern world, there appears to be no single locus of meaning and purpose constituting the basis of meaningful work. Persons are confronted with innumerable possibilities for life projects that rest on and aim at multiple, and sometimes incompatible, values. Lifelong projects committed to the production of wealth, for example, likely have different moral underpinnings than do those committed to the production of art or knowledge.

Calvin, of course, was not working in a world characterized by this kind of deep moral pluralism. The Reformation, however, represented an inbreaking of moral pluralism in the Western world, marking in many ways the transition from premodernity to modernity. No longer did the theological, political, and social priorities of the Catholic Church constitute the primary worldview informing social and political life in Western Europe. Led by their princes (who in turn were often led by their own political ambitions rather than profound theological commitments), Europeans in the Reformation period now had to negotiate multiple theological, religious, and moral worldviews that did not cohere.[44] Often these negotiations unfolded as violent battles on geographical, political, social, and conceptual fronts. Reformers like Luther and Calvin joined these battles in their theological reflection. Theological categories like vocation are pieces of larger arguments about the nature of God, human being, creation, and its destiny. Thus, Calvin's treatment of vocation is a theological argument situated in a historical context in which fundamental theological and moral commitments are in question.

For these reasons, the idea of vocation per se is problematic in a postmodern world. Vocation should therefore be viewed as a public argument in addition to a pursuit. It is an argument because it will never overcome its status as a possible framing, one among many others, in which to make meaning of work. To say that vocation is a *public* argument is to say that it is a claim made in public space about what makes life good. In the framing of vocation, good work makes for a good life, and work is good insofar as it contributes to the common good. Vocation is therefore ultimately a claim about the meaning of a person's life as it connects to the meaning of common life. This argument requires validation from public conversation partners—validation that it is not automatically granted and that the claimant may not receive.

The power of vocation as a public argument is that it both acknowledges the moral realities that different institutional settings create and the need to stretch those realities in the direction of God's intentions for creation. Because vocation is always a "calling in" a particular institutional space, it doesn't summarily dismiss the moral complexity of that space. Rather, as best as it can, vocation seeks to hold the moral complexity of institutional space in tension with the "calling to" participate in God's work in the world.

Vocation thus orients the moral meaning of work. In the theological perspective developed here, vocation is participation in God's project to redeem creation in a particular setting of work (the framing), conferring on the participant a sense of identity, direction, and purpose as she makes her way through the world (the pilgrimage). Vocation as framing and pilgrimage sets up the idea that vocation is also, inevitably, a moral argument. That is, in a pluralistic age, the notion that work participates in the project of another for the common good is problematic for the reasons cited above. To suggest that work of any kind is a vocation is to make a claim about the moral status of work that is imminently contestable. One task of this book is to understand in what ways the concept of political vocation is a moral argument about the common good.

Politics as a Vocation

A political vocation, as it is understood here, is a framing of the work of politics in reference to an external project that gives political work meaning and purpose. Politics involves the ways in which human beings and communities cooperate and compete with one another to sort out colliding purposes. To do the work of politics is to be engaged in some way in the practices of cooperation and competition involved in that work. The idea of an "external project" alludes to the normative center of vocation, which, in Calvin's rendering, has to do with God's redeeming purposes in the world. More will need to be said about what exactly constitutes the external project of political vocation and what it means for the work of politics. The rest of this chapter offers a preliminary description of the work of political vocation. This description will be expanded and given nuance in later chapters.

The most important reflection on political vocation in the modern age is Max Weber's seminal essay "Politics as a Vocation." In it Weber grapples with the moral ambiguity of political work. Political work is morally ambiguous, in Weber's account, because of the complex and often countervailing forces of power, money, bureaucracy, and idealism that render problematic the task of responsible political action. To have a vocation in politics, Weber argues, is to weigh these competing factors as best as one can, make a decision, and then claim responsibility for the consequences of one's actions.

On the evening of January 28, 1919, amid the revolutionary turmoil that rocked postwar Germany, Weber presented a lecture on politics to an audience at the University of Munich. Weber anticipated that his audience wanted him, a famous sociologist, to sort out Germany's uncertain political future. But he failed to deliver: "This lecture, which I give at your request," Weber said, "will necessarily disappoint you in a number of ways. You will naturally expect me to take a position on actual problems of the day." The actual problems of the day, however, had induced Weber to consider a different set of questions.

Weber had seen in the Great War the moral challenges that modern political systems pose to persons who work in them. The war had shown that modern states use political violence or its threat to implement policies through vast and impersonal bureaucracies with uncertain, imprecise, and morally ambiguous results. In the aftermath of the war, Weber observed communist, socialist, anarchist, and democratic elements all contending for control of that power, using violence to enforce their vision of political life.[45]

Weber aimed to construct a sociology of political leadership that would disabuse aspiring politicians of the fanatical idealisms that dominated political rhetoric in the immediate aftermath of the Great War. The "decisive means" of politics, Weber argues, is violence. And violent means in the hands of revolutionary elements who are unwilling to bear the responsibility of their actions is dangerous. Weber criticizes "Spartacism," a movement of revolutionary communism associated with the "Spartacist uprising," a general strike in Berlin (January 5–12, 1919), which had concluded only several days before Weber's lecture. Movements like Bolshevism and Spartacism prefer violent revolution to the peaceful maintenance of the status quo, even if a successful revolution isn't likely. For Weber, this inattention to the implications of revolutionary political action makes radical leftist politics morally no different from the politics of the imperial regime against which the revolution was directed.[46]

But Weber also wanted to avoid another extreme, a conception of politics as a job that reduces leadership to mere remunerated occupation, denuded of the weighty responsibilities of office. The problem with German imperial politics, Weber elaborates in his essay, was that it governed under the rule of officials rather than leaders. For Weber, officials act dispassionately and impartially on the instruction of leaders, who issue and bear responsibility for the policies and instructions they develop.[47] Officials are skillful administrators, but they make bad leaders because they are unable to act and bear the responsibility of their actions.[48] Politics for these functionaries tends to look more like an enterprise (*Betrieb*), a job by which one earns a living, rather than a genuine vocation (*Beruf*).[49] In the period leading to the Great War, Germany had been an officialdom, a "rule by officials." In fact, Germany, Weber remarks, "had the best officials in the world."[50] But Germany, for all its official prowess, lacked political leadership. In Weber's view, the result was government without responsibility.

Two kinds of irresponsibility, then, marked German political life: the irresponsibility of political idealists and ideologues who wouldn't claim responsibility for their actions and the irresponsibility of the administrators of the German empire who couldn't. Germany lacked politicians who could negotiate the moral complexity of the modern state with integrity. It lacked politicians, in other words, capable of doing political work well.[51] Weber wanted to know what kind of person is capable of navigating the moral perils of modern political life, not only achieving political success but also remaining a good person in the process.

The modern state, Weber writes, "claims a monopoly of the legitimate use of physical force within a given territory." Politics is that "striving" to "share" or "influence the distribution of violent power."[52] Not only are political judgments far reaching, in that they condition the lives of entire communities; they are also enforced by violent power, or the threat of its use. The combination of these two features of political work—the far-reaching effects of political judgment and the violent nature of political power—make the politician's work morally ambiguous.

The element of violent power magnifies the moral significance of political judgment. Observing the brutal and uncompromising politics of communist elements all around him, Weber warns that persons holding an "ethic of ultimate ends" enter politics only with disastrous effect. Such an ethic pursues ultimate values at all costs, justifying any means to achieve them. A person's dedication to ultimate values may make him virtuous apart from political life. But the use of political power to realize these ends without any regard for the evil that enforcement causes moral or religious virtue to turn into political vice.

The exercise of violent power, Weber argues, requires that politicians practice an "ethic of responsibility," according to which the politician anticipates and then takes responsibility for the consequences of his actions. The politician who exercises an ethic of responsibility is confronted with two dilemmas. First, he cannot determine exactly what the outcomes of his actions will be. Politicians make decisions that have unintended consequences. Even then, Weber argues, the politician must take responsibility for his actions. Second, harm caused by the exercise of power may outweigh benefits generated by the intended consequences of its exercise. Harmful means, in other words, may outweigh beneficial ends. Politicians need to judge when they are likely to go too far in the pursuit of their political goals. What separates responsible politicians from those who pursue ultimate ends is that responsible politicians know that compromise is often necessary to bring about the greatest good, even if it means that ultimate values are sacrificed.

Political power, in short, is fundamentally unwieldy and unstable. Any political judgment involves the risk that the exercise of political power will do more harm than good. The responsible politician does the best he can to anticipate the consequences the exercise of power will bring about. But at a certain point, he must simply act. Like Martin Luther, Weber writes, the politician "reaches the point where he can only declare: 'Here I stand. I can do no other.' "[53]

Wielding power in the face of uncertainty, responsible politicians engage something that is profoundly human: "however, it is immensely moving when a *mature* man . . . is aware of the responsibility for the consequences of his conduct and really feels such responsibility with his heart and soul." For Weber, the acceptance of responsibility for using political power "is something genuinely human and moving." To engage this "genuinely human" experience, Weber suggests, is itself an ultimate end. Therefore, an ethic of responsibility and an ethic of ultimate ends are not finally "absolute contrasts" but are instead "supplementary." Working "in unison," the two constitute "the genuine man," one who "can have the 'calling for politics.' "[54]

For Weber, the work of politics implies a profound encounter with human finitude. To be human is to experience and to respond to distinctively human limitations. Human beings are limited in moral perception and in power: they can neither anticipate the consequences of their actions with certainty, nor can they exercise complete control over their world and their own destiny. Politicians can respond either by accepting or denying their own finitude. Those who would practice an ethic of ultimate ends in political life ignore the limitations of their own capacities, both in imagining that they can achieve ultimate ends and in discounting the negative consequences that their actions will create.

A "calling for politics," by contrast, requires that the politician hold the tension between the responsibility to act and the responsibility for her actions. At bottom, the ethic of responsibility means that persons called to the political vocation must confront human finitude with integrity. For Weber, the responsible encounter with human finitude is the fundamental criterion of good political work.

Weber provides a complex account of the ambient conditions that make it difficult to have a vocation in politics. His account also shows that good political work is about the best one can do. The best one can do always falls short of the best that can be done, either because ambient political conditions will not allow the politician to do all she wants or because the politician's actions do not result in what she wants or both. At the heart of political vocation is the paradox that the politician wields great power and yet she must, at a certain point, surrender control of her own best efforts.

Weber frames the work of politics around the exercise of power. For Weber, persons called to the work of politics must take responsibility for the consequences of their actions. Weber answers the "why" of responsibility without offering a very full account of what responsible action is. The next chapter continues to inquire about the work of politics, exploring the relationship between responsibility and political action in more detail.

2

RESPONSIBILITY AND REPRESENTATION

"Something Genuinely Human and Moving": The Moral Integrity of Political Vocation

Weber's politician stands in a morally precarious position. The politician wields the immense coercive power of the modern state for which he (Weber, it is fair to say, has a "he" in mind) is responsible. Such responsibility means that the politician must often compromise to make incremental progress toward his goal. Even when he considers the use of power responsibly, the politician ultimately cannot be sure that his actions will produce desired effects; they may indeed backfire. Moreover, the politician works within, and often against, a huge political bureaucracy, many of whose officials live "from" rather than "for" politics. In the midst of complex, competing, and often countervailing powers and interests, the politician can only do the best he can and must claim responsibility for the results of his actions, whatever they may be.

The Weberian politician, in other words, works in an institutional setting characterized by profound moral ambiguity. Two conditions account for the moral ambiguity of political space. The first has to do with state-sanctioned violence, the medium of all political work. Violent power, Weber argues, is inherently unstable; with it, the politician can easily exceed his mandate, promoting himself to the detriment of the public interest. This threat is especially dire in the case of politicians who either act strictly to secure the goods of political office, including "adventure, victory, booty, power, and spoils," or strictly in service to an uncompromising ideal that gives no consideration to the moral meaning of the consequences of action. Hence, Weber writes that "[the politician] lets himself in for the diabolic forces lurking in all violence."[1] Anyone who would "seek the salvation of his soul, of his own or others," Weber asserts, should not pursue a political vocation. The holy and the violent, in his view, cannot cohere.[2]

The second, related reason for moral ambiguity in political life has to do with the moral achievements possible in politics. One cannot be a politician and achieve the good perfectly, even when one wills the good. Politics requires an "ethic of responsibility," valuing modest achievements that weigh the consequences of using binding power. An ethic of responsibility, however, falls short of the requirements of "an ethic of ultimate ends," a religious ethic according to which one pursues the good at all costs. In some ways, Weber thinks, these two ethics complement one another. Persons who seek religious perfection, however, should not work in politics.

From a religious perspective, as Weber imagines it, the political vocation is defective, because it denies the pursuit of absolute ends. For Weber, however, the political vocation has its own integrity, as evidenced by the politician's capacity to accept moral ambiguity and to act in the midst of it with a distinct ethical framework. Vocational work has integrity, Weber is suggesting, when it facilitates a distinctively human encounter with the world. Political vocation facilitates the achievement of "something genuinely human and moving," as Weber says.[3] That "something genuinely human," whatever it is, signals the integrity of vocational work. The political vocation, as Weber sees it, facilitates the formation of a self with a capacity to accept moral ambiguity, a confidence to act despite it, and an ability to accept responsibility for the consequences of one's actions. These qualities are achievements—one must actively work to cultivate them. Once cultivated, they distinguish the political vocation from other ways of being in the world. They are achievements, moreover, that, at least in Weber's view, allow a person more to be "genuinely" human.

A "distinctively human encounter with the world" has two different meanings in relationship to Weber's discussion. It means, first, that the skills developed in the pursuit of a political vocation allow a person to actualize herself in such a way that she lives a more fully human life. One becomes more fully human, that is, because one undergoes a particular human development that opens an expanded range of experiences.[4]

To have a distinctively human encounter with the world means, second, that the political vocation allows one to negotiate the limits of human agency in an authentic way. An ethic of responsibility, for example, empowers a politician to take responsibility for her actions, while at the same time disclosing the limits of responsible action. According to an ethic of responsibility, a politician must claim responsibility for the consequences of her actions. But a politician's capacity for responsible action is limited, since she cannot predict with certainty the outcomes of her actions. Cultivating a particular set of skills and dispositions enhances one's agency, but it also shapes the way one experiences and responds to the limits of agency. Weber's "Here I stand; I can do no other" therefore signals both the possibilities and the limitations involved in pursuing a political vocation. A vocation has integrity, then, in the distinctive way it facilitates possibilities for human experience and configures the encounter with human limitation. Said differently, the integrity of any vocation refers to the shape vocation gives to a particular way of being in the world, one that empowers human beings to flourish qua human beings in the delicate space between human possibility and human limitation. Flourishing in vocational work means that persons develop human capacities, but they also confront the limits of their agency, requiring negotiations with human finitude. In vocational work, then, human beings learn what it means to be human by pushing up against the boundaries of human experience.

Weber's analysis of the political vocation shows the important relationship vocation bears to institutional life. The differentiation of institutional life in modern societies creates a great many possibilities for experiencing the world. Different institutional settings have different (though not always radically different) moral logics that determine what good work looks like and, more generally, what the good life is about. The moral logic of the marketplace, for example, is an instrumental one, aimed at achieving concrete goals, usually on the basis of the rule of quid pro quo.[5] In the marketplace, persons are consumers, and consumers are encouraged to consume. For the consumer, the good life is about getting more of what one wants with the limited resources at one's disposal. The marketplace, therefore, shapes the experience of the consumer, a particular way of being in the world familiar to anyone who has shopped in a grocery store. The marketplace makes the consumer possible, and the consumer, by practicing consumption, reinforces the norms and practices of the marketplace.

The intelligibility and coherence of the consumer in the marketplace signals the distinctiveness of that role. Institutions like the marketplace render intelligible roles and the appropriate training for them. They sanction the performance of particular kinds of actions and the possible ends of action that can be pursued. Anyone who knows how to get the best deal in a supermarket has experienced the training the marketplace provides in forming persons to be good consumers. Institutions like the marketplace also provide moral logics according to which one knows what right action looks like (e.g., quid pro quo). The marketplace also gives shape to possible ends, or goals, of action. The goal of action in the marketplace is to get more of what one wants with the limited resources available.

Like the marketplace, political life, in Weber's view, is a distinctive institutional setting: it creates the conditions for particular roles, practices, norms, and values. Political life in modern societies also has a distinctive moral logic, the "ethic of responsibility," a particular way of making moral meaning of experience. Weber's key insight is that the shape any vocation takes depends in part upon the institutional setting in which it is situated. The politician's ethic of responsibility, therefore, is intelligible in an institutional setting in which persons are required to wield the coercive power of the state. The ethic of responsibility arises from the kind of moral agency politicians have. Institutions, then, condition the integrity of vocations.

Institutional settings facilitate distinctively human encounters with the world. Distinctiveness, however, is a necessary but not a sufficient condition of integrity. The market system, for example, creates the conditions for persons to experience the world as producers and consumers. These are distinctive roles, but they need not be judged to have integrity, at least not in every instance. That is because the roles of producer and consumer do not, in every instance, facilitate human flourishing; they do not expand a person's capacity to engage the world in a "genuinely human" way. Institutional roles, therefore, are morally ambiguous.

Weber is saying the same thing about political life. He is also arguing that at least there is such a thing as a political vocation that has integrity, in the sense that it creates the conditions for human flourishing. The modern state is an institutional setting making intelligible a particular kind of human experience in the context of political work. The morally relevant challenges and opportunities facing politicians in modern states exist because the institutional setting itself creates the conditions for them. To have a political vocation, to be able to do political work well, is to develop a particular set of habits and dispositions—virtues, in a word—with which one can negotiate the challenges and opportunities that political life in the modern state makes possible.

Weber likely exaggerates the disjunction between the political ethic of responsibility and the religious ethic of ultimate ends. Christian ethicists have long explored responsibility both as an ontological and a normative category, providing a foundation for Christian ethical reflection.[6] Still, Weber invites a consideration of whether there is a theological account of the integrity of political vocation—whether, that is, theology can make sense of the "genuinely human" that emerges in the political vocation.

Two prominent and related traditions of Christian political thought offer theological accounts of the ruler's work. Augustinian approaches understand the ruler's work in relationship to the eschatological reality that is the city of God. The political realist approaches of Emil Brunner and Reinhold Niebuhr emphasize the necessity of political life in taming the collective effects of sin. The following discussion shows that both approaches leave little room for thinking about the integrity of political vocation. The following analysis does not constitute a refutation of these views. It does, however, point to a gap in Christian theological reflection on political vocation. The final section, drawing on the work of Dietrich Bonhoeffer, proposes an alternative account.

Augustine's Wise Judge

One theological account of the ruler's work runs through St. Augustine and his contemporary exponents. Augustine has enjoyed renewed attention from political theologians in the last two decades, and Augustinian political theologies constitute a dominant current in contemporary political theology. Thinkers as diverse as John Milbank, William Cavanaugh, Stanley Hauerwas, Charles Mathewes, Kristin Deede Johnson, Luke Bretherton, Robert Dodaro, Eric Gregory, and James Wetzel all draw on Augustine to respond to challenges of political life in contemporary liberal polities.[7] Augustine is an attractive resource for political theologians for two main reasons. First, Augustine's city of God, the eschatological framework orienting his theological reflection, is a thoroughly political reality, lending itself to theological reflection on secular political life. Second, Augustine's contention that the eschatological reality that is the heavenly city represents the proper end of all political being offers a clear alternative to, and thus a critical resource for, secular political realities that theologians want to critique.[8] On the Augustinian view, secular political life, in whatever configuration, is at best only a poor simulacrum of the heavenly city, the genuinely real polity in which all things find their "final peace" in beatific communion with God. Augustinian political theologies get much purchase from this claim, though they differ as to whether it licenses constructive engagement with the earthly city or a repudiation of it.

In his *City of God*, Augustine famously divides the human race into "two orders," two cities, "allegorically speaking," which are created by two corresponding loves: "the earthly by love of self extending even to contempt of God, and the heavenly by love of God extending to contempt of self."[9] All of humanity is divided into "sheep and goats," "wheat and tares," elect and reprobate, separated in the way each orders its love, and "separated until the last judgment."[10] The earthly city creates the conditions of a provisional earthly peace, including all "things necessary for the support of the mortal life," which the heavenly city uses to aid its journey toward ultimate communion with God. "For as long as this Heavenly City is a pilgrim on earth," Augustine claims, it should use earthly peace where it is found, "directing the earthly peace towards heavenly peace." The pilgrim citizens of the city of God use earthly peace to cultivate a "perfectly ordered and perfectly harmonious fellowship in the enjoyment of God, and of one another in God."[11] Augustine recommends cooperation and even engagement with the politics of the earthly city. But for pilgrim citizens of the heavenly city, that engagement is instrumental: they are to use the goods of the earthly city to love and glorify God more completely.

In book 19, chapter 6, Augustine considers the work of judges in the earthly city. For Augustine, judging is a primary political act; judges judge, but so do other political officials.[12] "Social life" in secular time, Augustine writes, "is surrounded by darkness."[13] Judges search for the truth. But in the secular age, in the time between fall and ultimate redemption, "the wretchedness of man's condition" obscures the truth. Judges torture defendants and witnesses in an attempt to arrive at the truth. But judges cannot know for certain the consciences of those whom they judge. This ignorance, Augustine writes, "is very often a calamity to the innocent." Despite this dilemma, Augustine argues, judges should still "take their seat on the judge's bench." In the secular age, both ignorance and judgment are "unavoidable." The judge must do his work despite these conditions. If, in the course of carrying out his duty, the judge is in error, he will not be culpable. "But," Augustine asks, "is he also happy?" For Augustine, happiness—human flourishing—in its "final" form is beatific communion with God, characterized by an interminable and incorruptible peace. Obviously, the work of the judge, including the torture of persons whose innocence the judge can never know with certainty, does not reflect this final happiness. The wise man who would serve as judge would do best to "acknowledge that the necessity of acting in this way is a miserable one." The wise judge hates "his own part in it" and "with the knowledge of godliness . . . cries out to God, 'From my necessities deliver Thou me.'"[14]

Augustine's judge finds himself in a situation not unlike that of the Weberian politician. Both work in political offices that require the use of coercive power. Both run up against the limits of their own moral perception, the Weberian politician in his inability to know just what the consequences of his action will be, and the Augustinian judge in his inability to read accurately the consciences of those he judges. The Weberian politician's declaration, "Here I stand; I can do no other," captures a resignation to his own finitude that one hears in the Augustinian judge's cry, "From my necessities deliver Thou me." Both may not be morally or legally culpable for their actions, but both are required to live and work in a place of moral ambiguity and tension.

And yet there could hardly be a wider gulf between these two political figures. The Weberian politician has exercised his moral agency to the best of his ability and has exhausted all of his capacities for judgment and action. He runs up against the limits of his own finitude in a moment that renders him fully himself, fully human, "genuinely human and moving," as Weber says. The Weberian politician lives for politics, after all. Augustine's wise judge, by contrast, participates in the "wretchedness of man's condition" only by necessity. The judge is a decider, but he laments the tragic situation in which he finds himself, both knowing that he cannot know everything relevant to his judgment and yet accepting that judgments must be made. Though his judgments may bring harm to good people, the judge knows that it would in effect be "more wicked" to abandon "the claims of human society."[15] Judging for Augustine is not the kind of work in which one achieves one's own humanity. On the contrary, the judge risks putting his own spiritual well-being in jeopardy whenever he passes judgment on others.[16] No one, Augustine suggests, should want to carry the judge's burden.[17]

Augustine, of course, was not thinking about political vocation in the sense discussed in the previous chapter. He was, however, querying the moral and theological significance of political work. The judge's work is wretched because the judge, having "knowledge of godliness," knows that human beings love both godly and wicked things, but he cannot determine with certainty what each appellant loves.[18] Thus, the judge is doomed to commit the same evils as the wicked. Far from being "genuinely human and moving," the work of Augustine's wise judge is a necessary evil.

To say that a vocation has integrity is to say that it facilitates a distinctive way of being in the world in the context of which human beings flourish. Augustine's view seems to deny that political work in the secular age has integrity in this sense. Secular political life is not distinctive because it is eccentric; like all things in the world, political life has its center outside of itself, in God.[19] The secular political order, and the work that happens in it, is merely a simulacrum of the heavenly kingdom. The judgment of the wise judge always amounts to an imperfect rendering of God's judgment. God alone is the truly wise judge. Human beings judge only because judgment is necessary, but it is also always flawed. Indeed, the best judge is the one who paradoxically hopes that the secular polity, the very context in which the judge's work is intelligible, hastens to its end.[20]

In the messy confusion of the secular age, in which good and evil are, for the moment, inextricably mixed, the work of the judge is, as Charles Mathewes says, "fraught," because "only the sinless should judge. And the one sinless man who could judge—Christ himself—chooses not to."[21] Politics during the secular age is precarious work, not work in the context of which a person could become more fully human but work in the context of which she could only become culpable for falling short of Christ's judgment.

The precarious position of Augustine's wise judge points to a tension in Augustinian political theology more generally. The political arrangements of the eschatological city of God, since they are ordered to God, constitute the genuine, the "really real" polity. Augustine seeks to show, in other words, that "the spiritual is the *authentically* political" and thus "life outside the Christian community [fails] to be truly public, authentically political."[22] The political values of justice and equity, therefore, are meaningful only if God is their proper object. Worldly political arrangements are deficient to the extent that they fall short of the eschatological political norms and patterns of the city of God. Worldly political roles are deficient, in turn, to the extent that they participate, as a matter of "necessity," in the deficient arrangements of the secular polity.

Holding Evil at Bay

Political realists understand that political life amounts to a necessary evil, a mechanism required to restrain sinful human beings from wreaking havoc on one another. Indeed, some realists, including Reinhold Niebuhr, find in Augustine resources for developing this view.[23] Paradigmatically articulated by Martin Luther,[24] this view flourished in Protestant thought in the first half of the twentieth century. In the same way that the Great War oriented Weber's thinking about political vocation, theologians writing in the postwar context contemplated the profound ways in which the war disclosed the unparalleled power of the modern state. For these theologians, the distinguishing feature of the modern state is its use of violent, coercive power. On its own, such power is at best morally ambiguous, at worst simply evil. Such framings emphasize the paradoxical nature of political work: on the one hand, political life is necessary to keep evil at bay. On the other, persons who do political work must exercise extreme caution, lest their use of binding power reinforces the very evil its exercise is meant to restrain. Politics is therefore about paradox, a sentiment that Weber also understood. Weber saw both paradox and possibilities for the political vocation. Some of his theological contemporaries were less certain about its possibilities.

The Swiss theologian Emil Brunner characterizes the coercive power of the state as "contrary to love; it is evil." And yet, Brunner argues, such power is necessary. The state exists because of sin, and it exists to restrain sin. The state "represents human sin on the large scale. . . . In the State, we human beings see our own sin magnified a thousand times. The State is a product of collective sin." The state has a "divinely appointed purpose" to use the "daemonic, violent power of compulsion" to ensure that sinful human beings do not destroy one another.[25] The state's role is to create order. Christians, Brunner argues, have a duty to participate in the work of the state. But that participation is "paradoxical": Christians at once recognize the inherent evil of the state's purpose and function, and they also "thank God for it as a Divine gift."[26] This paradoxical tension in which Christian citizens do the work of politics is potentially crushing. Christians navigate the paradox of political life by maintaining the hope for the "new world that lies beyond history." Indeed, Brunner argues, that hope motivates the Christian's "joyful readiness for service" and also maintains "his sanity in service."

Reinhold Niebuhr's political ethic takes a similar approach. Niebuhr's Christian realism posits power as the fundamental social reality. According to Niebuhr, groups of people are constitutionally incapable of disinterested ethical comportment. Instead, groups pursue their own self-interest relentlessly. Public life is therefore characterized by the ongoing competition of group interests. Niebuhr argues that Christian social ethics can frame these social dynamics in theological perspective. It can also provide broad aims toward which social and political policies that regulate the play of group interest ought to aim. Beyond these two important tasks, however, Christian ethics has little to contribute to the minutiae of creating a balance of power between competing interests.

In his seminal early study *Moral Man and Immoral Society* (1932), Niebuhr famously argues that human reason enables "a capacity for self-transcendence. . . . [R]eason enables [man], within limits, to direct his energy so that it will flow in harmony, and not in conflict, with other life."[27] Human beings are able to create community with others precisely because reason checks self-regard and supports "those impulses which carry life beyond itself."[28] Because human beings are congenitally sinful, however, the individual's capacity for self-transcendence is not utterly reliable. Moreover, the rational capacity of the individual is diluted, and finally disappears altogether, as human beings aggregate into ever-larger groups, such as families, races, economic classes, and nations.[29] Groups are more likely to be given over to "impulses" toward self-interest. Thus, Niebuhr concludes, "group relations can never be as ethical as those which characterize individual relations."[30] The only way to control group interests is to keep them in check using coercive, countervailing forces. Ranging from war to control via formal legal and policy structures, coercive force can be more or less overtly violent.[31]

This view poses a problem for Christian ethics. For Niebuhr, the "ethic of Jesus" constitutes a moral "perfectionism" that demands "complete disinterestedness, religiously motivated." Christian ethics prescribes a moral life governed by the "law of love": "No one was to seek his own. . . . Evil was not to be resisted, the borrower was to be given more than he asked for without hope of return."[32] But such perfectionism is an unworkable paradigm for a social ethic.[33] At best, the ethic of Jesus supplies an ideal "vantage point" from which both to critique extant social policy and organization and very broadly to suggest directions in which to push present states of affairs. Indeed, a social ethic that seeks to balance contending powers in order to achieve relative justice needs broad ideals that define what relative justice will look like.[34] Still, justice as the attempt to preserve the "equilibria of power" is always only a mere approximation of the law of love.[35] Christian citizens and politicians are both obligated to win "proximate victories" for the good of their communities but cannot confuse proximate victories with "the final meaning of our existence."[36]

In their theologies of human institutions, both Brunner and Niebuhr posit a distinctive role for political life. Political life is that space where sin is in full manifestation, and political arrangements use necessary means to keep sin in check. For both Brunner and Niebuhr, the work of politics involves holding the tension between coercive power and social stability. Both Brunner and Niebuhr relate political justice to God's love, where the latter makes the former possible. The reality of divine love holds the paradox of political life together. In a way, both Brunner and Niebuhr affirm a version of Weber's distinction between the ethic of ultimate ends and the ethic of responsibility. For both thinkers, ultimate ends make political responsibility possible.

Weber sees the same moral ambiguity in political life. He also sees another kind of tension, a tension among the need to exercise political power, the responsibility that comes with its exercise, and the limited control politicians have to determine the outcomes for which they bear responsibility. Brunner, Niebuhr, and Weber all affirm the allure of political power and its potential to corrupt the persons who wield it. All three thinkers,

furthermore, affirm that political life manifests and magnifies human finitude and brokenness.

Unlike Weber, Brunner and Niebuhr see in political life the limits of
human possibility, a threatening situation that can only be managed. Politics for these thinkers is an arena in which human beings are least human—
for Brunner, because politics manifests a magnification of human sin, and
for Niebuhr, because politics manifests the inability of human beings to
transcend their own "egotism." Politics lacks integrity because it fails to constitute a space in which human beings flourish qua human beings. The
paradox of politics—that politics is a necessary evil—marks a threshold near
the lowest region of human being, below which human beings fail to be
genuinely human.

For Weber, the paradox of politics is not that politics is, as a social system, a necessary evil but that it entails the necessary use of morally ambiguous means. Politics both creates an unresolvable problem and then positions
persons called to political work to resolve it. Politicians take responsibility
for the use of violent power, even though taking responsibility is never sufficient to mitigate the unpredictable nature of power.[37] But taking responsibility is the best politicians can do. In that unresolvable tension, politicians
experience themselves as genuinely human.

Bonhoeffer on Responsibility and Representation

The German martyr and theologian Dietrich Bonhoeffer suggests a different way of thinking about the integrity of political vocation. Bonhoeffer
offers a theological account that grounds the experience of being "genuinely
human" in the context of vocational work in Jesus Christ, who is the genuinely human being. Participation in the life of Christ does not resolve the
moral tensions associated with vocational work in political life. Those moral
tensions, however, are revealed not merely as marks of human deficiency
but as the place where Christ is most present in the world.

Bonhoeffer did not finish his later text *Ethics* before his arrest, imprisonment, and ultimate execution at the hands of the Nazi regime. In the
extant manuscript, Bonhoeffer begins to address directly the challenges of
political agency. The section called "History and Good [1]" ends with an
intriguing suggestion about political ethics: "Political action," Bonhoeffer
writes, "means taking on responsibility. This cannot happen without power.
Power is to serve responsibility."[38] Bonhoeffer never developed this thesis in
Ethics, though, of course, the example of his life stands as its own interpretation of this argument.[39] Still, what Bonhoeffer says about the meaning of

responsibility and action in *Ethics* illumines the trajectory of his theological reflection on political vocation.

Jesus Christ is the locus of Bonhoeffer's theological and ethical thought. For Bonhoeffer, Jesus Christ is what is most real about human experience in the world, as Christ is where God and the world meet in a single reality.[40] The moral life is not therefore about following absolute principles that determine what is right and wrong.[41] Indeed, the moral life for Bonhoeffer is not fundamentally about right and wrong at all. Rather, it is about participation in Jesus Christ, the "true form" of humanity, who takes form in the world.[42] To be human, and to. live well, is to be formed in the life of Christ. Bonhoeffer's ethics is therefore an ethics of "formation" rather than an ethics of principle.

Jesus Christ takes form in the world to love, judge, and reconcile the world to God.[43] For Bonhoeffer, Christ's taking form in the world entails an "affirmation" of the world as it is. God in the person of Jesus Christ enters into the world and begins the work of reconciliation amid the concrete and messy realities of the world, within the "worldliness" of the world, as Bonhoeffer says. Being formed in Christ, then, involves a deep enmeshment in the messy worldliness of the world, with all of the moral complexity, brokenness, and ambiguity (of the sort discussed in this chapter) that it entails.[44] To say that God affirms the worldliness of the world, however, is not to say that the world-as-it-is is the same as the world-as-it-should-be. Bonhoeffer understands that the present "penultimate" reality will ultimately be "swallowed up" by the "ultimate" reality of the eschaton. But these two realities, the penultimate and the ultimate, are constitutive of one another.[45]

Ethics is about responsible action for the human good, the way in which human beings answer the calling of God.[46] Since Jesus Christ is the real human being, Bonhoeffer argues, Christ makes possible real human action, that is, "action that is in accord with reality."[47] The action of Jesus Christ to love, judge, and reconcile the world to God has two primary qualities: it is responsible and representative. To say that ethical action is responsible is to say that it bears a relationship to the other, namely, that it takes responsibility for the other for the purposes of loving, judging, and reconciling the other to God. In Jesus Christ, God is ultimately both the determiner and the agent of responsible action for the other. Responsible action is therefore always God's action, both "flowing into and springing from God's guidance."[48] Because responsible action is God's action, it is both free and good. It is free because it responds to and is not determined by the vagaries of the world. It is good because God alone, not absolute, inflexible rules, makes action in the world good. Thus, to act responsibly, one must "discern what is necessary . . . observe, weigh, and judge the matter" and thereby "enter the sphere of relativity, in the twilight that the historical situation casts over good and evil."[49] Responsible action therefore defies ordinary judgments about good and evil, for only God determines what is ultimately good for creation.

Closely linked to the idea of responsibility is that of representation. Responsibility, Bonhoeffer writes, is "based on" what he calls "vicarious representative action." Vicarious representative action is action on behalf of others; it is the action, Bonhoeffer says, of the "father," the "statesman," or the "instructor of an apprentice."[50] Bonhoeffer first develops the idea of vicarious representative action in his early work *Sanctorum Communio* and explores it further in *Ethics*. In the former work, Bonhoeffer argues that vicarious representative action is a theological concept that describes the nature of God's love. Jesus Christ takes on the sins of the world and is punished for them, dying on the cross as a criminal. As human beings are not able to carry the weight of their own sins themselves, God carries it for them.[51]

In *Ethics*, Bonhoeffer explores vicarious representative action as the substance of responsible action.[52] To act vicariously is to stand in the place of others and act on their behalf, to, in William Schweiker's formulation, "respect and enhance the integrity of life before God."[53] It is selfless action, requiring that one "[devote] one's own life to another person."[54] Vicarious representative action has "love as its content and freedom as its form."[55] It has love as its content because vicarious representative action "concretely enacts" God's love for human beings by drawing human beings into community with God.[56] Vicarious representative action has freedom as its form because God does not hold reality to an ideal, ahistorical moral standard that "despises" concrete historical situations that fall short of such a standard. Instead, God's love is "free from any unreal ideologies."[57] In the life, death, and resurrection of Jesus Christ, God enters into the reality of history, "accepts it as a given," and works within it to reconcile creature and Creator.

Vicarious representative action is the shape the life of Christ takes in the world.[58] Bonhoeffer is not saying that vicarious representative action achieves the restoration of sinful humanity in relationship to God. Only Jesus Christ can achieve this, and he has achieved it in his death on the cross. The moral life is not fundamentally about what vicarious representative action does; it is about one's formation in the life of Christ in the world. Indeed, since Jesus Christ is the real human, being formed in Christ is the most authentic way of being human. And being formed in Christ entails the work of vicarious representative action.

The "essence of responsible action," Bonhoeffer says, "intrinsically involves the sinless becoming guilty."[59] For Bonhoeffer, Christ, the One who was yet without sin, takes on "sinful flesh," becoming a sinful human being, indeed the "worst sinner" (*peccator pessimus*), who is crucified on the cross for his sin. The essence of Christ's humiliation is not that God became human and is at once both God and human. The "paradox" of Christ's humiliation is fundamentally that the sinless One took on the sin of the world, becoming both sinful and sinless. By virtue of Christ's taking on sinful flesh, Christ "robs" sin of its alienating power. The sinless One who has taken on sin is tempted by sin, anguishes because of sin, judges sin, is condemned because of sin, and finally redeems human beings from sin through death on the cross.[60]

As the "sphere of relativity, completely shrouded in the twilight that the historical situation casts upon good and evil," the moral world is not primarily of any one person's making.[61] The circumstances in which any person must act arrive as the culmination of the effects of judgments, which countless persons and communities have made over time and in space. The moral world is one of cumulative moral judgment; it is shot through with sin and guilt, beginning with the sin of the first parents. In such a world, human actors do not always have the luxury of making obvious choices between right and wrong. Instead, Bonhoeffer argues, "responsible action must decide . . . between right and right, wrong and wrong."[62] Moreover, God calls persons to discern God's ongoing calling to responsible action, a calling not beholden to fixed, universal moral laws.[63] The choice between right and right and wrong and wrong is responsive to the moral demands of the context of action as well as to the requirements of God's call.[64]

In Bonhoeffer's account, then, vocation, responsibility, and representation are inextricably linked. Responsible, representative action begins with and willingly enters into the sinful, messy spaces of the world not to despise them but to claim them as redeemed in Jesus Christ. Vocation, then, is the particular "place of responsibility," where one "responds to the call of Christ and lives responsibly."[65] In the context of vocation, Jesus Christ claims a particular space that "in every respect . . . is burdened with sin and guilt" and yet is the place in which God's redeeming work unfolds. Vocation is not just about one's work. Instead, it is about one's work in relationship to the ultimate calling to grace and redemption that is God's intention for the world. Vocation, like the particular setting in which it unfolds, is sinful and broken. Like the ultimate calling, vocation is also the "place" from which sin and brokenness are transformed and transfigured toward redemption and reconciliation.

While God's calling to act responsibly in a particular historical moment and vocational setting is specific and varied, it is not absolutely unbounded. Bonhoeffer argues that there are "limits" demarcating responsible from irresponsible action. Responsible action is limited both by human "creatureliness" and by the responsibility of the neighbor. As finite creatures, human beings are limited in understanding and moral foresight. One must seriously consider what outcomes are possible, which are likely, and what their moral status is; and one must also take into account one's own motivations for action. Moreover, persons are not utterly liable for one another. Others have their own responsibility, and to deny them this is to deny them agency, to patronize or infantilize them. Once one has negotiated these limitations, one is free to "completely surrender" a "deed" to God "the moment it is carried out."[66] These two limitations on responsibility affirm the permission God gives to human beings to be human (rather than superhuman) in the moral life. This permission exists, Bonhoeffer writes, because in Jesus Christ God became human, bearing responsibility for human beings within the horizon of human limitations.[67]

Bonhoeffer never fully fleshed out the connection among responsibility, representation, and political vocation. But his framing of the moral life in terms of these categories helpfully situates the moral complexity of political vocation. On one level, the political vocation is, Bonhoeffer recognizes, one of straightforward representation: political officials represent smaller communities to larger ones in a political system. In that role, the official enters into morally complex situations not entirely of her devising and makes morally fraught decisions. Political officials represent the good of their constituents by taking responsibility for them as best they can. But the moral complexity in which political officials do their work carries with it the burden of sin and guilt. To respond to any political circumstance is to work within parameters established by prior faulty and rebellious human judgments that politicians inherit as the precondition of their own judgments. In that sense, one takes on sin in the way of Christ by stepping into the political vocation. When they are doing their work well, political officials do the best they can to take responsibility for their constituents. In doing so, however, they inevitably run up against the limits, as Bonhoeffer calls them, established by their own creatureliness and by the creatureliness of others.

In taking the form of Christ in the world, persons become fully human in the midst of the unresolvable moral tensions of vocational work. Bonhoeffer provides a theological account of the integrity of vocation as a distinctively human encounter with the world, one that honors the relationship between human flourishing and the encounter with human limitation.

In taking responsibility for others, persons navigate complex moral space in which they must choose between relative goods and relative evils. For Bonhoeffer, what makes a choice good is not ultimately that it constitutes human action but that it constitutes God's action. Responsible actors discern, act, and give their action over to God, "who looks upon the heart, weighs the deeds, and guides history."[68] Vocation requires an ongoing negotiation of human finitude. In that negotiation, human beings find themselves in God.

To run up against human limitation in the responsible representation of the neighbor's good, and to bear the consequences for doing so, is to participate in God's redeeming work. Bonhoeffer argues that just as all participate in the sin of the first parents, so too must all participate in the redeeming work of Jesus Christ. Vocation in general, and the political vocation in particular, is where this participation happens. In Bonhoeffer's framing, Jesus Christ is the warrant of political vocation as a venture into human finitude on behalf of others. Though inevitably broken, and even at times unbearably broken (as Bonhoeffer's own life attests), the political vocation discloses the shape of God's redeeming work in the world.

Vocation, it has been argued, is a "framing" of work that holds in tension the institutional conditions of moral meaning and practice—the "reality" of work "on the ground," on the one hand, and the aspiration to work toward God's redemptive project, on the other. In his reflections on vocation and politics, Bonhoeffer teaches that this tension cannot simply be resolved. In a fallen world, there is no way of perfectly aligning the demands of ordinary moral sensibilities about right and wrong, the morally laden demands of work in any vocational location, and God's calling to take responsibility for the neighbor's flourishing. In the political vocation, as in any other, one must step into the "twilight" that the "historical situation casts upon good and evil," act, and then take responsibility for what comes of action. Precisely in the tension, in the brokenness and complexity of vocational work, the crucified Christ is present. In that place, human experience is genuinely real and profoundly moving.

The presence of Christ in the tensions of vocational work constitutes the integrity of political vocation. Every vocational setting is fractured in some morally resonant way—every setting, that is, requires difficult moral judgments between "right and right" and "wrong and wrong." The question, then, is, what are the moral contours of political space? What conditions account for the distinctive shape of the political vocation? Said differently, in what ways is the political vocation characteristically fractured? To the extent that vocation is a pilgrimage, that it entails a process of moral formation in the world, what are the characteristic pathways of that pilgrimage in the context of political life? The next three chapters explore the institutional conditions that characteristically shape political work—the moral terrain, as it were, of the vocational pilgrimage in the setting of political life. The final three chapters consider the ways in which a theological understanding of vocation responds to these conditions, reforming political work in the context of God's work.

3

VOCATION AND FORMATION
IN POLITICAL SPACE

For Bonhoeffer, a political vocation is one in which a person represents one political community to another, a smaller political community to a larger one, for example. The work of representation entails taking responsibility for that which one represents. The politician, then, takes responsibility for the community he or she represents. In Bonhoeffer's understanding, taking responsibility is itself a formative moment. In taking responsibility in the context of vocational work, a person takes the form of Christ in the world. To take the form of Christ is to work for the good of others and to accept whatever consequences such work may entail. It is also to become, to use Max Weber's phrase, "genuinely human." Political vocation, then, is Christ taking form in the world in the vocational place where persons take responsibility for the political communities they represent.

Bonhoeffer attends to the meaning of formation in the context of political vocation, offering a theological account of moral agency. Moral agency is the power to do work that is morally relevant or resonant in some way. Moral agents are persons, communities, or even nonhuman creatures that exercise moral agency. For Bonhoeffer, to be a moral agent is to take the form of Christ in a particular vocational setting. His account opens questions about what this formative process looks like on the ground.

Vocational work happens somewhere, in some institutional space; thus, the formation that vocational work involves is also located in that space. Institutional spaces are not simply empty containers for work; they give shape to work. Institutions, those patterns of action by which human beings organize social life, structure work by providing the norms and practices that determine what good work is, how it is done, and what it means. In doing so, institutions form persons capable of doing work well, however that is understood. Institutions, in short, make moral agents, and moral agents make and remake institutions as they exercise agency. Persons learn how to be customers when they participate in the marketplace, soldiers when they participate in the military, citizens when they participate in political life, children of God when they participate in faith communities, and so on.[1] In institutionally differentiated societies, persons are formed in multiple ways in multiple institutional settings.[2] These multiple formations, moreover, do not always cohere. A primary challenge of the moral life is determining how multiple and often-competing moral formations should hang together.

Institutional space therefore conditions moral formation. To understand how persons are formed in political work, therefore, one must know something about the structure of political space. The term "political space" has so far been used casually. To offer a formal definition, political space is any institutional location in which persons or groups do political work, that is, where they use power to achieve politically relevant ends in cooperation or competition with others who are doing the same.[3] The work of a U.S. senator happens in Congress and in the local communities the senator represents. The work of a community organizer happens in a broad-based community organization and in local government settings. The work of an ordinary citizen happens in a ballot box, at a rally, or at a fund-raiser. Political spaces determine what political work is done and which moral agents (senator, community organizer, ordinary citizen) are required to do it.

Institutions arrange political space in a variety of ways, according to different norms, practices, and procedures. The Senate is (ideally) a deliberative space, in which motions are made, arguments are offered to defend or challenge them, and measures are adopted or rejected as a result. A formal parliamentary process, of the sort one finds in *Robert's Rules of Order*, is used to structure the work done in such a space. Rallies constitute a different kind of political space. Rallies, as the name suggests, are meant to celebrate a particular candidate, party, or political effort. More deeply, rallies are about identity. They are opportunities for persons to acknowledge, celebrate, and commit themselves to a set of values that hold them together in a political community. The voting booth is yet another kind of political space. Quiet and earnest, the voting booth (again, ideally) fosters a citizen's private encounter with his or her own political conscience. That encounter issues in an act of political judgment that the citizen exercises as she casts her ballot. All political work, then, is institutionally conditioned.

Institutional spaces also condition moral agency, determining what morally relevant powers are appropriate in space, how to exercise them, and toward what ends. The focus here is on the way political institutions condition *political* agency, a particular kind of moral agency. Political agency means the capacities, skill sets, and practices (e.g., debating, compromising, mobilizing people and resources) efficacious in particular political spaces (a state legislature, a city street, a public hearing, etc.) in which agents engage in forms of political work (policy activism, community organizing, legislating, campaigning, protesting, etc.).

Political spaces structure political work and political agency variously. The work of the Senate, for example, is to govern through crafting and adopting legislation. One can exercise various forms of political agency to do that work: debate, compromise, and taking a stand, among others. In the voting booth, by contrast, ordinary citizens do the work of selecting political officials who will represent them. Citizens sometimes also do the work of governing in the voting booth, when, for example, they vote on a referendum. To do this work, citizens exercise the agency of deliberation and judgment. Political marches constitute yet another kind of political space. They aim both to shape public discourse and to influence political judgment. They require organization, the orchestration of public drama, and the use of prophetic speech.

The differences among these spaces are not necessarily radical. Voting happens on the floor of the Senate just as it happens in the voting booth. Deliberation happens in both spaces as well. But the meaning of work is different in each political space, in part because political spaces determine what counts as good work in them. To do good work in the Senate is to govern through passing legislation. How legislation is passed also matters. One could advance legislative measures against rival constituencies in zero-sum competition. Alternatively, one could compromise, developing legislation that a multipartisan coalition could endorse, ensuring that all factions get some (but not all) of what they want.

The meaning of good political work, then, depends in part on the shape any political institution gives to it. Institutions determine what agents are supposed to do, what kinds of agency they may exercise, what counts as acceptable and unacceptable behavior, and what virtues agents should strive to cultivate.

POLITICAL SELVES: MORAL FORMATION IN POLITICAL SPACE

Given the variety of political spaces, the very notion of "political life" is deceptive. The term posits a conceptual container holding all political configurations and activities in a particular cultural and historical setting. It is often conceptually useful to imagine such a container. Political life, however, is really a collection of diverse institutional settings that create multiple political spaces in which political agents do different kinds of political work.

Just as political spaces are multiple and diverse, the formative processes that happen in them are similarly multiple and diverse. Political spaces set the terms of moral formation. Persons who enter political space to pursue vocations in politics must be shaped into political selves capable of doing effective political work in the contexts in which they are working. There is, then, no such thing as a single political self. There are instead "multiple civic selves," multiple ways in which political selves are formed in different political spaces.[4] Ultimately, the focus of this analysis is most relevant to political officials who exercise formal political power by virtue of their location in government institutions. The official is the first figure examined below. An analysis of two additional political selves, the political activist and the citizen leader, and the political spaces they inhabit, will more clearly illumine the kind of self the political official is.

THE POLITICAL OFFICIAL: THE POLITICAL SELF AS PUBLIC SELF

Michael Ignatieff, the Canadian political theorist, politician, and public intellectual, is known both for his meteoric rise in Canadian politics and his even more precipitous fall. Ignatieff, a longtime expatriate academic in Britain and the United States, was coaxed into Canadian politics in 2006. By 2008 he was leader of the opposition and by 2009 leader of the Liberal Party of Canada. In 2011 both Ignatieff and his Liberal Party suffered an unprecedented electoral defeat, in which Ignatieff lost in his own constituency and his Liberal Party won the fewest seats in its 144-year history. The loss was devastating. But, because of his experience, Ignatieff is, among contemporary political theorists, uniquely positioned to reflect on the practice of politics, and particularly on "success and failure in politics."[5] In his public reflections, Ignatieff is in turns appreciative and affirming of the democratic tradition and also critical of the "degraded politics" of the contemporary moment in which opponents attack one another to avoid constructive debate.[6]

Ignatieff suggests that the national political stage requires the formation of a dual self. One aspect of the dual self, he writes, is the "private self," the self one has always been. The other is the "public self," a "strategic" presentation of the self that empowers the politician's political agency. The politician is not permitted the pleasure and luxury of spontaneous speech. Instead, the public self fits a "filter between [one's] brain and [one's] mouth," vetting all thoughts in light of the requirements of public speech. Dissimulation, Ignatieff suggests, is one of the filtering mechanisms. Good politicians do not lie, he is careful to say. But politics does require that politicians tell incomplete truths, particularly when speaking with the press or political opponents who are likely to manipulate one's public speech to advance their own ends.

The challenge, Ignatieff contends, is to hold the distance between the private, authentic self and the public self without confusing the two. As he negotiated the demands of Canadian politics, Ignatieff could feel the distance between the two closing: "as you submit to the compromises demanded by public life, your public self begins to alter the person inside." Soon, Ignatieff writes, "I had the disoriented feeling of having been taken over by a doppelgänger, a strange new persona I could barely recognize when I looked at myself in the mirror." Politicians must assiduously defend the private self, Ignatieff argues, lest they lose the private self to the politician's smile, the "fixed rictus of geniality politics demands of you."[7]

Politics on the national stage, in Canada and in any other modern democratic polity, Ignatieff is saying, requires the production of a public self that is a morally ambiguous creation. The good politician is able to form a public self while also maintaining a private self, holding each in tension with the other. The public self is a necessary condition of political agency, the capacity to act to achieve politically relevant ends. But the public self is not a sufficient condition of authentic selfhood; indeed, the public self may even be inimical to it.

The negotiation of the public self is related to the negotiation of political space. National politics happens just as much under the bar light as it does under the spotlight. Elected political officials move in and out of the formal political spaces in which their office is situated (Congress, Parliament, etc.) and into the more informal political spaces their formal office represents. For Ignatieff, the politician's capacity to navigate local political spaces is essential to a thriving democracy. Democracy is necessarily connected to place; as such, it demands "local knowledge" from politicians. "As soon as democracy loses its connection to place," Ignatieff writes, "as soon as the location of politics is no longer the union hall, the living room, the restaurant and the local bar . . . we'll all be in trouble."[8] Such local spaces, he argues, require that politicians be as candid as possible with their constituents, giving "straight answers to straight questions." In local political spaces, in which politicians work to build relationships with constituents, the distance between the public and private selves must be allowed to narrow, if not collapse.

Ignatieff's experience in Canadian politics helpfully illustrates how the political self is formed in the institutions of national politics. For Ignatieff, the official's political self is a dichotomous being, comprising both a public self and a private self. The public self is the political agent, enmeshed in the rigors of political life, a self-projection intended to contain as much of the moral ambiguity of political work as possible. The private self, by contrast, is the authentic self, the identity of the person behind the political agent. Ignatieff's public self resists the formative dynamics of political space by insulating the private self from the moral ambiguities of political life.

THE POLITICAL ACTIVIST: THE POLITICAL SELF AS PUBLIC FACE

The model of the public self and private self in tension represents one way in which political spaces form persons to participate in them as political selves. Political activists are formed as public selves in a somewhat different way. Sadie Fields, the former chairperson of the Georgia Christian Alliance, has been called "perhaps the most influential and polarizing woman in Georgia politics."[9] In 2004 Fields led a successful effort to pass an amendment to the Georgia state constitution banning same-sex marriage. Fields characterizes political activism as "combat."[10] Recounting her early activism, Fields says, "The first time you're in the fray of war, the fear is greater than the next battle." Though she continues to experience fear in the midst of political combat, Fields says that her opposition ultimately strengthens her resolve. Christian activists, she says, "do not operate out of fear, we operate out of faith. What opposition does eventually is make me even more dedicated and resolute."[11] Fields experienced politics as a battlefield, a space instilling fear in the newcomer. For Fields, politics is "combat," requiring that a person fearlessly enter the "fray" of political battle. Those who wish to pursue a political vocation must therefore develop a particular set of marshal virtues. A person must possess courage, resolve, and fearlessness to be a good activist.

Fields' activism also moved into political spaces that are less like a battlefield and more like a "mission field." In the 1990s Fields canvassed cities and towns across Georgia to build support for her work with the Christian Coalition. She discovered that it was difficult to mobilize some conservative Christians for whom religion and politics should not mix. Fields worked hard to present herself as a person who cherishes and can represent the values that conservative Christians care about and who can therefore be a leader worth following into unfamiliar political territory.[12] She wanted to "put a public face on the organization." That public face was of a "grandmother with a computer trying to start a revolution."[13]

The political self that Fields developed as an activist was the public face of the Christian Coalition, the organization she represented both to elected political officials in Georgia and to local communities. The public face of the political activist is something of a Janus face; it needs to represent the legitimacy and strength of the Christian Coalition in both directions. To elected political officials, Fields had to show that the Christian Coalition legitimately represented the interests of a sizable and serious voting constituency. That side of the public face showed a steely resolve that sustains engagement on the political battlefield. To local Christian communities, Fields showed another side of the Christian Coalition's public face, one that affirmed a particular understanding of southern, white, "traditional" culture, a trusted representative of the values of conservative Christian voters.

Activists carefully modulate their public face to respond adequately to the requirements of the political spaces in which they work. The public face of the political official has a representational function as well, both representing the office to diverse constituencies and representing constituencies in parliamentary spaces. In representing the organization's public face, the activist also attempts to earn legitimacy for the organization, both in the governmental bodies that might pursue the organization's agenda and in the communities that might support the organization. Unlike elected officials, who enjoy a measure of legitimacy by virtue of their election and office, activists must continually assert and maintain legitimacy, even as they represent constituents and advance their agendas.

THE CITIZEN LEADER: ORDINARY CITIZENS IN COMMUNITY ORGANIZING PROJECTS

Like activists, participants in broad-based community organizing projects do not occupy formal political office, nor are they situated in political spaces as rigorously delineated and normed as formal political offices. Instead, community organizing projects work to empower ordinary citizens to constitute political spaces that facilitate cooperative efforts for the common good.

In many organizing models, this space-constituting work is done through an intentional and structured process of cultivating public relationships. In public relationships, persons identify their own interests and the interests of those communities they represent, imagine how these interests can be advanced, and hold one another accountable for the work of doing so. The political space created in the ongoing development of public relationships allows ordinary citizens to work together to realize what the French political theorist Alexis de Tocqueville called "self-interest well understood," an understanding of "the individual advantage of citizens" oriented to "work for the happiness of all."[14] In building public relationships, citizens discern how their own self-interest works with the self-interest of others to advance the common good.

Community organizing creates opportunities for ordinary citizens to craft a public identity. Organizations like the Industrial Areas Foundation (IAF) use a one-on-one, face-to-face meeting format called a "relational meeting" to develop public relationships.[15] In "one-to-one" meetings, each conversation partner works to articulate her own self-interest and to explore the self-interest of the other. One-to-one conversations create space for persons to express the passion motivating their self-interest, often taking the form of anger around the violation of justice.[16] By participating in larger group discussions, called "house meetings," citizens experience themselves as public persons, capable of leading or being led by others in a community effort.[17]

A final space that community organizing projects create is the "accountability session" or "action meeting." The accountability session is a public meeting in which public officials are invited to pledge their support for the community organization's agenda. Accountability sessions are conducted on terms set by the community organization rather than the elected officials invited to participate in them. Public officials are required to listen to the citizen organization make its case for its agenda: "when the presentations have been made, and an IAF leader poses a yes-no question to [an official], the point is to determine whether the official is going to make a public commitment of some kind."[18] Accountability sessions are "rituals of commitment." Public officials are invited, in the presence of their constituents, to pledge their commitment to the community organization. A pledge of support marks commitment that can be evaluated and called to account. Failure to support the organization, however, constitutes grounds for future opposition to the official.

The political spaces created in community organizing processes—the one-to-one meeting, the house meeting, and the public action—form citizens who do more than vote in elections. Citizen participants in community organizing projects exercise a form of active citizenship in advancing their own projects for the common good and by holding public officials accountable to them. Community organizing projects at once create political spaces in which persons practice citizenship in a particular way and form participants to be skillful public leaders in them.

The public self formed in the context of community organizing is different from the public self of elected office. The political official's public self is accountable to myriad and often competing interests of constituents, allies, and opponents. For the political official, the public self is a production calculated to respond to these conflicting claims on his or her political power. As Ignatieff shows, the political official must work both to create the public self and also to hold that self in tension with the private self, lest the latter be subsumed under the former.

In the work of community organizing, ordinary citizens become public selves skilled in leading like-minded neighbors around matters of shared concern.[19] The publicity of the self in the community organizing context consists in a citizen's capacity to articulate from her own experience the passion she has about an issue that the organization is committed to advancing. Public selves in this setting are those to whom others look to represent the group's interests skillfully.[20]

The distance that separates these two public selves is related to the relationship each bears to political power. The work of political officials like Ignatieff is to wield political power to achieve political ends, advancing the interests of his constituents and party. Political officials represent and are accountable to diverse constituencies (such as, for example, community organizations) that want to determine how the official uses his power and to what ends. The political official's public self empowers the official to negotiate these competing claims while insulating the private self from the slings and arrows of political battle.

Ordinary citizens who participate in community organizing projects are oriented differently to political power. In democratic polities, ordinary citizens wield power not primarily to achieve political ends but to hold representatives accountable. They are among those who attempt to influence how officials use their power. The public leader is a development of the ordinary citizen, one who is ready to step out of the ballot box as the primary political space in which the citizen exercises agency. Public leaders working through community organizing projects take responsibility for agendas that reflect the aims of local communities and therefore advance shared goods.

Homogeneous Space: Political Space as Public Forum

Complex accounts of the relationships among space, agency, and formation are few and far between. In philosophical and theological literature, political space is often imagined homogenously, as though there is only one meaningful political space, and thus also one relevant conception of the political agent and of political agency. That homogeneous political space is what might be termed the "public forum," in which citizens, through reasoned debate with one another, articulate and defend proposals for law and policy affecting common goods. The primary form of political agency in the public forum is discourse, the use of rational argument to explain, analyze, and persuade others of a proper course of political action. In the framing of the political forum, citizens are not soldiers battling against adversaries whose goals and aspirations they hope to defeat. They are instead conversation partners, encountering one another in the public square as collaborators at best, and intelligible, even sympathetic, adversaries at worst.[21] Conversation partners will not agree on everything and may not even agree on fundamental commitments. But citizen–conversation partners are open to learning about the views of others and, in doing so, hope to learn more about their own commitments as well.

Liberal political theorists are skeptical that political societies can be organized around a single "comprehensive doctrine," as philosopher John Rawls famously called it. A comprehensive doctrine is a coherent, if not systematic, religious, philosophical, or moral worldview that any reasonable person might endorse.[22] Modern societies are marked by a pluralism of mutually incompatible comprehensive doctrines. Rather than organizing political society around a particular comprehensive doctrine, liberal theorists attempt to discern social and political structures sufficient to empower all persons to pursue whatever understanding of the good life they desire.

Some liberal theorists understand public discursive spaces to be ones in which citizens work out basic political arrangements that best empower persons to live out whatever understanding of the good life they think is most appropriate.[23] Others understand the scope of deliberation to extend farther down, forming the very basis of political legitimacy.[24] In deliberative theories of democracy, public deliberation is the means by which citizens identify common ends and the means to secure them.[25] In these theories, therefore, to enter into public discursive space is to be ready to participate in conversations with others in order to identify and advance shared social and political arrangements.

Public deliberation as a form of political agency poses some problems for citizens of faith. Religious citizens, some political theorists have argued, must be willing to speak in a moral language that is publicly accessible, so that others can understand and meaningfully engage them in public conversation. This means that Christian citizens will need to translate explicitly theological claims about the public good into a publicly accessible moral language that secular conversation partners can engage. In the 1990s and the first decade of the twenty-first century, philosophical and theological debates about how religious citizens ought to participate in public conversation in the liberal public sphere were manifold.[26] This debate seems to have settled in recent years.[27]

Still, the liberal conception of political space as a public forum, and its emphasis on political agency as discursive agency, has had a profound impact on contemporary theological understandings of political life.[28] Certainly, the public forum has much to recommend it as a model of political space. It enlivens and empowers citizenship, giving a voice to all who want one. All persons are to have access to public conversation or should at least have freely chosen representatives whose contributions reflect the views of their constituencies. Constructive public argument allows citizens to get to know one another. Conversation partners are required to take one another's contributions seriously, to imagine what it might be like to see the world through the eyes of others. Public argument is therefore a resource for political solidarity, and solidarity, in turn, builds up political community. A community of solidarity is better able to withstand disagreement, even impassioned, visceral disagreement in difficult times, and to weather other crises that threaten to weaken or undo community bonds.[29]

In both political theory and theology, the idea of the public forum functions as a norm: it describes how political space ought to function, not indeed how it actually does function. In practice, of course, political spaces do not often accommodate meaningful public debate and deliberation. As the discussion above indicates, political spaces are multiple and complex. They require different forms of political work, accommodate a range of political practices, and form political agents and political agency in a variety of ways.

A potential problem with the public forum framing is that it does not account for the normative complexity of political space. It can give the impression that political spaces are deficient to the extent that they do not accommodate public deliberation and debate. The public forum view can foreclose the possibility that political practices that do not feature or foreground deliberation are somehow morally deficient. The suggestion that political spaces are best when they encourage deliberation enforces a kind of normative hegemony in political space. This normative homogeneity extends in two further dimensions, to a particular view of the political agent as the scholar-citizen and of political agency as cooperation through public speech.

Homogeneous Agency: The Scholar-Citizen and Political Cooperation

It is difficult to imagine any form of political agency that does not involve some discursive aspect. Many political practices, particularly in the context of modern democratic polities, involve saying something implicitly or explicitly to a broader audience in order to articulate, argue, and persuade.[30] Aside from the ubiquity of discursive political practice, what makes public discourse appealing in philosophical accounts is that it affirms rationality as a criterion of human dignity. In the modern West, rationality has emerged as a dominant criterion of human identity.[31] To be human, in this view, is to use one's reason to recognize, analyze, and respond to the world. Rationality has also emerged as a primary marker of political agency in modern political life. To participate in public discourse is to deploy reason publicly to articulate, advance, and defend political arguments.

Immanuel Kant's 1784 essay "What Is Enlightenment?" is a classical statement of this modern vision of political agency. In the essay, Kant argues that enlightenment is a process of intellectual maturity in which persons learn to think for themselves, without, that is, the "guidance of another."[32] Kant asserts that the necessary condition of enlightenment is the freedom "to make *public use* of one's reason in all matters."[33] One uses public reason as a "scholar," or a "man of learning" (*ein Gelehrter*), particularly in the context of the scholar's "writings."[34] The public use of reason is addressed to a "reading public" (*das ganze Publikum der Leserwelt*). The reading public is an audience of persons who are similarly learned, capable of critical thought, and concerned about the ongoing enlightenment of an entire people. In the Kantian picture, the "man of learning" uses reason to address matters of public concern before a similarly capable audience.[35]

In the frame of the public forum, citizens take on a scholarly identity. Like the scholar, the citizen's primary role is to formulate ideas about politically relevant issues and to present public arguments others can engage. Giving and asking for reasons, scholar-citizens work together to determine which ideas best capture the public good. Kant's scholar-citizen captures the modern notion that reason is the ground of human dignity. In political settings, citizens affirm the dignity of one another as rational creatures through the public use of reason.

As a norm of political agency, public discourse recommends a particular form of political power. Political power entails two kinds of capacities: the capacity to achieve desired ends and the capacity to influence the will of persons and communities to work toward the achievement of such ends. Political power ordinarily has an instrumental quality in that it is always aimed at achieving some goal. That political power has an instrumental quality does not mean that it always entails instrumental relationships in which parties use one another to achieve desired ends. The framing of political agency as public discourse intends to maximize political encounters in which persons reach mutual understanding in order to cooperate.

Scholars, in other words, strive to treat one another as ends, not as means to ends, in political space. In the frame of public discourse, politics aspires to move toward mutual understanding, even if consensus is not always possible in practice.

The scholar-citizen's task is not only to articulate and advance public arguments; it is finally to persuade others to act on them. Public discourse might lead to robust forms of cooperation, in which all parties agree to work actively on a common goal. It might instead lead to more passive arrangements, in which all parties consent to allow a lead party or parties to advance a shared goal, or at least a tolerable one. Short of consensus, public argument could lead to some form of compromise, where each party gets some of what it wants and must tolerate some of what it does not. In short, public discourse aspires to mutual understanding in order to prepare the cooperative exercise of political power.

The framing of the public forum therefore emphasizes cooperative uses of political power to nurture politically relevant relationships while also achieving politically relevant ends. In giving and asking for reasons to support and critique public arguments, a citizen learns about her conversation partner: her passions and motivations, her fundamental commitments, and her desired goals. When the time comes to move beyond mutual understanding toward persuasion—when, in other words, the instrumental purposes of politics emerge more clearly—interlocutors, now understanding something of their conversation partner's worldview, can enter into the other's concerns and engage her empathically. If persuasion is necessary, conversation partners will have a better understanding of the kinds of ends others might support in light of their fundamental commitments.

The cooperative use of political power, especially when it begins with discursive attempts to reach mutual understanding, lends itself to theological affirmation. In the examination of the other's point of view, interlocutors acknowledge the inherent dignity of the other as a person who bears the image of God. For theologians who understand that human identity is constituted in relationship to others, discourse is an obvious medium for creating and nurturing such relationships.[36] Cooperative political action that emerges from relationships forged in mutual respect and understanding can be interpreted theologically to anticipate the political realities of the kingdom of God.

While most forms of political agency have a discursive dimension, some do not create mutual understanding as an initial step or do not aspire to use political power cooperatively. Political power is sometimes used competitively, as when one constituency aims to achieve its objectives, even at the expense of another constituency's aims. Political power can even be used aggressively, to force one constituency to act according to the wishes of another.

Competition is one form of the binding use of political power. In political competition, vying parties aspire to win in fair and legitimate contests of political will. Having won, the victorious parties may enforce their will, even if such enforcement contravenes the desires of the losing parties. But the binding use of power following victory will be understood to be legitimate, all other things being equal, since the use of power is in this case the result of fair competition. The winning party cannot proceed unchallenged; there will always be follow-up competitions in a properly functioning political system. And if the winning party oversteps its mandate to enforce its will in the meantime, it might weaken its position in ensuing political contests.[37]

Compared with cooperation, competition might seem to be a deficient modality of political agency. Political theories that value public argument in the public forum as a primary mode of political agency see in it a way of affirming the dignity of others as autonomous, rational agents capable of reasoned deliberation about issues that matter most to them. To engage in public argument is to take seriously the arguments of others as worthy of consideration and response and thus to acknowledge others as fully empowered political agents. While fair and legitimate competition entails affirmation of the political standing of competitors, it need not entail a robust respect for the other's political agenda. Indeed, deep disrespect might fuel political competition. From the perspective of theories that value cooperative discourse as the primary modality of political agency, political competition can appear to be a deficient or second-best strategy. It is to be used when all else fails, allowing political actors to proceed in the political process but falling short of full affirmation of opponents as worthy political agents.

Michael Walzer suggests that political competition is worthy of moral approval. He argues that deliberative theories of politics have not adequately accounted for a range of political practices beyond deliberative communication. This is in part because deliberative theories primarily value a particular conception of cooperative reason that aims at consensus. But politics has other "values," too, Walzer writes, and these are "often in tension with" deliberative reason: passion, commitment, solidarity, courage, and competitiveness.[38] Several political practices have discursive elements but often do not foreground cooperative or public deliberation: political education, organization, mobilization, demonstration, statement, debate, bargaining, lobbying, campaigning, voting, fund-raising, corruption, "scut work," and ruling.[39]

All of these practices are marked by "a permanence of conflict" rather than a trajectory toward reasoned consensus by way of public discourse. They show that politics includes cooperation but is in large measure about power, conflict, and victory. For Walzer, "rational agreement" is not realistic in politics. Instead, what is needed is a modus vivendi to ensure that political conflict is constructive. In deliberative democratic theories, reason is the locus of human dignity. These theories hold that we honor the inherent value of other citizens when we engage in reasoned deliberation in public spaces. But passion, Walzer argues, is just as much a source of human dignity.[40] Passionate competition is a form of recognition and respect, just as much as reasoned deliberation.

Walzer's suggestion—that passionate politics is aimed at competition rather than cooperation—poses a challenge to theologians. It is not obvious what theological sense should be made of politics understood, as Walzer says, as an "endless return to disagreements and conflicts, the struggle to manage and contain them and, at the same time, to win whatever temporary victories are available."[41] In Walzer's conception, the emphasis on cooperation relationally, prominent in the public forum framing, is undercut. The focus here is not on the persons involved but on issues and, importantly, on winning the issue at hand. Winning might mean that one side uses another as a means to the end of winning. In quid pro quo compromise, for example, one side might yield its opposition to some issue on the condition that competitors yield their opposition to a different issue in return. Each side uses the other as a means to different ends without changing position or point of view.

For Walzer, competition is the condition of political agency that makes the setting of political vocation more like a battlefield than a public forum. But for theologians the political battlefield can be a difficult space to inhabit. Theologians want to affirm relationality, rather than partisanship, as a standard of human flourishing; the inherent dignity of persons, rather than instrumentality, as a standard of moral worth; and cooperation, rather than competition, as a standard of good political work. But politics is often a competition resulting in victories, or partial victories, rather than a cooperative undertaking resulting in consensus and mutual understanding. Theologians have yet to offer a nuanced theological framing of political space that includes an adequate treatment of political competition—of political space as "battlefield," to echo Sadie Fields' characterization. The battlefield metaphor, as Fields uses it, captures the moral complexity of political competition. Other features of political space make it morally treacherous terrain. The next chapter examines these in detail.

4

THE MORAL AMBIGUITY OF POLITICAL SPACE

CONTRACTING WITH "DIABOLICAL POWERS"

Weber warns that political vocation requires a constant struggle against corrupting powers: "He who lets himself in for politics, that is, for power and force as means," Weber writes, "contracts with diabolical powers and for his action it is *not* true that good can follow only from good and evil only from evil, but that often the opposite is true."[1] There is something about politics, he recognizes, that has the potential to corrupt otherwise good persons. That something—whatever it is—is not inherently evil; otherwise, it would be odd to suggest that politics could be a vocation at all. But it is "diabolical" in that it conspires to pull persons in the direction of evil.

One way of thinking theologically about the "diabolical" quality of politics is to consider how politics plays on human limitations. Christian traditions have long held that human limitation emerges in the complex interplay between finitude and sin. To invoke finitude is to signal the ways in which human experience is defined by the limitations that make human beings human, what defines them, in other words, as creatures rather than the Creator. Human beings are vulnerable rather than invincible. Human lives have limited rather than infinite duration. The human capacity for moral perception is also limited: human beings cannot know with certainty what the outcomes of their actions will be and thus cannot eliminate the possibility of unintended consequences. Additionally, humans are bound to act within and to respond to situations not entirely of their own making. They have limited powers to change situations that are already morally complex, if not tragically constituted.

Christian traditions also hold that human beings are limited by the condition of sin. Because of sin, humans find themselves unable to know the good perfectly. They do not, in other words, know the good the way that God knows the good. Human beings can, perhaps, catch glimpses of the good in the structure of nature, in the discernment of God's call, or through internal moral awareness. At best, however, humans know the good only impartially. Moreover, because of sin, they are unable to will the good perfectly, even when they think they know what the good is. Christians have used the term "pride" to describe the human tendency to overstep the boundary between creature and Creator, to put themselves in the place of God and imagine that they exercise sovereign control over creation as God is often understood to do. Thus, human beings, Christian traditions have held, sin when pride induces them not to do what they ought to do in the attempt to be like God.

Politics is diabolical in the sense that political dynamics play on human limitations in the overlapping dimensions of finitude and sin, pulling political agents in the direction of evil. But whatever it is that makes politics "diabolical" also makes politics what it is. The features and dynamics that distinguish politics from other institutional settings, in other words, constitute the very same conditions that pull political work in the direction of evil.

Political space is therefore morally ambiguous. To say that political space is morally ambiguous is to say that it imposes a set of conditions that, when combined with human limitations, potentially undermine the good. The word "potentially" is key here: moral ambiguity does not exist if a situation or set of conditions is, in any ordinary moral calculus, plainly evil. A way of signaling the potential undermining of the good is to say that the good is elusive. Moral ambiguity, then, exists when the good is elusive.

In theological perspectives, the good is elusive in the combined effects of finitude and sin. The features that distinguish political life from other institutional settings conspire against human limitations in a number of distinctive ways. Politics plays on the limits of moral perception, requiring political agents to make decisions between competing goods, resulting in inevitable sacrifice, and to make decisions vulnerable to unintended consequences. It also plays on the limits of human agency: political agents often cannot change the situations in which they work and to which they must respond. Yet responses are required. Politics also plays on pride: political power tempts political agents to overstep appropriate boundaries of human agency, inducing what Augustine called the *libido dominandi*, the drive to wield dominating power, to rule rather than to be ruled.[2]

The encounter with moral ambiguity in the political vocation raises questions about the status of the political self. The idea of vocation, it has been argued, is not only about work; it is also about the worker, since vocation entails a formative process for the self. In the framing of vocation, work changes a person: a person becomes a particular kind of self by virtue of participating in vocational work (the "pilgrimage" of vocation). Vocational work therefore makes a person into the self that God intends for her to be.

If vocational work entails a pilgrimage, a process of self-formation, and that formative process is in some way morally ambiguous, then the self formed in that process will need to negotiate moral ambiguity. It is even possible that the political self, the self that emerges from the formative process political vocation entails, will itself be morally ambiguous. The political self develops skills and qualities of character that are not straightforwardly good, at least not from a theological point of view. These qualities include dissimulation, aggression, and self-promotion, among others.[3] Such a self also becomes adept at using the moral logics that politics requires, including compromise, negotiation, and competition, which might, in some circumstances, strike some as morally problematic. Finally, political selves aspire to achieve goals that will be contentious, such as laws and policies that some constituencies will endorse and others will oppose.

The relationships among political vocation, self-formation, and moral ambiguity pose a challenge to theological reflection. Christian theologians typically want to affirm unconditional rather than instrumental relationality, cooperation rather than competition, humility rather than self-promotion and glory, a wariness of coercive power rather than a readiness to use it, truth telling rather than dissimulation, and the like. It may be difficult for theological framings to validate the political self. The challenge for a theology of political vocation, then, is to respond theologically to the complex and morally ambiguous ways in which political spaces form political agents. To respond to this challenge, an account of the moral ambiguity of political space is necessary.

Anatomy of the Unsavory

A word often associated with politics is "unsavory." Politics is often imagined to be an inherently corrupting endeavor. Politics makes for bad persons because it pushes good persons to act in morally problematic ways. Therefore, politics, it is sometimes thought, is one way to live life poorly. The idea that politics is unsavory constitutes a commentary on the moral contours of political institutions. To say that any institution has "moral contours" is to signal that there are features that distinguish it from other institutions and that these features have a normative quality. The features that make politics what it is encode commitments about the nature of agents and of agency, appropriate forms of moral reasoning, and a sense of the proper aims of judgment and action. For the purposes of this analysis, these features can be divided into five categories.

The first has to do with questions about who agents are in political space and what qualities make them good or evil. The word "virtue" is used to describe discourse about these questions. The second has to do with the kind of power that political agents exercise, what they can or cannot do in political space. The word "agency" signals considerations of these matters. There are questions, third, about the moral logic that governs actions. The term "moral logic" refers to the calculus by which persons make morally relevant decisions in particular institutional spaces. Fourth, moral ambiguity arises around the question of the proper ends of action in political space, what political agents should aim to do with their power. Considerations of this kind are indicated by the word "ends." Finally, there are questions about the moral status of nonpolitical goods that exercise influence in political spaces. A key consideration here is the role of money in politics. Money is properly an economic, not a political, good. It is at home in the marketplace, not political space. Of course, the influence money can buy bears on political space anyway. This influence must be assessed.

To summarize, five features account for moral ambiguity in political space: (1) political virtue, (2) political power, (3) political logic, (4) competing goods and loyalties, and (5) money in politics.

Agents: The Moral Ambiguity of Political Virtue

When Sadie Fields talks about how her fear was conditioned from one experience of political battle to another, she is in effect describing a process of moral formation. That is, she is describing not only an experience of doing work but also a process of becoming a certain kind of self as a result of doing such work. In her first encounters with political opposition, Fields suggested that she was a fearful person. But then she learned to chasten her fear by anchoring her public presence in her faith, enabling her to operate out of faith instead of fear. Fields casts herself as a person who has become capable of readily engaging her faith in her political work.

Such a capacity is a morally relevant one because it informs how one comports oneself in political life. Political vocation is not simply a task, not just a kind of work one does. It is rather simultaneously task *and* training, a process by which one becomes a certain kind of self. Through training, a self develops certain qualities of character—virtues, in other words—that empower her to do the work, in this case, political work. Christians have long recognized faith as a central theological virtue. If Fields' reflection about her political activism is truthful, it would seem that operating out of faith rather than fear indeed attests to the attainment of virtue (the virtue of faith). But it is far from clear that work in politics conduces to the development of virtuous character.

Many prominent political personalities demonstrate the ambiguity of political character. Lyndon Johnson was in many ways an effective politician, one of the savviest political operators, and also one of the most morally ambiguous figures ever to hold the office of the president. In the immediate aftermath of President Kennedy's assassination, Johnson was faced with questions about when and how he should be sworn in as president and how the public at large would view the legitimacy of his ascent to the office. Johnson had an additional concern: he wanted Robert Kennedy, the president's brother and attorney general, to endorse his succession to the presidency.

To these ends, Johnson called Kennedy only minutes after the latter was informed of his brother's death. Johnson had several questions about what should happen next: Could he be sworn in in Dallas? What was the exact wording of the oath of office? Who could administer the oath?[4] As attorney general, Kennedy was the highest-ranking legal officer in the administration, thus qualified to answer such questions in such a crisis. But any number of officials could have answered them. And Kennedy, as Johnson well knew, was in a place of utter shock.[5] Johnson understood that by answering these questions, Kennedy would in effect be endorsing Johnson's immediate succession to the presidency, demonstrating continuity, order, and stability in that process. Johnson would also have the endorsement of a rival.

By all accounts, Kennedy did not explicitly endorse Johnson's plan to be sworn in in Dallas. But he also did not oppose the plan, which, Johnson reasoned, would constitute assent should questions be raised later.[6] The oath was famously administered in Dallas on Air Force One. Johnson further succeeded in persuading officials that the former first lady, Jackie Kennedy, should be at his side during the swearing in.

Lyndon Johnson's response to President Kennedy's assassination offends ordinary sensibilities about how persons should treat others in a time of tragedy and grief. Johnson quite straightforwardly exploited the situation in Dallas for his own political gain. Even more striking is the ease with which Johnson seemed to transition into the role of political operative in a moment of tremendous political and emotional crisis. Whatever else can be said about Johnson's behavior in this moment, he did make a tactically sound political judgment. His move was effective in helping him to secure his hold on the presidency. Johnson saw what political advantage required in the moment, and he responded accordingly. One might condemn Johnson for his callousness and selfishness, but one must also conclude that he exercised the political virtues of shrewdness and calculation.

Different conclusions can be drawn here about the nature of the political virtues. It might be that politics requires persons to develop qualities of character, like shrewdness and calculation, that are vices rather than virtues, and thus no persons should strive to develop them. Or it might be that qualities like shrewdness and calculation, which enable persons to excel at politics, are virtues in political spaces but are incompatible with virtues persons might develop in other institutional spaces. That is, the qualities required for successful political leadership are not vicious per se, but they might preclude the development of other kinds of virtues. The Renaissance political theorist Niccolò Machiavelli suggests precisely this.[7]

For Machiavelli, the Christian and the republican virtues are fundamentally at odds with one another.[8] The ancient religions of Greek and Roman antiquity located the highest good in the context of the world, training persons to develop worldly virtues and esteem worldly goods. The ancient religions, which ground the republican tradition, value "greatness of spirit, strength of body, and all other things capable of making men very strong." Christian religion, by contrast, teaches persons to despise the world, to strive toward an ultimate good that resides beyond the world. "Our religion," Machiavelli writes, "has glorified humble and contemplative more than active men." Christianity values as the "highest good" virtues like "humility, abjectness, and contempt of things human." For this reason, Machiavelli saw a relationship between the political corruption of his age and the worldly indifference that Christianity teaches: "this [Christian] mode of life thus seems to have rendered the world weak and given it in prey to criminal men, who can manage it securely, seeing that the collectivity of men, so as to go to paradise, think more of enduring their beatings than avenging them."[9]

Machiavelli and theologian Stanley Hauerwas have much in common in seeing intractable differences between Christian and worldly virtues, except that Hauerwas suspects that the latter are not virtues at all. Hauerwas is famous for his thesis that the church is the most authentic polity. The church's mandate is to witness to the broken political communities of the world that stand in need of redemption. The church forms persons in the virtues befitting of a redeemed people, "peaceableness"—the rejection of violence—chief among them.[10] For Hauerwas, the liberal democratic regimes of "the world" are morally bankrupt because they claim there are no shared stories, practices, or virtues in relationship to which citizens constitute a common identity as a community. The Christian vision, by contrast, offers a vision of what it means to be genuinely human.

Drawing on Augustine, Hauerwas argues that only when Christians learn disciplines of attention to place and enduring patience possible in the "alternative political ethic" of the church will they be worthy of authentic participation in radical democratic movements. For Augustine, Hauerwas explains, the politics of the world trades on a death-denying "rhetoric of glory"—the desire of the Roman statesman to cheat death by memorializing personal glory. The politics of glory is therefore driven by the fear of death. Augustine posits the martyr as an important counterfigure to the Roman statesman. The glory of the martyr is not a heroic but a "reflected glory—a reflection of the glory of Christ."[11] Freed from the fear of death, the martyr faithfully discloses the glory of Christ's lordship over life and death. Thus, the martyr works with patience and humility born of an awareness that political being is finally the work of God, not of human beings. Precisely these political virtues—patience and humility, Hauerwas asserts—are needed to sustain radical democratic politics.[12]

Machiavelli and Hauerwas both affirm that the virtues of the worldly and heavenly polities do not cohere, but for utterly different reasons. For Machiavelli, the Roman statesman possesses a "greatness of spirit" that sustains a politics of strength and worldly achievement. Hauerwas, by contrast, recommends the Augustinian martyr who yearns to reflect the glory of God in the practices of patience and humility, two virtues of the heavenly polity where citizenship is most real. The question is whether the Machiavellian-Hauerwasian disjunction between the politics of this world and those of the next constitute the only way to think about Christian engagement in political life, whether the choice to be Christian entails a choice to reject political engagement in political spaces that require formation in worldly political virtues.

Agency: The Moral Ambiguity of Political Power

Weber argues that the distinctive means of modern politics is legitimate violence, the coercive power of the state to compel its citizens, on pain of punishment, to order their lives according to law and policy.[13] To choose a political vocation, Weber contends, is to make "a pact with the means of violence."[14] Wielding coercive power, politicians must claim responsibility for the consequences of wielding it. But, Weber asserts, this could have dire consequences for the ultimate disposition of a politician's soul. Political power has a dark side, even when it is the legitimate violence of state power.

The politician threatens to endanger the "salvation of his soul" no matter what he does.[15]

Political life in modern states, in other words, is distinguished by a particular understanding of political agency. Agency per se is the power to bring about or change states of affairs. The term "moral agency" signals that the exercise of agency is in some sense morally relevant, that the forms agency takes or the ends its exercise brings about relate in some way to an understanding of the good and the good life. Political agency, in turn, is a kind of moral agency; it is moral agency exercised in political space. Political agency, as it is defined above, includes the capacities, skill sets, and practices efficacious in particular political contexts in which agents engage in forms of political work (e.g., policy activism, community organizing, legislating, campaigning, protesting).

Political power is morally ambiguous, owing to three features: it is binding, legitimate, and amplified. Political power is binding to the extent that it requires participation in states of affairs. Of course, this binding quality is not an exclusive modality of political power. Indeed, political agents also cooperate in a number of different ways. But binding political power is distinctive in political space because it is, within limits, a legitimate form of power in that space; it is sanctioned in political space.[16] Thus, laws are, in essence, formal and, all things being equal, legitimate expressions of binding power that create norms and structures for social life. One can choose to break the law if one wants—but then one should expect to be punished by the state in some way as a result. In many other institutional settings—families, religious communities, educational institutions, health care systems, and so on—binding power certainly exists, but it is not understood to be normative in the same way. By contrast, binding power belongs to the "moral logic" of political life, the calculus by which one may make legitimate decisions about the exercise of agency in political space.

Political power is also an amplified form of power. Amplification means that the consequences of exercising political power are weightier than consequences of exercising agency in other regions of the moral life. Ordinarily, individual persons intend their actions to have limited effect on others. Political actions, however, are intended to shape the lives of entire human communities (towns, cities, states, nations, etc.). Of course, the exercise of power in any form and context to achieve particular ends is always susceptible to unintended consequences. To the extent that unintended consequences of the exercise of political power are problematic, they are even more so because of the amplified quality of political power.

Amplification, it is important to note, is not only the effect but also the precondition of political agency. When politicians make decisions about law and policy, they are responding in part to the amplified effects of precursor policies and laws that have shaped the lives of human communities, for better or worse. Politicians, in other words, are often required to intervene in messes not of their own making. Indeed, in any region of the moral life (not just political life), persons must make decisions about situations not of their own making. But the amplified character of political power intensifies the complexity of situations in which politicians exercise political agency. Moral judgment, in short, is always broken, but this brokenness takes on additional weight in political life because it is amplified through the tremendous power that politicians wield.

Of course, political power is not always experienced as imposing. Laws and policies, even though they require persons and communities to live their lives in certain ways, are often appreciated, at least tacitly. They are, however, sometimes opposed rather than appreciated. When they are, opponents and proponents alike feel the binding force of the law—opponents because they must live their lives according to coercive standards they do not endorse and proponents because they might feel conflicted about the discord that laws they support have created.

In May 2012 North Carolinians voted on a referendum to amend Article XIV of the state constitution to limit "the only domestic legal union" valid or recognized in the state to marriage "between one man and one woman." In addition to banning state-sanctioned marriages between persons of the same gender, the amendment was thought to undercut a broad set of legal protections available to both same-gendered domestic partnerships and married heterosexual partners.[17] In the end, 34.66 percent of the North Carolina electorate participated in the May 8, 2012, election in which voters passed the referendum.[18] A fraction of these voters voted for the amendment. In effect, a relatively small percentage of the North Carolina electorate voted to restrict civil rights and legal protections for their LGBTQ neighbors and, potentially, also for themselves. Right or wrong, the exercise of political power of this kind is imposing: some North Carolina citizens have forced others to go without legal protections that they themselves enjoy.

The North Carolina amendment, it should be noted, was later overturned by a U.S. district judge, opening the way for same-sex marriages.[19] But the North Carolina example illustrates the way binding force, ironically, can attenuate the bonds of political community even as it enforces them. Certainly, LGBTQ citizens felt excluded from full participation in the political community as a result of the 2012 referendum. They would likely have claimed that the referendum represented an abuse of power; citizens who voted for the referendum, of course, would have argued the contrary.

There are also situations in which politicians use power in clearly dubious ways to achieve ends that most would endorse. Politicians, in other words, must sometimes do wrong in order to do right, getting their hands dirty in the process and raising the possibility that they have abused power. In June 2013 former National Security Agency contractor Edward Snowden, through a series of articles published in the UK newspaper *The Guardian*, revealed classified information about National Security Agency and Central Intelligence Agency spying programs. Snowden's leaks revealed U.S. surveillance operations in European capitals and spying on European Union officials. Snowden was subsequently charged on several counts relating to the illegal disclosure of classified information.[20] Asked about Snowden's disclosures at a press conference in Tanzania, President Obama, without confirming allegations of spying, explained that countries, even allied countries, spy on one another.[21] Spying is just what countries do, Obama asserted. At the time of this writing, the full import of Snowden's whistle-blowing is uncertain. It seems as though the U.S. government has engaged in activities that violate a range of international norms, if not laws, and has perhaps even compromised the privacy of U.S. citizens.

Obama's defense of spying turns on the claim that it is practically an acceptable activity in all capitals. Any outrage that European heads of state have expressed about the Snowden affair is, therefore, disingenuous. An implicit claim is that spying is also necessary: it helps to protect U.S. interests. That argument is probably true in some ways. The questions of which interests, whose interests, and at what cost to relationships with allies abroad and political liberties at home need to be clarified before a judgment can be made about whether the ends justify the means. That is precisely what the debate about the Snowden affair is about. Still, the administration might argue that it sometimes needs to act dubiously in order that good may come. That is what politics requires, some would say, and if one cannot stand the heat, then one should get out of the kitchen.[22] Of course, the fact that questionable moral behavior happens in politics is not enough to excuse it, even if the setting of such behavior in political life does mitigate it in some way.[23]

Dirty hands would be less problematic if political power were not so seductive. There is something about power, as Augustine and others have noted, such that it tends to become an end in itself. Political power can operationalize human pride, theologians have long argued: it induces human beings to transgress the boundaries of human agency, putting themselves in God's position. Power that is binding, amplified, and legitimate runs head-on into the weakness of will that human beings experience by virtue of their enmeshment in sin.

Moral Logic: The Moral Ambiguity of Instrumentality and Political Expediency

The moral logic of politics, the calculus by which morally relevant decisions are made, is an instrumental one. Whatever else they are doing, politicians exercise power to meet certain needs and realize certain desires.[24] Politics, in short, is about "getting it done." Moreover, moral agency and moral logic go hand in hand. Politicians get it done by using forms of binding instrumental power.

The problem of dirty hands is an example of how politicians use the instrumental logic of politics properly toward the achievement of particular ends, while at the same time using political power, the characteristic means of politics, in morally ambiguous ways in the name of getting it done. Another kind of moral ambiguity arises around political expediency, when instrumentality conflicts with political principle. Politicians often say they are committed to principles that guide their political judgment. Presumably, principles are not to be compromised even if they stand in the way of achieving desired ends. But as the dominant moral logic in political space, instrumentality makes demands that pressure politicians to compromise their principles. Expediency names the implicit demand that the moral logic of instrumentality be honored in political life, even at the expense of principled commitments.

Whatever else they want, politicians almost always also want to maintain and expand their political power. Without power, politicians cannot achieve anything. Politicians therefore are always concerned about their hold on power, a concern that takes the form of asserting and defending, in explicit and implicit ways, a politician's claim on the office he holds. There are often times when politicians have to decide whether they will risk compromising or even losing entirely their hold on political power for the sake of defending a principled commitment. Politicians must, in other words, determine how flexible principled commitments are and when their principles draw a line that cannot be crossed.

On September 14, 2001, three days after the September 11 attacks, Rep. Barbara Lee, then the Democratic congresswoman from California's Ninth District, voted against the congressional Authorization for Use of Military Force (AUMF). The AUMF empowers the president to prosecute what has since been called the "War on Terrorism."[25] The AUMF passed 420–1; Lee's was the only no vote. Lee's opposition to the AUMF was not only incomprehensible but also enraging to many of her colleagues, her constituents, and to the American electorate broadly. Lee viewed the power that the AUMF conferred on the president to be too broad, a "blank check . . . to attack anyone involved in the Sept. 11 events—anywhere, in any country, without regard to our nation's long-term foreign policy, economic and national security interests, and without time limit."[26] She urged Congress and the American people to "step back for a moment," fearing that the actions of Congress in that moment of emergency could "spiral out of control."[27]

Lee agonized over the vote. She believed she had to vote against the AUMF, but her conscience was unsettled. On September 14, 2001, just before the House was scheduled to vote on the bill, Lee joined her congressional colleagues at a noon prayer service at the National Cathedral. The priest, reflecting on Jeremiah 31:15, urged the legislators gathered in the congregation to consider the consequences of their action. The words of the priest's prayer resonated with Lee in a way that provided a rationale for her decision. The priest prayed, "as we act we not become the evil we deplore."[28] In her speech on the floor of the House later that day, Lee cited the words of that prayer.

Lee took a stand on principle. In the early days of the War on Terror, she paid for it in hate mail. Congressional colleagues worried that Lee's stand would compromise her ability to work on issues that mattered to her in Congress.[29] Looking back on the American response to terrorism since September 11, however, Lee's concerns seem plausible. With thousands of combatants and civilians dead and injured in the intervening time, the indefinite detention and even torture of persons assumed to be enemy combatants, revelations of privacy violations by American intelligence agencies, among other developments, Lee's decision to vote against the AUMF could be seen as prescient.

In politics, lines sometimes need to be drawn, even when drawing them risks the loss of political capital, or even the loss of political power altogether. Drawing lines around nonnegotiable principles is not an easy task. Indeed, politicians are known for drawing lines and then crossing them. President Barack Obama found himself caught between politics and principle in the wake of the *Citizens United* decision.[30] In that decision, the Supreme Court ruled that while corporations and other entities cannot make direct contributions to political campaigns, they can engage in unlimited fund-raising and spending on political messaging to support or oppose candidates. For many, this ruling represents a decisive entry of money into political life.

Early in his presidency, President Obama opposed the interests of money in politics by consistently supporting campaign finance reform. For a time, Obama discouraged his supporters from contributing to super PACS, partisan political entities funded by corporate and private monies. But in the 2012 campaign, the president found himself in a tough spot.[31] He was caught between his desire to advance campaign reform (and, more generally, to distance himself from big business), on the one hand, and, on the other, his need to raise campaign funds on a political landscape redefined by *Citizens United*. By the summer of 2012, Republicans were closing in on an $800 million fund-raising effort, fueled to a great extent through the collateral support of conservative super PACs. Ultimately, Republican fund-raising efforts pressured Obama to back off his commitments to campaign finance reform.[32] In the end, the Obama campaign began actively to encourage donations to liberal super PACS.

In this situation, Obama chose politics over principle. One can ask whether such a decision makes Obama a hypocrite. Obama, of course, would argue that *Citizens United* changed the rules of the game, and he therefore needed to change his strategy. Obama cannot be entirely to blame for playing a game the rules of which he did not devise. His tactical hypocrisy might be viewed as a relatively minor moral failing, particularly in political space, in which a politician must do the best he can to uphold his principles and still perpetuate his tenure in office.

There are indeed times in political life when it is appropriate to draw lines and burn bridges, but these times should be very judiciously considered. The moral logic of instrumentality demands results, and results can only be generated with power. Political space requires both, but having both often entails collisions between principled commitments and strategic expediency.

Ends of Action: The Moral Ambiguity of Competing Goods and Loyalties

Politicians often make hard choices between competing political goods. Caught up in the commitment to competing goods are often commitments to multiple and competing constituencies. Politics is never simply the straightforward representation of a particular constituency's interests. A constituency may want goods that are incompatible with one another. Politicians may want goods that their constituents do not. Politicians must inevitably choose which goods they want most to pursue and thereby also the constituencies with which they will ally themselves.

Ruling in the 2013 case *Shelby County v. Holder*, the Supreme Court effectively struck down a provision in the Voting Rights Act of 1965 known as "preclearance." Preclearance requires state and local governments, mostly in the American South, which have long legacies of discriminatory voting practices under Jim Crow legislation, to submit to the Justice Department any proposed changes to election procedure for review and approval. In this arrangement, the federal government effectively controlled the ability of certain state and local governments to determine local electoral procedures.

Since the 1960s, preclearance was justified as an extraordinary measure of congressional power to ensure that historically disenfranchised communities have fair access to the electoral process. *Shelby County* ruled that preclearance was based on outdated assessments of electoral discrimination in the affected areas and that, therefore, Congress cannot justify its extraordinary assertion of power over against state and local governments and its unequal treatment of the same.[33] Thus, the Supreme Court judged that the measures of the Voting Rights Act constitute an unwarranted assertion of congressional power, undermining both the principle of federalism (that state and local governments should have maximal authority over their own jurisdictions) and state equality (that the federal government should treat the states equally). The court did not overturn all of the checks that the Justice Department has vis-à-vis jurisdictions affected by the Voting Rights Act. The ruling will, however, make preclearance more difficult.[34]

Shelby County v. Holder puts both the Obama administration and Republican congressional leadership in difficult political positions. The president is obligated to uphold the law, as made by Congress and interpreted by the Supreme Court. But the Obama administration wants to champion the rights of disenfranchised citizens. For that reason, in the summer of 2013, on the heels of the *Shelby County* decision, the Justice Department took steps to enforce preclearance in Texas. The grounds on which the administration would enforce preclearance after the Supreme Court overturned it, however, were unclear.[35]

Republican congressional leaders also find themselves in a political quandary. Republicans have lost ground to Democrats in garnering the support of minority electorates. Minority communities tend to identify with the Democratic Party, and their allegiance has made a difference in electoral support of Democratic candidates in recent national elections.[36] Some even say that Republicans need more minority support if the party is to be relevant in the future.[37] Out of a desire to maintain and expand power, Republicans want to develop a more expansive voting base among minority communities. But state sovereignty is also an important Republican principle. Local constituencies that strongly identify with the Republican Party are suspicious of far-reaching federal authority and defend the sovereignty of state and local governments. Some state governments, with strong Republican support, have passed voter identification laws reinscribing, opponents argue, minority discrimination that the Voting Rights Act was meant to protect. The Voting Rights legislation, in its original configuration, opposes some of the core principles that Republicans defend. Republicans are faced with a hard decision, then, either to support proposed overhauls of the Voting Rights Act, which could alienate the Republican base, or not and risk continuing to distance minority voting constituencies.

Important differences distinguish the interests of the Obama administration and Republican congressional leadership in this situation. The Obama administration is in a tough spot because it is tasked with enforcing an interpretation of the law that it does not want to enforce. Executive responsibility and political loyalty work at cross-purposes, in that the administration's duty to enforce the law (by abandoning preclearance) contravenes what the administration takes to be the salutary political objective, to protect the civil rights of minority citizens by enforcing a review of state voting procedures.[38]

Republicans, meanwhile, want to attract a minority electorate while also empowering local and state governments with as much autonomy (over against the federal government) as possible. Here it seems, at least on the face of things, that they cannot have it both ways. To advocate for what state and local governments want—to be able to determine for themselves their own election practices—threatens to reinforce a dominant image of the Republican Party, namely, that it does not care about historically disenfranchised constituents. That tension might be mitigated if state and local governments in the American South were unquestionably responsive to the concerns of minority voters. But many Southern jurisdictions have put into place stricter voter identification requirements, a measure that smacks of Jim Crow-era discrimination to many minority voters.

Republicans face a hard decision and may need to choose between two competing values—defending the political sovereignty of local communities that may, now or in the future, arrange their electoral procedures unfairly or defending the citizenship rights of persons historically excluded from the political process.[39] Also in the mix is political calculation, having to do with which course will most preserve and expand the Republicans' political power and their capacity to govern.[40]

Republicans are faced with a kind of hard decision regarding political loyalties that politicians negotiate all of the time. Politicians step into situations not of their own devising, in which obligations to multiple communities compete, so that politicians find it difficult to advance all of them simultaneously. Hard decisions are not, of course, unique to political life. In moral life generally, persons sometimes find themselves in situations not of their own devising, in which they cannot have all of what they want. The distinctive manifestation of this problem in political life is bound up with the desire to maintain and expand power while also advancing a political agenda.

External Pressures: The Moral Ambiguity of Money in Politics

Money is a condition of political space that both enhances and constrains political agency. It is an external condition to political life in the sense that money belongs properly to a different institutional setting, the marketplace. In the marketplace, money is used to mediate relationships of exchange between persons or other entities. Persons engaging in exchange relationships in the marketplace understand that they are getting something from others by virtue of giving something to them. The moral logic of the marketplace is quid pro quo—the this-for-that—and money facilitates the functioning of this moral logic.

Dominant understandings of properly functioning democratic polities do not imagine that political life is simply reducible to the marketplace or that political relationships are simply reducible to quid pro quo exchanges. Some would say that there is a role for quid pro quo in political life. "Horse trading" and forms of political compromise depend on it. But few think that political goods, such as public education; police, fire, and other emergency services; infrastructure; and the like, should simply be for sale, accessible only to those who can pay a competitive price for them.[41] Instead, politics is thought to provide for the common good of a political community, even if some of its members would not be able to secure the goods of political community were they for sale to the highest bidder in a marketplace.

Still, money finds its way into politics. Politicians need money to fund their campaigns. Private citizens give money to support preferred political agendas and candidates. Sometimes citizens are so influential in their financial support that they are not only able to support preferred political agendas and candidates; they are able to use their wealth to set political agendas, select candidates, and, more or less directly, determine policy. The *Citizens United* decision is seen by many to have removed some of the important legal barriers that prevented money from exercising an undue influence on politics. The debate around the *Citizens United* decision belongs to a larger set of concerns about the proper role money should play in political life.

In the U.S. context, there are many signs that money may be exercising an undue influence on politics.[42] Fund-raising is never far from the minds of members of Congress, who spend an estimated 30–70 percent of their official time raising campaign funds.[43] Newly elected representatives learn at their orientation meetings that they should expect to spend three to four hours each day on "fundraising and call time," along with additional time attending fund-raising events.[44] To do the work of fund-raising, both parties have established off-site call centers, since congressional representatives may not conduct fund-raising activities from their Washington offices. With congressional representatives spending so much of their official time in call centers raising money and therefore absent from the legislative chambers, some commentators are concerned that they are distracted from the work of deliberation that undergirds the legislative process.[45]

Politicians anxious about raising money can lean on lobbyists for help. But there is an obvious problem with this: forms of lobbying that provide financial support to politicians threaten to introduce the logic of quid pro quo into political relationships. Lobbyists channel money to politicians, and politicians feel obligated to provide something in return. There is little evidence that politicians directly exchange votes for money in most cases. The law strictly regulates lobbying to prevent quid pro quo from infiltrating political life. Though the work of lobbying is not overtly transactional, lobbying may create a culture of gift exchange in political systems, obligating politicians to return favors in due time, if not directly for gifts given and services rendered.[46]

Wealthy citizens may also use money to exercise undue influence on politics. John Snow, a politically conservative Democrat, was a former judge and a three-term state senator from North Carolina. In the 2010 election, Snow was thought to be the likely winner as an incumbent candidate against a relatively unknown challenger. But he lost the election by the narrowest of margins. Losing was one surprise; another was the ferocity with which Snow was attacked in seemingly unending TV advertisements.[47]

Snow's opponent was not his downfall. What Snow did not see coming at him was the political will and financial resources of Art Pope, chair and CEO of Variety Wholesalers, and multimillionaire exponent of conservative politics in North Carolina. Real Jobs North Carolina and Civitas Action, two organizations heavily funded by Pope, were responsible for the attack ads that seemed to make the difference in Snow's defeat. In the 2010 election cycle, civic organizations funded by Pope targeted twenty-two Democrats, of whom Snow and seventeen others were ultimately defeated.[48] By 2012, owing in part to these victories, Republicans had seized control of the

North Carolina General Assembly and the governor's office for the first time in nearly 150 years and made sweeping changes to the tax code, voting rights, and education policy, among other areas.[49]

Even before the *Citizens United* decision loosened restrictions on corporate political donations, Art Pope very skillfully channeled his money into political arenas. Pope has helped to found several 501(c)(4) organizations ("social welfare" groups[50]), like Real Jobs North Carolina and Civitas Action, to which he has channeled large amounts of corporate and family foundation money with the benefit of a tax write-off.[51] In this way, Pope and his family have contributed in the neighborhood of $40 million to state politics in the last decade.[52] Pope joins David and Charles Koch, George Soros, and other singularly wealthy citizens who exercise tremendous, some would say disproportionate, influence on American politics through financial contributions. In all of these cases, money can function as a condition of political space that threatens to import the norms of market exchange into political life, rendering the goods of politics among those that can be bought and sold.

In sum, political space is morally perilous for four related reasons. First, secular political virtues do not neatly cohere with the Christian virtues, and may even be incompatible with them. Second, political power is a morally ambiguous instrument. Political power is a modality of binding force: it is warranted and constrained by law, but political power is ambiguous nonetheless. Third, politics requires an ongoing negotiation of moral principle in light of the demands of expediency. Politicians need to know when to take a stand on inflexible principles and when principles can be compromised to maintain or advance political power and interests. Finally, money in politics threatens to transform political goods accessible to all citizens into market goods accessible only to persons willing and able to pay the price.

❈ ❈ ❈

This chapter has argued that the moral contours of political space structure human limitation, creating the conditions for moral ambiguity. As a framing of work, vocation proposes to take seriously the institutional structures in which work happens, since institutions belong to God's redeeming work in the world. To "take institutional structures seriously" does not imply an unqualified endorsement of institutional life. Seen in the framing of pilgrimage, in which God's project of redemption begins to unfold in secular time, vocation both honors the particularity of human institutions as redemptive spaces, and, to the extent that institutional settings fall short of God's redeeming purposes, vocation also works to reform them in that direction.

5

THE JOURNEY OF POLITICAL VOCATION

So far, the argument has suggested (1) that the institutional settings constituting political life are distinctive from other settings in institutionally differentiated societies; (2) that what distinguishes political life from other institutional settings are the "moral contours" of political space—that is, the particular ways in which political space makes morally relevant demands on the formation of agents, the structure of moral agency, the "moral logic" appropriate to political work, and the relevant ends of action; and (3) that, at the same time, the features that distinguish political space from other institutional spaces create the conditions for moral ambiguity when viewed in theological perspective.

The task of this chapter is to argue, from a theological point of view, why political vocation is meaningful, even though it is steeped in moral ambiguity. The chapter fleshes out a claim that has so far functioned as a premise of the argument: that institutional life, in the context of which any vocation is intelligible, participates in God's project of redemption that is unfolding in the world. As such, the moral contours that define institutions, distinguishing them from others, are theologically significant, even though, under the conditions of sin and finitude, they generate moral ambiguity. A theological understanding of vocation as a "calling in" place values the institutional shape of vocational work. Such an understanding holds that part of the way God redeems creation is in and through the institutional structures that organize social life and provide the conditions of human flourishing. The task of this chapter, then, is to describe how the moral complexity of political space is theologically significant and thus why politics is a worthy calling.

To develop this argument, this chapter fleshes out a claim about the structure of vocation already introduced in the discussion above. The idea of vocation acknowledges a creative tension between the structure of work as it is and the structure of work as it should be. Vocation, in other words, acknowledges a tension between the "is" and "ought" of work. As a "calling in" place, vocation affirms that patterns and practices that constitute political institutions have theological integrity—that there is a distinctive way that political institutions facilitate possibilities for human experience and configure the encounter with human limitation. Thus, it will not do simply to disparage political institutions because they require an engagement with moral ambiguity. In this world, there is no way of configuring political work to resolve moral ambiguity. The idea of vocation, however, aspires to pull political work in the direction of God's redemptive project. Vocation, in other words, tugs at the tension between the "is" and "ought" of political work, nudging it in the direction of God's project with a full recognition that this Godward movement always happens in the space of moral ambiguity.

THEOLOGIES OF INSTITUTIONAL LIFE

Christian theologians and ethicists have long offered guidance for political processes in the modern world, recommending laws and policies that they think reflect God's intentions for human persons and communities and critiquing others that do not. However, Christian political theology mostly lacks careful theological attention to the institutional structures of political life. It has also largely failed to reflect on the meaning of good political work with an awareness of the moral complexity of political institutions. Christian political theology has failed, that is, to consider how the institutional shape of political life informs a theological understanding of what politics is and what it means to do the work of politics well.

Some theologians think this is no failure at all, taking the view that political institutions in liberal democracies are inherently deficient.[1] It is no mystery why theologians might come to such a conclusion. Not only do worldly political institutions seem to be functionally ineffective; their very structures appear to be morally corrupt when viewed from a theological perspective. The discussion above addressed the use of binding power by one constituency to get what it wants in ways that preclude other constituencies from getting what they want. At other times, politics entails a compromising of principle to secure goods. Politics may also involve the use of dubious means to achieve desired ends. The presence of money in politics, finally, threatens to reduce political life to a marketplace, if it has not already.

To take seriously the institutional structures of political life, one would need to imagine that they are theologically significant, even though they are often functionally deficient and always morally ambiguous. One would need to think, that is, that there is theological value in the distinctive patterns of meaning making and practice that make political institutions what they are and make them different from other institutional settings.

To ascribe theological value to political institutions is to understand that they play a particular role in God's project of redemption. Strands of both Protestant and Catholic traditions have affirmed such a view. An exponent of the Social Gospel movement, Walter Rauschenbusch recognized that different institutional settings—family, church, educational systems, political life, and the economic order—have distinctive roles to play in the unfolding of the kingdom of God in the world. With the exception of the recalcitrant marketplace, each of these "orders," he argues, has already been "Christianized," remade in the ethic of Jesus Christ, one that emphasizes democratic equality, human actualization, and brotherly love. For Rauschenbusch, institutions in the modern world are plural, each making a distinctive contribution to social life. But all are converging on a single moral logic uniting all in the purposes of the kingdom of God.[2] Though each institutional setting has different roles to play in the unfolding kingdom, all will be patterned on a uniform social ethic. Rauschenbusch's theology of institutional life therefore constitutes a kind of reductionism: ultimately, the moral contours that distinguish institutions from one another will give way to a uniform moral logic in the unfolding of the kingdom of God in the world. In Rauschenbusch's perspective, the distinctive moral contours of any institutional space only mark the distance from the coming kingdom. As God redeems, institutionally located moral pluralism will dissolve.

Reinhold Niebuhr's Christian realism offers another kind of reductionist analysis of modern institutional life. Writing through two world wars, the Great Depression, and the Cold War, Niebuhr's story about institutions is very nearly the opposite of Rauschenbusch's. For Niebuhr, human beings have a limited capacity for self-transcendence, empowering individuals to some extent to set aside egotistical self-interest to practice the other-regarding love of Christ. That capacity for limited self-transcendence is obviated whenever persons form groups (nations, industrial organizations, racial groups, etc.) united by common interests. Groups, Niebuhr argues, have no capacity for self-transcendence and therefore no capacity to critically evaluate and hold in check their own "egotism." Left unchecked, groups are sure to pursue their own self-interest over against the interests of others. The only way to hold collective egotism at bay is to use the coercive force of law and policy to restrain groups and to find ways to pit group interests against one another. Institutional settings, especially economic and political life, are arenas in which the balancing of competing powers plays out. Unlike Rauschenbusch, institutions for Niebuhr are not being perfected in the social ethic of Jesus. But institutions are theologically significant as the necessary condition of the work of justice, understood as the incremental and ever-elusive movement toward the ideal of Christ's other-regarding love.[3] Institutional life for Niebuhr represents a deterioration of human agency; it is the context in which human sin is most obviously manifest. For Niebuhr, there are no theologically significant distinctions among institutions. All institutions evidence the divisive dynamics of group egotism. All therefore require the use of counterbalancing power to establish a modicum of justice in the world.

Beginning with Pope Leo XIII's encyclical *Rerum Novarum* (1891), the body of literature known as Catholic Social Teaching (CST) sets out the most sustained theological treatment of modern institutional life available in Christian literature. Informed by the natural law tradition, CST holds that human institutions play a critical role in providing for the common good, the "sum total of those conditions of social living, whereby men are enabled more fully and more readily to achieve their own perfection."[4] Modern social life is distinguished by ever-increasing opportunities for social configuration as well as an ever-deepening awareness of the interconnectedness of all human communities with one another and with the earth. Because of institutional complexity and the realities of interdependence, providing for the common good becomes more and more challenging.

CST's fundamental commitments to the values of dignity, solidarity, and participation motivate its response to the conditions of institutional complexity and interdependence in the modern world. The commitment to dignity affirms that human beings are created in the image and likeness of God and therefore have inherent value. The institutions of family, church, polity, and economy honor human dignity when they provide resources required for human flourishing. States should therefore develop regulatory measures ensuring the fair and sufficient provision of social goods. CST further affirms solidarity, the basic human need to exist in community with others, and therefore argues that institutions should work to empower persons to participate fully in social life.[5] Finally, in the dual principles of subsidiarity and socialization, CST develops a framework for responding to institutional complexity. According to the principle of subsidiarity, the work of social provision should be left to the smallest possible associations capable of effective provision.[6] At the same time, the principle of socialization holds that social configurations must be adequately regulated if they are to provide for the common good.[7]

Unlike Rauschenbusch's Social Gospel or Niebuhr's Christian Realism, CST validates as a social good the multiplication of distinctive institutional arrangements that modern social life makes possible. Institutional differentiation reflects the human drive to live in community with others. The development of new social arrangements—in markets, political settings, and civil society—is therefore a good that corresponds with theological commitments to human dignity, community, and local moral agency. The problem with social and institutional differentiation is that it renders more complex the project of providing for the common good. Modern societies need to provide enough freedom for persons to organize themselves as they see fit, but they also need to provide enough structure so that human organizations effectively serve, rather than undermine, the common good. CST both prescribes broad norms for the arrangement of social life in institutionally differentiated societies (of the sort described above) and also tackles specific problems in different institutional settings (polity, marketplace, family, etc.).

Rauschenbusch, Niebuhr, and CST represent three different theological strategies for addressing the condition of institutionally determined moral pluralism in modern social life. Rauschenbusch and Niebuhr both take reductionist approaches, albeit drawing radically different conclusions. Rauschenbusch attempts to reduce the moral pluralism generated in multiple institutional settings to a moral monism that arises with the kingdom of God. Niebuhr, by contrast, reduces institutional pluralism to the interrelated dynamics of sin and theological anthropology. Institutional differentiation for Niebuhr is not per se theologically interesting. All institutional settings, no matter how distinctive their patterns, are occasions for group egotism. Niebuhr, then, reduces institutional differentiation and the moral pluralism that it generates to a more fundamental, theologically resonant condition in the structure of group egotism. CST, finally, provides a theological framework that acknowledges and values institutional complexity in modern societies. It does not aspire to reduce such complexity to a more fundamental condition. Rather, CST recognizes institutional complexity as a potential human good and provides both broad guidelines for structuring institutional life and responses to specific social issues so that institutions are more reliably oriented to the common good.

All three theologies of institutional life contain valuable insights for the way Christians should think about the modern world. Rauschenbusch provides a faithful account of the trajectory in which institutions ought to develop when they are at their best: institutions should embody the norms of neighborly love and equality that create the conditions of human flour-ishing in the world. Indeed, the idea of the project of political vocation, developed in detail in the following chapters, retrieves something of Raus-chenbusch's insight about the unfolding of the kingdom of God in the world and appreciates Rauschenbusch's insistence that God's redemptive work happens both in the world and within human institutions.

Niebuhr offers a clear-eyed view of the way institutions actually work to advance the interests of powerful groups at the expense of other compet-ing interests. Niebuhr's view offers a realistic counterbalance to Rauschen-busch that obligates theological reflection to account for the operation of sin in institutional settings. The idea of vocation, again, intends to affirm Niebuhr's realism to a degree, by holding the project of political vocation in tension with the complex realities of institutional functioning. The tension between norm and reality that the argument here ascribes to the idea of vocation pays tribute to Niebuhr's realism.

CST, finally, provides the insight that institutional complexity is a good that, with appropriate structure, contributes to human flourishing. CST affirms the development and maintenance of institutional patterns as a dimension of the human need for community. It also affirms that insti-tutions play a role in the divine structuring of creation moving all created things toward a natural end. CST, in other words, represents a way of affirm-ing the integrity of differentiated institutional settings as particular ways of structuring human experience and work. At the same time, CST offers a model of how to respond to the particularity and diversity of institutional settings that holds them accountable to the common good. CST, in short, understands that the complex connection between the "is" and "ought" of institutional life belongs to the structure of creation.

None of these three models, however, offer a clear theological account of what is to be done with the unresolvable moral ambiguities that institu-tional structures create. Niebuhr's approach comes the closest to provid-ing a theological treatment of moral ambiguity in institutional settings. For Niebuhr, moral ambiguity is to be expected in institutional life, since the latter is a context in which group egotism is managed as best as it can be. Niebuhr, however, finally consigns moral ambiguity to the dynamics of sin and human brokenness. His strategy is to contain moral ambiguity, to keep it in check. But a close look at the work of politics in which moral ambiguity exists shows that it is not simply a reflection of human brokenness, though it is surely also that. Politics is not just a context in which groups pursue their own desires at the expense of the common good, though it is surely also that as well. Political work occasions the cultivation of virtue as well as vice on the part of individual political agents, as Machiavelli and Weber both recognize—virtues like passion, responsibility, and proportionality (in Weber's case) and "greatness of spirit" and "strength of body" (in Machiavelli's). Niebuhr provides a helpful assessment of the dangers of politics, and his caution needs to be taken into account. But a theology of political vocation also needs to affirm a particular way of being human in the world that political life makes possible.

Christian social ethics in the U.S. context developed, in part, in response to the peculiar institutional arrangements of modern industrial societies, as the examples of Rauschenbusch and Niebuhr clearly show. As a collection of traditions and subtraditions, Christian social ethics has attended in multiple and richly revealing ways to modern political life, the goods it creates, and the ills and evils it perpetrates. On the whole, however, Christian social ethics has not parsed the moral complexity of political institutions in a nuanced way. Theological responses to political life in contemporary literature mostly prefer to render it as any of a variety of normative monoliths: "the state," "liberalism," "democracy," the "context" of politics, and so on. Theological treatments have not responded to political life as a set of morally laden patterns and practices, which not only create social goods and perpetrate evils but also proffer complex moral logics, normative schemes, and formative experiences for the persons that inhabit and work in them. The institutional patterns of political life are morally ambiguous: they are not completely good, but they are not completely deficient, either. And they have something of normative significance to offer that other institutional settings, including the church, do not. While the tradition of Christian social ethics is a theological response to modern institutional life, it has ironically not pushed *far enough* into the structure of political institutions to provide an adequate theological account of the role they play in the work God is doing in the world.

The theology of political vocation that this chapter begins to develop, and that the following chapters explore in more detail, constitutes an attempt to reckon theologically with political life as a morally complex institutional space. The primary thesis of the following chapters is that the concept of vocation both values the normative particularity of political institutions and endeavors to stretch the institutional patterns of political life in the direction of God's project to redeem creation.

From Time in Space to Person in Place

Weber envisioned ambiguous political spaces that responsible politicians are able to negotiate, at least within limits. For Weber, the problem of moral ambiguity in political space has more to do with human limitations than with the nature of politics per se. In the Weberian vision, violent power is simply a given feature of modern political systems; the problem is with those who use it. Human beings have limited moral perception; they can only anticipate, without knowing for certain, what the consequences of their actions will be. The problem Weber explored is how politicians can exercise responsibility in using power under the conditions of human finitude. Though he certainly recognized that there are systemic problems associated with the modern state, such as the role of money in politics and complex political bureaucracies, he did not think these problems are utterly intractable.

Perhaps Weber got it wrong, or at least he was not able to anticipate how utterly crippling systemic problems in modern political systems would be. In the current moment, one could reasonably conclude that money has irredeemably corrupted politics in the U.S. setting. If political spaces are corrupt, there is nothing morally ambiguous about them. The main job of politicians, at least Washington politicians, it seems, is to raise money to fund their next campaign. When politicians have time to engage in the actual work of politics, no one can be certain that they are representing their own constituents meaningfully. Instead, politicians represent the interests of lobbyists and wealthy contributors who have paid good money for such representation. Such a view feels cynical to be sure, but it hardly seems inaccurate.

Indeed, the corruption of political space may extend far beyond the workings of Washington. In both explicit and implicit ways, many have argued, political spaces in the United States and other contexts have lost their institutional integrity. Political life is now simply an extension of the complex movements of capital in a globalized market system. Real power rests in a decentralized constellation of coordinated institutions—multinational corporations, military organizations, some nation-states, among others—that benefit from domestic and international structures hastening the flow of globalized capital. American political institutions are no longer republican in the original sense of the term.[8] They are no longer a "public thing" that advances a common good. Rather, they are imperial, in that they advance the economic interests of the most privileged by exploiting global economic resources. In this view, the United States is more accurately described as an oligarchy (rule by the few) or a plutocracy (rule by the wealthy) than a democracy.[9]

In this view, or some version of it, there is not much hope for political vocation. If vocation includes an emphasis on formation, and the institutional space in which vocation takes shape is itself corrupted, then the person being formed in the context of political work will likely also be corrupt. Unsavory politics makes for unsavory people.

One theological response to the problem of irreducibly corrupt political space is to anchor genuine politics in a different political setting. Augustinian theologians understand that the eschaton, the city of God, is the authentic and ultimate political reality. Augustine's notion of the city of God defines an era more than it identifies a place; it is the presence of the ultimate time in the *saeculum*, the secular, penultimate time. The city of God is the ultimate time, the time that follows the world, but it is also concurrent time, time in the world.

The political spaces that structure the penultimate moment known as "the world" are mere shadows of the eschaton. The eschaton represents the end and destiny of creation, an ultimate moment that not only sits at the end of history but reaches into history and makes claims on moral and political life in secular time. In the city of God, God, not the self, is the proper end of all loves. Therefore, in the secular moment, human beings are to work to orient all of their loves to God. To the extent that secular political spaces fail to acknowledge God as the source and end of all things, they fall short of "real" politics.

Augustinian framings make possible different responses to political life in the secular age. One Augustinian approach emphasizes the complementary relationship between the secular city and the city of God. The eschaton, the ultimate political time, always relativizes the best human attempts to create political space in secular time. Citizens should therefore welcome public dialogue with conversation partners who represent diverse viewpoints. Public dialogue is the medium in which citizens work with one another to better understand and always continually revise their understanding (however always imperfectly) of the good that God intends for creation.[10] At the same time, rulers, like Augustine's wise judge discussed above, should be aware that their actions stand under the judgment of God. Therefore, rulers should approach the work of political judgment with care and reservation.[11]

Another Augustinian view pits eschatological political time against secular political time. Secular political configurations (the nation-state and the globalized market system in particular) advance the power and privilege of elites, opposing the reality of the ultimate peace and unity the eschaton represents. The responsibility of the church is to form citizens of the heavenly city in its performance and practice of the Christian faith.[12] The church creates an alternative political space that stands opposed to the self-serving orientation of secular political life.

Both approaches contrast the ultimate reality of eschatological political time with the penultimate reality of secular political space, using the former as leverage to ground or oppose the latter. Both approaches, in other words, relate, in both critical and constructive ways, a deficient ontological reality to a complete one. The critical leverage, however, comes at a cost. In Augustinian framings, secular political space must be less real than its eschatological counterpart. The moral ambiguity of secular political space, then, is a sign of ontological deficiency. In its ontological deficiency, secular political space points to the reality of eschatological political space. Politics in the secular moment is at best a foil for the real.

The analysis of Augustine's wise judge discussed above suggested that Augustinian framings leave political vocation in a difficult position. In the context of ontological deficiency, it is difficult to know what theological sense to make of a calling to politics. Moral ambiguity is a condition of political work that persons must negotiate continuously. It is also a condition of the formative process persons undergo as they negotiate political work. If moral ambiguity is not fundamentally real, if it has a merely deficient ontological status, then political vocation in secular political space has little theological import. Augustinian framings can abandon secular political space to the forces that threaten to corrupt it, since secular political space is not ultimately real.

Dietrich Bonhoeffer's theological ethics offers a different approach. For Bonhoeffer, the locus of reality is not ultimately a space or time per se; it is in the person of Jesus Christ who takes form in worldly places. The place where Christ takes form in the world, wherever it is, is ontologically authentic because it is where reality is manifest. But its ontological authenticity is not a feature of the space itself. Rather, it is conferred by Christ's presence in place. Since the broken Christ takes form in worldly places, the world is not ontologically deficient, though it remains broken: "Christ has died for the world, and Christ is Christ only in the midst of the world. It is nothing but unbelief to give the world . . . less than Christ. It means not taking seriously the incarnation, the crucifixion, and the bodily resurrection."[13] Vocation, moreover, is the place of responsibility, where Christ takes form in the world. To live into vocation, then, is to participate in the real.

Bonhoeffer understood that participation in the real requires negotiating moral ambiguity. In his presence in the midst of brokenness, Christ transfigures moral ambiguity into the very texture of reality. By shifting the ontological focus from political space to the person of Christ, Bonhoeffer's ethics provides a theological rationale for taking the moral ambiguity of political life seriously. His theology of vocation does not resolve the problem of corrupted political space; more will need to be said about how vocation responds to worldly politics in this regard. But Bonhoeffer's ethics also does not cede political space to the powers of corruption. Instead, in the person of Christ taking form in the world, Bonhoeffer creates a place for the negotiation of moral ambiguity in secular political life, making vocation a viable framework for political work.

Bonhoeffer's approach shifts the locus of the real from eschatological time to the presence of Christ in the context of vocation. For Bonhoeffer, the real just is the place where Christ takes form in vocational work. That Christ takes form in the context of vocational work does not resolve the moral ambiguity that comes along with work. But Christ's presence does show that vocational work, in any institutional space and in whatever degree of moral complexity it entails, belongs to God's project of redemption.

VOCATION AND THE FORMATION OF THE SELF

The shift from time in space to person in place as the locus of the real raises a question about the status of selves formed in political space. The moral ambiguity of political space stems both from the features that distinguish political space from other institutional spaces in which persons live their lives as well as from the way these features condition political agency. Selves inhabiting political spaces encounter moral ambiguity not only in the exercise of political agency, in making decisions that inform action. They also encounter moral ambiguity in the ways political spaces form them as moral agents. Vocation is a framing of work that acknowledges that selves at work are also selves being formed in particular ways as workers. The problem is that if political spaces exercise a formative influence on persons who work in them and political spaces are marked by moral ambiguity, then it is not clear how one should evaluate the self formed in the political vocation.

Bonhoeffer was aware of the moral challenges that institutional settings pose to vocational work. He does not, however, dwell on the way institutional contexts condition both worker and work in complex ways. For Bonhoeffer, the primary role of institutions is to support human beings in the life of Christ. He develops throughout the corpus of his work a theological response to human institutional life, which in his mature theology issues in the notion of the "divine mandates."[14] In *Ethics*, Bonhoeffer defines the divine mandates as "the concrete divine commission grounded in the revelation of Christ and the testimony of scripture; it is the authorization and legitimization to declare a particular divine commandment, the conferring of divine authority on an earthly institution."[15] The divine mandates are the institutions of work, marriage, government, and the church in the context of which human beings live their lives before God. The mandates are brought into being by God's command and therefore have the character of "divinely imposed tasks."[16] Bonhoeffer explains that the mandates are divine because, like the orders of preservation, their end is Christ. That is, the mandates are the concrete form in which human beings participate in creation reconciled to God in Christ.[17] In the context of the mandates, God's command to human beings becomes intelligible.

The divine mandates, Bonhoeffer argues, are finally united in human persons conformed to Christ. The mandates aim not to "wear people down through endless conflicts" but to foster "the whole human being who stands in reality before God." The mandates may not be "unified" with one another either actually or "theoretically," but, Bonhoeffer writes, "the human person is not the place where the divine mandates" show their disunity. The mandates are instead unified in the human person because the human person is the place where the reality of Jesus Christ takes form in the world. Thus, the mandates work to build persons up in the life of Christ, not divide them.[18]

Bonhoeffer's point is that the mandates exist to provide human beings with the goods necessary for flourishing. Though multiple institutional settings create, maintain, and distribute a variety of goods, all of which are required for life, institutions should not compromise the integrity of human being. Writing in the midst of his active resistance to the Nazi regime, Bonhoeffer understood that totalitarian systems expect persons to serve political institutions rather than vice versa. The subordination of person to polity amounts to the destruction of human integrity. For Bonhoeffer, institutional differentiation and the moral pluralism that comes along with it stop at the doorstep of the person. In the person, the diversity of goods are united in service to human well-being: "the irreducible variety of goods makes possible a wholeness of life, in which all goods can be enjoyed in appropriate relations to each other and to God."[19]

Bonhoeffer's worry about the totalitarian violation of human integrity is well taken. It seems, however, that through participation in a variety of institutional contexts, persons are multiply formed as moral agents. They are formed as citizens in political life, consumers and producers in the market system, parents and children in family systems, students and teachers in educational settings, beloved neighbors in faith communities, soldiers in the military, patients in health-care systems, and so on. All of these settings have different, though not always radically different, norms, practices, and moral logics. The identities that each confers upon persons (of citizen,

soldier, patient, consumer, etc.) therefore have different, and often competing, expectations about what makes for human flourishing.

Contrary to Bonhoeffer, these multiple and institutionally located
moral formations and the "endless conflicts" between them live in each
person. Indeed, much of the moral labor persons do happens in sorting
out these conflicts and in determining how to inhabit all of these identities
with integrity. Anyone who walks into a supermarket knows exactly how he
is supposed to behave in that space. The space itself is set up for customers.
Customers are economic agents motivated to acquire as much of what they
want and need with the limited resources they have. They practice an instrumental moral logic, a utilitarian calculus that seeks to maximize desired
ends with limited means. Customers respond to branding and marketing,
as well as to bargains, discounts, and deals. They encounter supermarket
employees as sellers; the expectations each has about the other are formed
through the moral logic of quid pro quo, the this-for-that of economic life:
one gives something one values and receives something of value in return.
Buyers and sellers are typically polite to one another, but they are not bud-
dies; their relationship is not emotionally forged in the way persons relate to
family members or congregants in their community of faith.

Persons who wander into a supermarket step reflexively, and largely
unconsciously, into the morally laden role of customer. Indeed, it is jarring
to practice an alternative moral logic in the marketplace. Persons who want
their purchases to satisfy a criterion of responsibility imported from some
other form of moral training, say, from their communities of faith, find that
it is not easy to be a good consumer at the same time. Buying an organi-
cally farmed apple will mean paying a higher price for the same (and often
smaller) product. Such a decision requires conscious and counterintuitive
decision making.

Similarly, persons formed in political space will acknowledge, struggle
with, and respond to the morally ambiguous qualities of that space from
the perspective of the many other ways in which they are formed. The self
that emerges from this struggle is, as Weber acknowledges, one who can
act responsibly, though without having resolved the moral ambiguity that
surrounds the political vocation. Such a self, having made "a pact with the
means of violence," carries in herself the moral ambiguities associated with
that pact. If that moral burden is carried with integrity, Weber argues, something "genuinely human and profoundly moving" is disclosed in the work
of political vocation.

Since the concept of vocation includes an awareness of moral formation, it is important to expand Bonhoeffer's understanding of Christ's

presence in the world to include an account of self-formation in the crucible of moral ambiguity. John Calvin's view of sanctification is helpful in this regard. Calvin saw a connection between vocational work and the process of self-becoming, which he calls "sanctification." For Calvin, God's grace is both justifying and sanctifying. Grace both mitigates God's judgment of sin and transforms persons, regenerating the distorted image of God in them as they make the pilgrim's journey through the world. The journey of sanctification itself unfolds first with the "general call," the "outward preaching of the Word," and then with a "special" calling, the "illumination of the Spirit" that induces the elect to respond in faith to the general call.[20] The special calling initiates a transformative journey by virtue of which the image of God is gradually, but never completely, restored in the elect.

Calvin calls vocational work a "calling" as well, but the calling of voca-tional work plays another role in the journey of sanctification. The voca-tional calling gives shape and structure to the process of regeneration, establishing a "sentry post" that orients persons to the transformative pro-cess of sanctification, so that each individual "may not heedlessly wander about through life." While the self undergoes a regenerative process doing vocational work, Calvin is not suggesting that the work itself is the medium of regeneration. Rather, Calvin is aware of "the great restlessness human nature flames, with what fickleness it is borne hither and thither, how its ambition longs to embrace various things at once."[21] The sentry post of vocational work provides structure for the pilgrim's journey through the fallen world. It holds the elect to a "straight path," delineating the "duties" of each, thus empowering the elect to participate in the journey of sancti-fication. The journey of faith is therefore both enlivened and structured by different callings. Thus, for Calvin, sanctification is a pilgrimage. It is not a haphazard wandering through the world but a formative journey that prepares persons for participation in redeemed creation. The gradual resto-ration of the divine image expands one's capacity to recognize and respond in love to the divine image in the neighbor.[22]

Calvin, like Bonhoeffer, understood that the moral life unfolds in the way persons conform to the being of Christ in the world. Calvin emphasizes that the journey of sanctification takes a cruciform shape. To be formed in Christ is to be formed as the One who bears the cross in the world.[23] To bear the cross, Calvin argues, is to negotiate trials and tribulations that God imposes. The moral ambiguity of the world always has a hold on human being and human work. Vocation in Calvin's view provides structure for pilgrims to engage the moral ambiguity of the world through work.

Of course, Calvin neither experienced nor theorized a world characterized by the kind of deep institutional differentiation and moral pluralism
explored here. But Calvin's model of the moral life provides a helpful way
of understanding what moral formation in a vocational context means in
the modern world. Human beings negotiate the complexities of multiple
and competing moral formations in terms of one another. Christians, of
course, will prioritize their formation in Christian communities of faith
and thus will identify fundamental moral commitments and make moral
judgments from that perspective. But vocation as a "calling in" means that
God is present and works in the spaces in which persons find themselves.
In the modern world, those spaces are formative spaces; political life is one
among these.

The challenge of the moral life is to negotiate multiple and competing moral formations in the place in which the vocational call comes. That
negotiation is not as simple as rejecting all others in favor of just one. Christian citizens cannot simply engage in political life as though their formation
in the church is the only one that is operative. On deep, visceral levels, multiple formations claim us—in the church, the market, the polity, and the like.
And each of these multiple formations is neither utterly morally authoritative nor utterly morally bankrupt. As Christ takes form in the place of vocation, any institutional setting can be the occasion of reality in Christ. Thus,
the moral logics and languages particular to any institutional setting are not
to be summarily rejected, nor are they to be uncritically embraced; any and
all of them constitute the contours of Christ's presence in the world.

The Augustinian conceit that human beings are either among the sheep
or the goats, the wheat or the tares, citizens of Jerusalem or Babylon, the
city of God or the earthly city, is one that Calvin shared. As a description
of human formation, the conceit is not helpful, because it does not account
for the multiple, complex, and conflicted ways persons are formed within
and across institutional spaces. Though human beings should strive to order
their loves properly to God, there is no escaping, in this world, the multiple and competing orders in which human goods exist in institutional life.
Disorder of this sort is not just "out there" in moral judgment and action;
it goes all the way down into the identities, motivations, impulses, energies,
and worldviews that make human beings human. In this sense, we are all
sheep and goats, wheat and tares, citizens of the divine and earthly cities.

The formative journey that happens in vocational work reflects, in Calvin's image, the cross-bearing Christ in this sense: vocational work requires
a difficult and ongoing negotiation among competing normative demands,
a negotiation that has implications not only for human work but also for

human identity. To be formed in the context of moral ambiguity is to wrestle with the finitude and brokenness of the world, a wrestling that goes unresolved in this life. That place of wrestling is nevertheless utterly real, because it is the place where Christ takes form. That wrestling goes all the way down, into the very constitution of the self.

Being conformed to Christ in the space of vocation, then, is not only a matter of representing others and taking responsibility for their good. It also entails an ongoing encounter with a morally ambiguous world, especially in political space. Moral ambiguity is not just "out there," a condition of the world that persons negotiate in and through their work. Rather, moral ambiguity works its way into the self as condition of self-formation. Political agents may not be able to avoid "dirty hands" in all situations, since, as Bonhoeffer suggests, responsible action often involves a choice between "right and right, wrong and wrong."[24] And dirty hands do not always wash clean; they become part of the political self.

Vocation therefore requires a concept of the self in negotiation. Rather than the hierarchical conceptions of the critical "I" posited by Freud and others, Michael Walzer argues for a dialogical conception of the self. "The order of the self," he writes, "is better imagined as a thickly populated circle, with me in the center surrounded by my self-critics who stand at different temporal and spatial removes (but don't necessarily stand still)."[25] The self does not dissolve in the circle; rather, the circled order is always maintained, and the self is in constant dialogue with the different moral voices that bring critique to bear on her. In the modern context, self-formation is a process that involves continual dialogue with a great many sources of moral authority that encircle the self. The circle that surrounds the self includes some authorities the self did not choose to include in the first place. Their presence is simply given. And some sources exercise more authority than others. In crafting a vocational identity, persons are not able to step outside of the circle. But neither is the self at the circle's center subsumed by any authority that stands on its periphery. In short, the self exercises agency in responding to the many normative voices that make claims on it.

In institutionally differentiated societies, some members of the circle represent institutionally located moral languages—those of the marketplace, political life, faith communities, the family, and so on. Others represent the voices of structural dynamics that make morally relevant demands on the self: the voices of race, class, sexual and gender identities, among others. All of these make various and often competing claims on the self, both in terms of the self's moral commitments and its identity. The primary task of the moral life is to order these competing claims as best as one can, to determine

which voices will take priority and when. All of the voices to which the circled self responds have some legitimate claims to make; all therefore need to
be taken seriously. Under the conditions of sin and finitude, however, the
self will not be able to reconcile all of them.

The idea of vocation as a "calling in" place values the dialogical process
of self-formation, as Walzer describes it. This chapter has argued that God
is present and working in that cacophony of voices. But vocation is also a
"calling to" participate in a project for the common good. From the perspective of vocation, the project is the circled self's orienting voice, the one in
terms of which the self evaluates and responds to conversation partners in
the circle. The tension of vocation, then, arises in the work of both taking
seriously the formative voices that encircle the self and responding to them
in terms of the project of vocation. In the person of Christ taking form in
the world, the concept of vocation holds the tension between the claims of
the place of vocation and the claims of the project of vocation, pulling the
former in the direction of the latter. The project of political vocation is the
subject of the next chapter.

6

THE PROJECT OF POLITICAL VOCATION

"We live through institutions," declares Robert Bellah and his colleagues, a claim that sums up a good part of the argument here so far.[1] Political life is one among many institutional settings that together compose modern social life. Political life itself comprises a number of related institutional settings marked by distinctive patterns of moral meaning and practice. Political institutions make distinctive demands on moral formation, moral norms and values, moral calculus, and aspirations for goals and ends of action. In their way, political institutions create the conditions for moral ambiguity with which political agents must reckon as they go about the work of politics.

It is easy for Christian theologians simply to dismiss the complex institutional patterns that make up secular political life as morally vacuous or pernicious and to propose the church as the only meaningful alternative political arrangement. The point of view of this book is that all human institutions participate in God's project to redeem creation. There is something therefore about institutional structures, however morally complex and ambiguous they are, that is salutary to and integral in the work God is doing to create the conditions of flourishing for persons and communities. The idea of vocation is a "calling in" place that values the distinctive ways institutions condition human experience. At the same time, vocation is a "calling to" transformative work that pulls both worker and work in the direction of God's redemptive purposes.

The first several chapters focused on vocation as a "calling in" place. The next three turn to vocation as a "calling to" transformative work. The two dimensions of vocation—as "calling in" and "calling to"—exist in a tension that goes unresolved in secular time. In this tension, vocation both affirms and complicates the institutional patterns giving shape to political life. Vocation affirms that the distinctive moral logics, languages, and formations that political institutions make possible are constitutive of political work and of the goods created and maintained in political institutions. But vocation also gestures beyond the horizon of secular political life toward a vision of creation redeemed and reconciled to God, a vision that discloses radically different ways of being in the world that reflect God's commitment to abundant life and the flourishing of creation. Owing to the combined effects of sin and finitude, the tension-filled space between the "calling in" and the "calling to" of vocation does not ever completely collapse in secular time. But the space does narrow, as God's project to redeem creation reaches from the eschatological into the secular moment to claim and orient human work until the final destiny of creation unfolds. A theological understanding of vocation therefore invites a reorientation of political work in the direction of God's redemptive purposes.

Ethicists often consider the anatomy of the moral life around three primary categories: agents, actions, and ends. Agents are the persons, communities, or even nonhuman realities that exercise morally relevant powers. Power, in this sense, is simply the capacity to influence or change states of affairs. Action refers to power exercised, the way in which agents go about influencing or changing states of affairs. Ends, finally, are the results of actions, intended or unintended. Ethicists ask questions about the moral status of each of these categories: the moral status of agents and formative processes by which persons become moral agents, often considered in the framing of virtue ethics; the moral status of actions in terms of the rules and principles that guide them, often explored in the framing of deontological ethics; and the moral status of the ends of action, treated in the framing of consequentialist ethics.

The normative center of the idea of vocation, it will be argued here, is the vocational project, the redemptive reality that God is bringing about both in the world and in the eschatological time in which the ultimate destiny of creation unfolds. The project of political vocation, then, is both the point of reference in relationship to which the status of virtue and actions are considered as well as the proper end of vocational work, the state of affairs that vocational work intends to bring about. The discussion in these last three chapters, rather than beginning with agents, moving to actions, and concluding with the ends of action, begins instead with a consideration of the project of political vocation, the end and normative reference point of vocational work. The last two chapters, then, focus on the moral status of political agents (virtue) and of political actions (agency), respectively, in relationship to the project of political vocation.

THE NORMATIVE CENTER OF GRAVITY OF POLITICAL VOCATION

The argument above suggested that the "calling to" of vocation is not only an invitation to participate in God's project; it is also a calling to self-formation. In the doing of vocational work, a person becomes a particular kind of self, one who cultivates an identity and sense of purpose in relationship to the work to which she is called. Vocational work, then, goes beyond the simple performance of certain tasks; it calls persons to a way of being in the world in the context of which they become a certain kind of worker.

The framing of vocation therefore requires stereoscopic consideration both of the kind of work vocation requires and, at the same time, the ways in which the doing of vocational work always also entails formative processes for the worker. The attention of vocation, in other words, is always on both work and worker, on the tasks accomplished and on the moral capacities persons develop as they commit themselves to vocational work. Following Aristotle and other classical thinkers, one might call such qualities "virtues," the habits of excellence that enable a person to live and work well.[2] To have good character is to possess a range of virtues. The idea of virtue focuses attention on the aspect of the moral life relating to moral formation, addressing questions about what makes for good persons and communities.

It might be true that in *any* understanding of work—a job, a career, a profession—persons undergo some morally relevant change by virtue of engaging in the work. What makes vocation as a framing of work distinctive in this regard is that moral development in a vocational framework happens in relationship to the kind of project that is the object of vocation. That project relates to a common good, one that both includes but also transcends the good of persons called to participate in it. Therefore, the kind of self one becomes by virtue of pursuing vocational work is one capable of understanding and participating in a project for the common good.

The same is true for the structure of vocational work. Ethicists use the term "deontological ethics" to denote the area of moral inquiry addressing the rules, principles, and guidelines determining how judgments are made and what actions, as a consequence, are to be performed. The deontological dimension of political vocation will be defined in relationship to the project of political vocation. That is, in a theology of political vocation, right moral judgments and actions will be those that best reflect the moral structure of the vocational project—those, in other words, that best reflect vocational work's commitment to the common good.

It has been suggested that two related conditions, institutional differentiation and moral pluralism, shape moral experience in modern societies. Such societies are institutionally differentiated in the sense that many different patterns of action organize human experience. They are morally pluralistic in the sense that these different patterns express different moral logics, placing differing, often competing, expectations on how persons conduct their lives. Thus, some virtues are appropriate in some institutional settings but not in others. Certain qualities of character might be virtuous in the family, others in politics, still others in economic life, and so on. In the market system, it is appropriate to exercise strategic judgment according to which persons treat their own resources, available goods, and, to an extent, even other persons as means to their own happiness. In religious life, by contrast, such strategic reckoning is very likely inappropriate, especially in the way persons treat others. Christians, for example, understand persons as children of God and neighbors to one another to be offered unconditional love, not as a means to an end. Many problems of the moral life arise when institutionally located value systems, including expectations about virtue, come into conflict. In such times, persons must decide who they are going to be.

For Aristotle, virtue is situated as a mean on a spectrum between poles defined by vices of deficiency and excess.[3] One way of thinking about Aristotelian virtue in institutionally differentiated and morally pluralistic societies is to imagine that different institutional settings situate virtues in different ways. A degree of self-promotion might be virtuous in political life but a vicious habit in the context of faith communities. The spectra of virtue shift, in other words, from one institutional setting to another. In modern and postmodern social and political experiences, virtue is on the move.

Another possibility is that different framings of work might reconfigure spectra of virtue *within* any particular institutional setting. Since vocation is oriented to a project for the common good, a vocational framing of work will configure the spectrum of political virtue in relationship to the common good, however it is defined. Virtue in political life, in other words, will be measured in relationship to the worker's commitment to and ability to bring about the common good that is the focus of vocational work. Were political work considered in the framing of a job or a career, by contrast, the spectrum constituting political virtue would be defined differently. Those for whom political work is just a job, those who, in Weber's term, "live from" politics, would likely consider earning a living a primary end of work.

Political virtue for such persons will be defined in relationship to the end of earning money.

It is not enough, then, simply to explore the moral structure of agents, actions, and ends discretely, as though each has its own normative scheme defined apart from the others. Instead, in the framing of vocation, understandings of agents and of agency are defined in terms of their relationship to the project of political vocation, the end of vocational work. In a vocational framing, therefore, the goals of political work (the project to realize a particular vision of the common good) in an important sense constitute the formative process work involves. Similarly, the moral logic of vocational work—the principles that determine what good political work looks like—is defined in relationship to these goals. The project of political vocation is in this sense the normative center of gravity for a theology of political vocation.

THE COMMON GOOD ON SHAKY GROUND

Political vocation as a framing of work, it was suggested above, includes the idea that work in an important sense does not belong to the worker. In the theological framework developed here, God, not the worker, initiates the vocational project and invites others to participate in it. To say that God's work is a "project" is to signal that it is work unfolding in the world—that in secular time God's work is not yet fully realized, though in eschatological perspectives it is paradoxically already completed. The vocational project, moreover, constitutes a center of value: it determines why work is meaningful, it orients work to ends that the project determines, and it provides a pattern for lives well lived. To say that the work that constitutes the normative center of vocation is God's project to redeem creation is to suggest that God is bringing about a destiny that is good for all of creation. Creation flourishes when it is reconciled to God and restored in relationship to God, since God is the Creator and Sustainer of life. The project of vocation in any vocational context, then, is a project for the common good, not only the good of human persons and communities but the good of the entire created order.

The claim that political vocation is oriented to a common good is problematic for a number of reasons. First, the notion will strike many as obviously absurd. As has been noted in the discussion above, politicians, in the U.S. setting at any rate, do not seem particularly concerned to promote any conception of the common good. Instead, they appear to be focused on advancing the good of their constituents (at best) or even simply the good of their own careers. It is telling that there is currently no coherent public discourse about the common good in American political life—no "live conversation," in other words, about what the common good is and what it might mean to pursue it as a political goal.

Discourse about the common good is problematic, moreover, because it does not travel well in a postmodern age. In theological traditions, the idea of the common good, it is fair to say, is most prominently featured in Catholic thought. In that context, the common good typically belongs to a conception of a stable moral order inherent in the very structure of creation, existing independently of human experience of it. In the context of this moral order, all things move toward a "natural" end. Human beings similarly move toward a final end, the beatific vision of God, a condition that constitutes the ultimate grounds of human flourishing. Political societies provide the means necessary to aid human beings in the movement toward their natural end. Theological frameworks of this sort advocate moral realism, the view that there is a moral order existing independently in some way from human experience.

The postmodern milieu is characteristically suspicious of moral realisms of any kind. Instead, postmodern worldviews value the constructed nature of moral meaning and value. Persons and communities create conceptions of the good; they are not discovered through the operation of reason. Thus, postmodernity is characterized by a loss of normative frameworks understood and experienced to be ontologically durable and axiologically comprehensive.[4] Finally, and relatedly, discourse about the common good is understood to encode the values, norms, and preferences of dominant groups, reinforcing structures that marginalize, exclude, and disempower subaltern communities in social life. Goods held to be "common" can, in more and less explicit ways, reinscribe racist, classist, heteronormative, and patriarchal ideologies.[5]

Each of these problems poses legitimate concerns to which any political understanding of the common good must respond. Together, they raise significant questions about whether discourse about the common good is meaningful or helpful at all. It might be, as Reinhold Niebuhr's realism suggests, that public discourse about the common good is not likely to respond in effective ways to the problem of "group egotism" in political life. Indeed, Niebuhr urges, discourses that invoke the common good in the U.S. setting often serve to conceal the ulterior motives of dominant groups, often in ways that proponents of such discourses do not even recognize themselves.[6]

These objections point to the way that the framing of vocation, whatever else it is, is also a contestable, public argument about the meaning of political work. It is a public argument in the sense that, in a "secular age," vocation is one among many ways of understanding the meaning of work, no one of which can claim unquestioned normativity. As a public argument, therefore, vocation will need to clarify, in response to these objections, how the common good is both genuinely common and genuinely good.

❀ ❀ ❀

The project of political vocation has three primary features. Each recommends a virtue enabling capacities needed to sustain work on the project. First, the project of political vocation is God's project; it is not a human project. God invites persons and communities to participate in it. But God's redemptive purposes exceed the human capacity to know them adequately in any particular moment. The demands of God's project must therefore be an object of ongoing and careful discernment. Political agents must continually work together to understand how God is inviting participation in the project and what that invitation means for the ongoing work of political life. Discernment, then, is the first virtue related to the project of political vocation. In the discussion here, resources from the Reformed theological tradition are engaged to understand the work of discernment.

Second, the project of political vocation includes but also transcends the good of the particular individuals and communities that participate in it. God's project determines the destiny of all of creation; it constitutes the end toward which all of creation moves in secular and in eschatological time. Political agents committed to the project of political vocation must therefore cultivate a capacity to identify goods that transcend narrow self- and group interests, broadening to concerns for more expansive publics and the natural world, and to imagine how local interests are served in relationship to common goods. Solidarity is the virtue that names this capacity. The traditions of Catholic social thought offer insights about the virtue of solidarity in relationship to commitments to the common good.

Third and finally, political agents need to understand that past actions by themselves and a great many others have obstructed the project of political vocation. Once understood, political agents must further claim responsibility for these impediments and be willing to work to change conditions to better enhance human responses to God's redeeming purposes. The virtue associated with these capacities is repentance. Dietrich Bonhoeffer offers helpful insights into the role of repentance in social and political life.

The project of political vocation demands the cultivation of these three virtues, but they do not name clearly what exactly that project is. In the theological perspective developed here, the project of political vocation—the common good in which God calls all of creation to participate—is God's commitment to the flourishing of creation. To say that God is committed to the flourishing of creation is to say that God intends for all created things to develop along trajectories in which they become what God intends for them to be. Fundamentally, God intends for all created things to exist in relationship to God. Indeed, creation cannot become all that God intends for it to be—it cannot flourish, in other words—unless it exists in relationship with God. Sin disrupts and distorts the relationship between creature and Creator. But the life, death, and resurrection of Jesus Christ signals God's commitment to right relatedness. God's commitment to the flourishing of creation is therefore a redemptive project, one that restores and advances the trajectory toward flourishing that God intends for all created things. Thus, God's project for the flourishing of all creation reflects God's redeeming purposes.

The flourishing of creation is right relationship with God. Flourishing is not only an eschatological condition; it is a possibility that unfolds in the context of history and culminates in the eschatological moment. For human beings, flourishing means the development of physical, social, spiritual, emotional, intellectual, and psychological capacities that empower persons to participate in God's redemptive project. God's redemptive project is therefore both the condition and the end of human flourishing.

The above paragraphs amount to a simple naming of a particular view of God's vocational project. That naming is not an argument, or at least not a very good one; such an argument could only be developed in the context of another book-length project. Instead, this naming reflects the author's fundamental commitments, rooted in his formation in both Reformed and Catholic traditions. It functions, therefore, like a faith statement that the following discussions explore and illumine. There are, of course, other ways of naming the meaning of God's redeeming purposes. It is hoped that other approaches find resonance in the discussions that follow.

DISCERNMENT AND PUBLIC ARGUMENT

The Reformed tradition compounds challenges to the common good by adding an epistemological concern. Sin causes congenital deficiencies limiting the knowledge of God and God's work. It is understood to disfigure, though not to obliterate completely, knowledge of God and God's being. Since God is the ground of the good, human knowledge is also limited with respect to moral perception. John Calvin holds that, even after the fall, the "seeds" of a primitive moral awareness remain among the "natural endowments" of human beings. With classical sources, Calvin affirms that human beings are social animals "by nature." Through "natural instinct," Calvin argues, human beings perceive "universal impressions" of "certain civic fair dealing and order." All human beings understand that any human association must be regulated by laws.[7] He later claims that the "moral law," which requires the worship of God and "sincere affection" for other human beings, is the "testimony of the natural law . . . engraved on the minds of men." The moral law prescribes equity as the "goal and rule and limit of all laws."[8] Calvin, a trained medieval jurist, often invokes the legal concept of equity, classically understood as the rectification of positive law when its generality fails to treat similar cases fairly. For Calvin, equity also has a theological valence, as a divinely sanctioned norm that both enforces punishment and penalty in fair and reasonable ways and also instructs and empowers to promote human flourishing.[9]

Human beings therefore have a natural, though incomplete and inaccurate, sensibility about the requirements of justice.[10] In the face of incomplete and inaccurate moral and theological perception, Calvin famously argues that Scripture aids in the understanding of divine things, serving as "spectacles" that "clearly [show] us the true God."[11] Scripture shows that magistrates are to "provide for the common safety and peace of all" and are thus are empowered, through mechanisms of punishment and reward, to restrain the wicked and "give aid and protection to the oppressed."[12] Magistrates, moreover, are to serve as a "pattern," a model of justice and equity for their subjects to emulate.

For Calvin, the purpose of civil government ultimately is to provide the means of support for the church and, more generally, for the pilgrim's journey through the world. The "appointed end" of civil government, Calvin argues, is "to cherish and protect the outward worship of God" and "to defend sound doctrine of piety and the position of the church."[13] Civil government, in other words, provides the necessary legal and material conditions under which persons flourish as they negotiate the moral life and the process of sanctification it entails. One can view sanctification as Calvin's description of God's redemptive project for human beings. Political life, then, participates in a vital way in God's redeeming work in the world.

The Reformed strand makes two important contributions to an understanding of the common good. The first is an awareness that political society properly provides the basic conditions for social order and peace. Calvin sees this mandate both in the purpose of the law and in the roles and responsibilities of the magistrate. Basic political justice includes provisions that empower the weak and suffering and punish the wicked. Political life, at its best, empowers persons and communities to participate fully in the ultimate common good, understood as the operation of God's grace to redeem and restore the integrity of creation.

The second contribution is a wariness, what Douglas Ottati calls a "circumspect appreciation," for human renderings of the common good in political society.[14] Because of the limits on moral perception, human understandings of a divinely ordained moral order are inevitably approximate, incomplete, and always, in some respect, erroneous. The Reformed tradition values ongoing discernment, particularly in the context of community, about what the common good is and what it means for corporate life.[15]

The practice of discernment, then, holds persons and communities accountable for interpreting moral judgments in relationship to an understanding of and commitment to the common good, with an awareness that understandings of the common good must be continually revisited and reimagined. As a mode of knowing, discernment pushes against the boundaries of human finitude to grasp something of the transcendent normative reality in the being of God. Discernment is considered judgment reflecting both a careful account of available information and an awareness, based on prior experience, of how judgments will stand up to the rigors of lived experience; it is, James Gustafson writes, more about "certitude" than it is about "certainty." Discernment is not "the conclusion of a formally logical argument, a strict deduction from a single moral principle, or an absolutely certain result from the exercises of human 'reason' alone." Rather, discernment is "informed intuition," involving a capacity to see "parts in relation to a whole" and to express "sensibilities as well as reasoning."[16] In the mode of discernment, particular judgments are evaluated in relationship to fundamental commitments, which, for Christians, are articulated in Scriptural, theological, and practical traditions. A person's own life experiences, multiple formations in families and communities of origin, and significant relationships inform the evaluation of broad commitments and particular judgments alike.[17] Persons are therefore said to be discerning when they make informed judgments that are fitting to a particular issue in a particular historical moment.

Discernment contrasts with other modes of public knowing. It was suggested above that theorists of democratic practice often promote public argument as the primary discursive practice in public space. Argument, Scott Aikin and Robert Talisse argue, is "the attempt to make clear the reasons why we believe something that we believe."[18] Everyone wants to know that they believe what they believe for good reasons and that actions informed by beliefs and commitments are well founded and well ordered. No one enjoys the discovery of his own error or confusion, and no one wants to be "duped" by himself or others. Argument therefore helps persons to "manage" their "cognitive lives," allowing them to exercise "control over the processes by which we form, evaluate, sustain, and revise our beliefs."[19] Argument, Aikin and Talisse argue, is therefore the active maintenance of one's "cognitive hygiene." In public contexts, argument serves much the same purpose. Citizens articulate arguments to advance and defend proposals in order to discover the best reasons for social and political arrangements. Through responsible argumentative practices, democracy becomes "the political and social expression of our aspiration to cognitive health and rational self-control." Public argument is the primary way in which democracy functions as a "system of self-government."[20]

Aikin and Talisse articulate a view about the centrality of public argument that resonates in much of contemporary democratic theory.[21] The practices of public argument, as articulated in this body of literature, and the practices of discernment described here look similar to one another on the ground but contrast significantly in orientation to understandings of moral agency and the proper ends of action. As in Aikin and Talisse's framing, the idea of public argument as a discursive practice emerges from a modernist sensibility about the agency of individual rational agents. As in the discussion of Kant's scholar above, the locus of political agency in the modern context is the individual political agent, and, more locally, in the individual's rational capacity to identify and interrogate the good. Such beliefs need to be "maintained," "controlled," and vetted through rational analysis to ensure that they are sufficiently sound. The vetting process, both in the individual's own mind and in the evaluation of ideas in public argument, maintains the "cognitive hygiene" of individuals and democratic political spaces as a whole to guard against confusion and the possibility of being "duped."

The practices of discernment, by contrast, are oriented not primarily to the individual agent but to the reality that is being discerned, a reality that creates the conditions of the common good. In acknowledging that discernment inevitably runs up against the contours of human finitude, discerning persons and communities expect, in a way, to be "duped" and to exercise only limited "control" over their understanding of the common good that is the object of discernment. Discerning communities know that their "cognitive hygiene" is always a little shabby. The object of discernment is not securing and maintaining the integrity of belief in the individual mind and corporate moral consciousness. Instead, discernment is a continual approach and reapproach to the common good that expects and is comfortable with insecure belief. Discernment is not preoccupied with security; rather, it is an invitation to a continual learning process about the common good and what it requires in social and political life. Discernment, then, points to the magnitude of the reality that is its object.

The practice of discernment entails an active encounter with tragic judgment. The next chapter explores Reinhold Niebuhr's understanding of tragedy and irony, focusing on the latter as an orientation to the politician's ambition and drive. The virtue of discernment pushes in the direction of tragedy rather than irony. The idea of the project of political vocation holds that there is a transcendent source of good, that the good is found instead of made, but that human beings, in the complex interplay of sin and finitude, cannot see clearly what goods entail and how they relate to other goods. Because of their limited moral perception, human beings are sometimes required to make tragic choices between competing goods, any of which are affirmed to have value but that together preclude one another.[22] The moral weight of tragedy is intensified in the choices political agents make, because of the quality of amplification discussed above. Discerning political agents do the best they can within the boundaries of limited moral vision and must learn to live with the consequences of tragic choice.

Discernment, then, is a virtue of political comportment issuing in a distinctive attitude about the purpose of public deliberation. Discerning political agents are not concerned primarily to "win" or score points in arguments; they assume that a diversity of voices illumine different dimensions of the common good, no one of them seeing the object of discernment with utter clarity. To be sure, as the discussion above indicated, political agents sometimes need to win, or appear to win, arguments in order to please constituents. But those who view politics as a vocation will imagine that winning in public argument is a very limited, although sometimes necessary, good. They will look for opportunities to explore the common good with public conversation partners in order to best serve the communities for which they are responsible.

Solidarity and Human Flourishing

A second virtue that an orientation to the project of political vocation encourages is solidarity. The tradition of Catholic Social Teaching has illumined the virtue of solidarity in relationship to an understanding of the common good in particularly helpful ways. In CST, solidarity is the virtue of passionate commitment to the common good, reflecting a recognition that the flourishing of creation happens in the interconnections of all created things. Solidarity, Pope John Paul II writes, "is a *firm and persevering determination* to commit oneself to the *common good* . . . to the good of all and of each individual, because we are *all* really responsible for *all*."[23]

The idea of the common good in Catholic social thought reflects Thomistic commitments about the patterning and movement of all created things toward natural ends in the unfolding and development of creation.[24] The common good, Pope Paul VI famously wrote in Gaudium et Spes, is "the sum of those conditions of social life which allow social groups and their individual members relatively thorough and ready access to their own fulfillment."[25] For human life to develop appropriately, to flourish according to its particular end, human beings and communities must have access to goods that create the conditions for human flourishing.

The common good, CST argues, arises in the well-ordered and complementary schemes of distributive, contributive, social, and commutative justice. Distributive justice is concerned with questions about what communities owe their members, with respect to goods that exist only by virtue of community organization (like defense, infrastructure, public education). Contributive justice, by contrast, is concerned with questions about what community members owe their communities, in terms of commitments to work, public service, familial obligations, and so on. Social justice attends to the conditions that empower persons to participate fully in social life, including the basic provision of food and shelter, civil rights, education, health care, and the like. Commutative justice, finally, ensures the fairness of contractual and exchange relationships between community members. Conditions that undercut any of these obligations marginalize persons and communities in social life. Inequitable access to work, housing, the goods of health care, and civil rights, among others, all block participation in the common good.[26]

Solidarity is that virtue that empowers persons and communities to order social arrangements in ways that create the conditions for the common good. Solidarity goes beyond charity, the unilateral provision of goods by an empowered party to a disempowered party. In its affirmation of interrelatedness, solidarity is a "social virtue," inviting the participation and equal collaboration of parties that work in solidarity with one another.[27] Solidarity requires the difficult work of recognizing and exploring difference, forming the foundation of genuinely cooperative work.[28]

Solidarity responds to the moral contours of the redemptive project in which God calls persons to participate. God orders creation to an end (telos), an ultimate destiny that constitutes the basis of creation's flourishing. Human flourishing means that all persons have access to goods that enable the full development of human potentialities, participate fully and equally in social and political life, have opportunities to contribute to the many communities in which they are members, and enjoy fair and equitable relationships with other persons. Of course, it is often unclear exactly what arrangements will best promote the common good. Practices of discernment are required to make (always provisional) decisions about what common goods look like in any particular historical and cultural moment and what it will mean for persons and communities to access common goods adequately.

As a political virtue, solidarity pulls commitments away from particular constituencies, partisan allegiances, and money in politics toward commitments to broader human communities and the natural world. To practice the virtue of solidarity does not imply the wholesale abandonment of commitments to particular constituencies. But it is the active consideration of how commitments to constituencies advance or undermine the good of all. Politicians often must make hard decisions about how they will maintain power while also serving the common good. Constituents, moreover, often perceive that commitments to the common good do not directly advance their interests, and indeed, in some ways, actively undermine them. As a passionate commitment to the common good, solidarity encourages politicians to educate their constituents about how common goods are indeed *common*—that they benefit all citizens in a basic sense, even if the pursuit of common goods undermines constituent interests in the short run.

The reality of political practice is that politicians will sometimes make decisions that undermine the common good and thus oppose the demands of solidarity in order to maintain power. Politicians who wish to cultivate the virtue of solidarity will need to consider whether, in such situations, it is best to take a stand in the name of the common good and, by doing so, risk the partial or complete loss of political power. An alternative is to make decisions that undermine solidarity in the short run in order to maintain power but thereby open possibilities for long-term commitment to the common good. There is no clear and easy way to make decisions in such moments.

The virtue of solidarity, at minimum, shifts the spectrum along which political agents evaluate the virtue of good political work. In the U.S. context, the inflexible representation of partisan and constituent interests is often taken to be virtuous political agency. Skills and practices that enable parochial forms of representation, in other words, are understood to produce virtue. But one could imagine a spectrum along which solidarity is understood to be the primary virtue of political agency, with, perhaps, parochial representation being the vice of deficiency and paternalism being the vice of excess. Parochial representation, on the one hand, is vicious because it lacks a capacity both to imagine and to attend to the common good, focusing narrowly on the interests of local constituencies, partisan commitments, or moneyed interests. Paternalism, on the other hand, is vicious because its excessive zeal to provide for the "disadvantaged" eschews meaningful partnership with the persons and communities taken to be disadvantaged.

Even if politicians decide that they cannot practice solidarity in particular situations, opting instead for parochial representation, the virtue of solidarity itself makes possible a critical evaluation of such comportment. In such situations, an orientation to the virtue of solidarity discloses the conditions of viciousness and tragic choice in political life, and it reveals the horizon toward which political agents should aspire.

PREPARING THE WAY: POLITICS AS REPENTANCE

The project of political vocation, finally, demands attention to the habits and practices of repentance. Repentance recognizes that past political judgments have caused both intended and unintended harm and seeks to provide remedies for such harms as an expression of care for the created order.[29] Bonhoeffer's reflections on the nature of "ultimate and penultimate things" reveal the political character of repentance.

For Bonhoeffer God's grace extended to creation provides the purpose of all vocational work. The justification of the sinner by grace achieved in the life, death, and resurrection of Jesus Christ marks the decisive entry of God into the human experience. "The event of justification," the place and time Christ takes form in the world, positions human life before God. To be justified is to live life before God and thus to live a genuinely human life. It is also to experience genuine freedom "for God and for one another."[30] In the event of justification, the ultimate condition of reality effects a "complete break" with the time before it. That complete break reveals the preceding time as a penultimate moment, "a dark tunnel of human life, which was barred within and without and was disappearing ever more deeply into an abyss from which there is no exit."[31] The sinner is "torn out of imprisonment in [her] own ego" and anchored on a foundation outside of herself.[32] Thus, the event of justification transfigures the human experience, ushering it into a radically novel qualitative and temporal context.

Penultimate time is revealed to be penultimate only in relationship to the complete break that the ultimate effects. The break between penultimate and ultimate raises an obvious question: Can the penultimate moment, that is, "all that precedes the ultimate," be "taken seriously in its own way"? Since the ultimate "determines" the penultimate and since the penultimate loses its "self-sufficiency" in relationship to the ultimate, in what way, if any, can the penultimate moment have value? Should the penultimate simply be despised?

Bonhoeffer's answer to this question is a decisive no. For Bonhoeffer the "penultimate must be preserved for the sake of the ultimate." "Arbitrary destruction" of the penultimate can "seriously hinder" the ultimate.[33] Abuse of the penultimate threatens to undermine the ability of persons to hear and respond to the word of justification. Instead, Bonhoeffer argues, the penultimate must be actively "cared for" because "the way for the Word must be prepared."[34] Christians are obligated to active engagement for the good of the penultimate. To prepare the way for grace is "a matter of concrete intervention in the visible world," Bonhoeffer writes, "as concrete and visible as hunger and nourishment."[35] Preparing the way entails feeding the hungry, sheltering the homeless, freeing the slave, righting injustice, alleviating "disgrace, desolation, poverty, and helplessness," disrupting the privilege of the "well-fed and the powerful," and empowering those who have "lost self-control" and those "who are disappointed by a false faith."[36]

Preparing the way for persons to receive grace, however, is not a necessary condition of their receiving it. God's decision to enter into human experience cannot finally be prevented or ensured by human action: "No one can oppose Christ's coming," Bonhoeffer writes, but we can "hinder the receiving of grace."[37] The responsibility of Christians is to smooth out the way of grace. The smoothing and clearing, however, are always ultimately preparatory and, therefore, always penultimate actions. The proclamation of the Word of grace and its reception happen through divine agency, and thus the move from the penultimate to the ultimate moment is always ultimately a divine movement.

The work of preparing the way is not "simply a matter of creating certain desired and conducive conditions, such as creating a program of social reform." Rather, preparing the way is finally an expression of repentance.[38] In their sinfulness, human beings have created a world in which persons and communities are demeaned, degraded, and dehumanized. Human beings "become things, commodities, or machines," crippling the "orders," the institutional structures and settings that create the conditions of human flourishing.[39] To prepare the way is to respond to the neighbor who languishes and suffers because of human sinfulness. Such a response constitutes repentance, a "concrete changing of one's ways," both because it confesses guilt for hindering the Word of grace in the world and because it turns away from apostasy, acknowledging Jesus Christ as the source and standard for what "being human" and "being good" mean.[40]

Human efforts to work for the good of the neighbor as repentance constitute a kind of undoing: the undoing of harm human beings have caused to one another in their sinfulness, a leveling of the places made uneven through human-caused destruction, degradation, and violence to persons, communities, and the ecological contexts in which all creation flourishes. Though preparing the way does not cause "the event of justification," it empowers sinners to receive the grace of God as Jesus Christ makes his way to humanity.

Seen from Bonhoeffer's perspective, then, to participate in God's redemptive project is to prepare the way for the event of justification in the world. Preparing the way amounts to the work of repentance that undoes evils that hinder human flourishing.[41] As a political virtue, repentance recognizes that political agency often intentionally and unintentionally falls short of a passionate commitment to the common good. It understands evils caused by law and policy to degrade the capacities of persons and communities to participate fully in the event of Christ's taking form in the world. Thus, repentance shows that the common good that is at the heart of God's project is not simply a matter of worldly provision. The common good is not just about providing persons with the material, social, and political goods that create the conditions of human flourishing in the world. Rather, the common good that is the project of political vocation is more fundamentally about empowering persons and communities to participate in life before God. The virtue of repentance, then, fills out the theological meaning of "human flourishing."

Discernment, solidarity, and repentance work together to reorient political agency toward the common good, the project of political vocation. The project of political vocation, God's work to reconcile creation and Creator, is that condition that ultimately makes human flourishing possible. There are multiple conditions, explored in the previous chapter, that obstruct the realization of the common good in political life. At minimum, God's redemptive project constitutes the context in which the "genuinely human and profoundly moving" quality of political work is intelligible. For political agents who understand their work in the framing of vocation, political work is good—it engages something of the "genuinely human"—to the extent that it aspires to the common good, even when it fails to realize it.

7

IRONY AS A POLITICAL VIRTUE

Gov. Andrew Cuomo of New York, the *New York Times* observes, is "making history." Most everything the governor does, according to the governor himself, is "historic": The governor "has called a loan program for energy-efficient home improvements historic, as well as the creation of a new application process for economic development grants. The establishment of a Medicaid spending commission? That was historic, too."[1] Cuomo's penchant for claiming that his political achievements are "historic," the article reports, has caught the attention of many in Albany. Some wonder whether this bad habit undermines Cuomo's political credibility.

Of course, it is not surprising that politicians work hard, sometimes too hard, to promote themselves and cast their achievements in the best possible light. To govern, one has first to attain and then maintain power. To do both, one must, among other things, persuade relevant constituencies that one possesses qualities that make for good political leadership. By claiming that his achievements are "historic," Cuomo is saying in effect that he is a leader that history will remember favorably and thus that he possesses qualities enabling him to make historically significant contributions as a political leader. The governor wants to show, in other words, that he possesses political virtues—those habits that make him a good politician—and therefore exhibits good political character. Ironically, Cuomo was later embroiled in a controversy involving his alleged interference in an ethics commission that he himself established, an episode that for many belied the governor's aspirations to root out corruption in New York state government.[2]

The *New York Times* article is poking fun at Cuomo's overreach, that his claim to historical significance stretches the bounds of plausibility. It also points to the ways in which this overreach may actually serve to undermine Cuomo's effectiveness as a politician. Exaggeration, the article is suggesting, is evidence of political vice, a bad habit that impedes Cuomo's ability to do his work well. Cuomo's claim to political virtue turns out to be a vice. Aristotle understood vice to be either a deficiency or excess of virtue, while virtue exists as a mean between two vices of deficiency and excess.[3] Therefore, following Aristotelian logic, one might argue that veracity, truth telling, is a virtue, with exaggeration as its excessive form and disingenuousness as its deficient form.

The discussion above noted that some virtues are appropriate in some institutional settings but not in others. It might be that some measure of self-promotion is virtuous in political life. Politicians have political power when they have the backing of their constituents. To gain this support, politicians must show their constituencies they are worthy representatives. That is exactly what Cuomo was trying to do in celebrating his various "historic" achievements. In other settings, in faith communities, say, self-promotion may not be embraced as a virtue.

In political life, one could imagine, healthy self-promotion is a virtue lying between the vices of self-deprecation (a vice of deficiency) and self-aggrandizement (a vice of excess). On this continuum, Cuomo seems to have run afoul of the vice of self-aggrandizement, rendering his claims to historical significance unbelievable. One could argue that in religious life, by contrast, the continuum shifts, so that neither self-promotion nor self-aggrandizement is appropriate. Religious communities often call upon persons to develop the virtue of humility rather than self-promotion. Indeed, self-promotion might be the vice of excess on a continuum in which humility is the mean virtue.

The idea of virtue focuses attention on the aspect of the moral life relating to moral formation. The dual conditions of institutional differentiation and moral pluralism mean that moral formation is an experience of being pushed and pulled in different, sometimes competing, and sometimes even opposite, directions. If a politician were an adherent of a religious tradition that values the virtue of humility, he or she might find it difficult to reconcile that virtue with the habits required for self-promotion in political life. On a deep level, moral formation in institutionally differentiated societies is a fractured and fracturing process. Persons have to negotiate different moral identities that belong properly to different institutional settings: citizen, customer, soldier, patient, child of God, student, and employee, to name a few.

It might be that these differing moral identities are simply not reconcilable, and persons must learn how to live in the tensions that exist among them.

Niccolò Machiavelli was among the first theorists to articulate the problem of deep moral pluralism in the early modern West.[4] For Machiavelli, the classical exponents of republican politics urged that statesmen develop the virtues of "rage, vigor, fortitude in adversity, public achievement, order, discipline, happiness, strength, justice, above all assertion of one's proper claims and the knowledge and power needed to secure their satisfaction."[5] By contrast, Christians required the virtues of "charity, mercy, sacrifice, love of God, forgiveness of enemies, contempt for the goods of this world, faith in the life hereafter, belief in the salvation of the individual soul as being of incomparable value."[6] For Machiavelli, the this-worldly orientation of the republican virtues conflicts with the otherworldly orientation of the Christian virtues. One can be a good Christian or a good republican, Machiavelli seems to be saying, but one cannot be both.

Machiavelli raises a possibility worth querying in more detail. His suggestion is that political life requires a certain kind of self, whose virtues and dispositions are incompatible with those a person develops in Christian religious life. Michael Ignatieff proposes another possibility in the discussion above. For Ignatieff, politics requires a political self that is a projection for public audiences. But the political self is not identical with the politician's genuine self, the "private self," as he calls it. It is critical, Ignatieff argues, that politicians have the capacity to project a public self in political space. The public self does political work, but a politician must not allow the private self to be subsumed in it. Ignatieff's proposal implies a set of virtues that not only empowers a politician to do political work well but that also maintains the integrity of the politician's private self, holding it in tension with the public projection of the self that political life requires.

Ignatieff's idea of public self-projection speaks to the precariousness of political agency. Because it is an amplified form of moral agency, political agency is excessive in its very nature. Political agency also bears a complicated relationship to accountability. Statecraft consists in large measure in the work of founding and maintaining institutions that bring order to social life and enforce that order through accountability structures. Standing outside of the institutions it creates and maintains, political agency as statecraft is to some extent self-authorizing. Statecraft is itself a condition of political accountability. But that curious power—the power to create the conditions of political accountability—also renders statecraft a volatile form of moral agency. What holds statecraft to account?

The excessive and self-authorizing qualities of political agency threaten to corrupt the politician, to distort the politician's estimation of herself as a moral agent. The politician can get lost in the self-projection, conflating the public good and her own good.[7] Traditions of Western political thought endorse two characteristics of good political leadership, both demonstrating the volatility of political agency. The first is a salutary love of glory, which motivates the politician's dedication to and persistence in complex political projects. The second, from Machiavelli's account, is his complex idea of *virtú*, the set of characteristics that embolden political leaders to establish and maintain political institutions, despite the risks involved in doing so. Good political leadership requires both a love of glory and Machiavellian *virtú*. Both require counterbalance if the distance between the public and the private self is to be maintained. The argument of this chapter is that a theological understanding of irony provides a counterbalance to the volatility of political virtue.

PRECARIOUS GLORY

In book 5 of his *City of God*, St. Augustine criticizes classical thinkers who urged the love of human praise as a legitimate political drive. Augustine was aware of Cicero's insistence that the statesman thrives because of his desire for glory: "What stimulated our ancestors to so many remarkable and splendid deeds," Cicero wrote, "was their desire for glory, and it is on glory that the leading man of the state must be nourished."[8] Augustine argues Cicero's "pestilential opinion" obscures the proper object of human love, the "love of righteousness" and the "love of truth." The more a person resists the desire for "human praise," Augustine argues, "the more nearly does he approach the likeness of God."[9] Genuine glory, Augustine argues, is God's alone; the martyrs who suffered mightily because of their witness to God did not themselves earn glory. Rather, they reflected God's glory in their witness.[10] "True virtue," moreover, is incompatible with the pursuit of human glory, for true virtue is oriented away from the self and toward the "worship of the true God."[11] The "heroes of Rome," by contrast, ultimately fear death. Their pursuit of earthly glory is an enfeebled attempt to mitigate the finality of death.[12]

Cicero stands in a long tradition of classical republican, Renaissance, and later thinkers who recommended the love of glory or fame as a motivational "spur" for politicians to found and lead enduring political institutions.[13] In this tradition, the durability of politicians' glory parallels the durability of the political institutions they found and lead. To the extent that the state, as Cicero argues, secures "a happy life for its citizens, supported by resources and material wealth, renowned and respected for integrity," the "statesmen" responsible for it will be esteemed in the memories of civic descendants.[14] Glory is therefore a political passion that induces concern for the common good by way of self-interest; it transforms "ambition and self-interest into dedicated effort for the community."[15]

The desire for glory "nourishes," as Cicero says, the virtues of political imagination and constancy.[16] Alexander Hamilton, a later inheritor of the republican tradition, famously argues in *Federalist* No. 72 that the presidential office should not be constrained by term limits because such constraints dampen a prospective officer's desire to "plan and undertake extensive and arduous enterprises for the public benefit, requiring considerable time to mature and perfect them." Presidents, like all politicians, Hamilton argues, are motivated by "the love of fame, the ruling passion of noblest minds," prompting commitment to difficult and long-term political projects that extend beyond the president's tenure or even his lifetime.[17] The desire for fame, whose object is the enduring memory of political achievements, induces politicians not only to think beyond their own self-interest but to dare to imagine institutions of human artifice that aspire to do what human beings cannot: to endure indefinitely.

In the classical conception, then, the desire for glory is not simply an end in itself, fame for the sake of fame. Rather, it has a distinctive political telos, the advancement of political institutions. Glory is a precondition of good statecraft. To some extent, glory stands outside of the norms and practices of political institutions, because it precedes them. The desire for glory, however, has a dark side: it can be ruinously hubristic and self-serving, and it can motivate a desire to dominate others.

Augustine does not see the point of glory as a political virtue. To earn the "glory of conquest," Augustine argues, Rome needed to wage war to advance the imperial project. That project "would indeed have been accomplished more successfully had it been done by agreement," but in that case the glories that accompany victory in war would not have been available. Bellicosity, Augustine is saying, is the precondition of "human glory." But what difference does it make, he asks, "that some men should be conquerors and others conquered?" It is true that some citizens of Rome earned glory by human standards. But from the perspective of the citizens of the heavenly city, the boasting of "men" has no ultimate significance; it is only so much "smoke, which has no weight."[18]

Augustine's argument has the advantage of accounting for the volatility of fame. There is a thin line, one can imagine, between, on the one hand, the desire to earn fame for having made meaningful contributions to effective and durable political institutions and, on the other, the base drive for fame for fame's sake. The desire for glory, Augustine recognizes, can devolve into a straightforward "lust for mastery" (*libido dominandi*).[19] His argument, however, does not appreciate the ruler's role as "statesman," the leader motivated to found and actively maintain the institutions of the state. Indeed, to the extent that he acknowledges that rule involves state-craft, Augustine disparages it.[20] "Even certain worshipers of demons," he says, enjoy the rewards of earthly rule, which are ephemeral. Earthly rul-ers have already received their reward, Augustine refrains. The good Chris-tian emperor, by contrast, will be happy if he is just, humble, god fearing, merciful, gentle, benevolent, loving, contrite, and prayerful, among other qualities.[21] Augustine does not contemplate the ruler's role as institutional architect; thus, the political virtues he ascribes to the happy emperor do not account for this work. Augustine's happy emperor is ruler and judge, not founder and statesman. Earthly political institutions, in Augustine's vision, are necessarily fleeting. They are features of a penultimate moment that ultimately gives way to the eschaton. As in all regions of the moral life, good political administration in Augustine's view reflects virtue rightly ordered to God. The good ruler's political virtues flow from God, whose heavenly city is eternally founded. The political institutions of the heavenly city, whatever they may be, need no maintenance. Statecraft is not done in the city of God.

But here below, there is no happy emperor, or ruler of any kind, who can govern at remove from the complexities and vicissitudes of political institutions. Ruling in the earthly city inevitably entails the active mainte-nance of institutions, with an investment in their durability. It may be that a healthy ego is the necessary precondition of a vital political imagination and the resolve to push ahead with work that is, as Weber said, the "strong and slow boring of hard boards."

Precarious Virtú

Machiavelli approached the political virtues with a keen awareness of their ambiguous status relative to political institutions. With classical republican theorists, Machiavelli understood that the mark of good political work is the glory politicians earn in the memory of their posterity.[22] Glory is merited in particular for the work political agents do to establish and maintain durable political institutions.[23] To be successful in this work, political agents must develop certain virtues, which Machiavelli identifies with his elusive con-cept of *virtú*. Machiavelli's *virtú* departs in significant ways from the classical understanding of moral virtue. In classical framings, moral virtues are those habituated dispositions of the soul that orient a person toward the human end *eudaimonia*, happiness or flourishing. Unlike its ancient counterpart, *virtù* responds in Machiavelli's rendering to necessity rather than a natural or divinely created moral order.[24] *Virtù* is more often deliberate rather than habituated, more responsive to occasion and context than an expression of stable moral integrity. Finally, Machiavelli picks out a considerably different set of virtues than are found in classical examinations of moral virtue. *Virtù* for Machiavelli includes "flexibility, shrewdness, decisiveness, resolution and cunning," among other traits.[25]

For Machiavelli, politics often operates outside the boundaries of ordinary morality because politics is in part the activity involved in setting up the institutions and structures in which ordinary morality is nourished. To found a republic or a kingdom with good institutions, or to reform malfunctioning institutions, Machiavelli argues, one person must exercise sole responsibility: "A wise legislator when establishing a republic," he writes, "if he wants to serve not his own interests but the public good . . . should make every effort to ensure that all power lies in his own hands."[26] Political leaders should not be criticized for "extralegal actions" they may need to take in order to found republics. However, Machiavelli argues, power should not remain in the hands of a single ruler, if republican institutions are to thrive: one "person alone may be best at drawing up plans, but the institutions he has designed will not survive long if they continue to depend on the decisions of one man."[27] Therefore, Machiavelli absolves Romulus, who wished to found Rome on the Palatine Hill, for murdering his brother Remus, who wished to found the city on the Aventine Hill. Romulus, after founding the city of Rome, established a senate "to whose views he listened and advice he took." Therefore, Romulus' actions, in Machiavelli's interpretation, "were aimed at the public good and not at self-advancement."[28] Machiavelli continually commends the use of "ruthless methods" in the founding, re-establishing, or reformation of political orders, particularly in cases in which the populace is not yet trained to be good citizens or subjects.[29]

The exceptional actions that individuals take to found or re-establish a republic, Machiavelli emphasizes, must be in service of strong institutions that form good citizens. The *virtù* of the founder is not sufficient to sustain a political order. Instead, "the strength of the population as a whole . . . is what is needed to maintain good institutions." A populace must be "well ordered," as was the ancient Roman citizenry who "were in love with the glory and the common good of their homeland." Indeed, Machiavelli argues, a well-ordered populace is even wiser than individual rulers, or at least is no less wise, contrary to popular opinions suspicious of popular rule.[30]

Machiavelli criticizes "our religion" (Catholic Christianity), which, to the extent that it prepares persons for republican citizenship, he finds deficient in comparison to the religion of the ancient Romans. The former teaches persons to be "less concerned with their reputation in this world" than the next. It also "glorifies men who are humble and contemplative," regarding "humility, self-abasement, and contempt for worldly goods as supreme virtues."[31] "Classical" Roman religion, by contrast, valorized persons who had "already been heaped with worldly glories," especially "men such as generals of armies and rulers of states." It encouraged virtues like "boldness of spirit, strength of body, and all other qualities that make men redoubtable."[32] Roman Christianity, in other words, attenuates the formation of a strong citizenry.

In the formation and maintenance of strong political institutions, Machiavelli sees an asymmetry in the conduct of rulers and the conduct of the ruled. In times of institutional founding, re-establishment, or reformation, rulers are not to be constrained by ordinary standards of moral conduct. Indeed, in such times, it will be necessary for rulers to act in morally outrageous ways in order to found or reform strong political institutions. In order for these institutions to last, however, political institutions must occasion the formation of good citizens, those who possess a "strength of character," enabling them to endure the slings and arrows of fortune.[33] The ruler's license to act in morally ambiguous ways when strong political institutions are absent contrasts, therefore, with the moral integrity of a citizenry formed in well-ordered political institutions.

Machiavelli's insight is that rulers always stand with one foot outside of the institutional boundaries of political life that make ordinary moral and political conduct intelligible. That is because the work of rulers constitutes the precondition of strong political institutions. Machiavelli is not saying that rulers are devoid of ordinary moral awareness or are absolutely unaccountable to moral norms. He is affirming that political work by its very nature bears an ambiguous relationship to ordinary moral standards, which Machiavelli would affirm bind citizens in well-ordered political institutions.

Machiavelli is not, of course, the first theorist to notice the volatile nature of political agency. But, unlike many who recommend taming political agency through the cultivation of virtue, Machiavelli understands that the ruler's *virtù* depends on his relationship to political institutions.[34] Rulers are accountable to well-ordered political institutions to the extent that such institutions empower citizens to hold their rulers accountable. But that is a contingent arrangement, one to which rulers should aspire to create. In an absolute sense, however, rulers are accountable only to fortune, Fortúna, over which they exercise limited, but never total, control.[35]

There is certainly much in Machiavelli's political ethic that is deeply problematic; the argument here is not intended to recommend Machiavelli's statecraft in every aspect. But his wisdom about the nature of political virtue, its inherent moral ambiguity, is salutary. Statecraft as the art of building and maintaining political institutions works at some remove from the normative frameworks political communities provide. At times, statecraft calls upon virtues—dispositions that inform skillful practices—that conventional norms do not endorse.

STANDING OUTSIDE OF ONESELF

Both the love of glory and the political skillfulness associated with *virtú* are in some measure necessary to do the work of politics well. Both, however, threaten moral viciousness, and neither has an internal mechanism to forestall vice. The politician's commitment to building durable political institutions is supposed to direct the desire for glory toward the common good, since glory is earned only in making lasting contributions. But the desire for glory is often shortsighted, easily duped, and, as Augustine understood, only a short step away from the desire for domination. The politician who cultivates *virtú* to respond skillfully to political necessities will likely get her hands dirty—that is, she will break a moral code for the sake of a political good. But there is nothing to ensure that *virtú* does not devolve into despotism, in which rulers break moral codes for their own good. In short, these two qualities threaten to undermine what Weber calls the politician's "sense of proportion," his ability to recognize the limitations of power's constructive use.[36]

It may be necessary to establish external mechanisms that ensure that these drives issue in virtuous dispositions, that is, that they capture an appropriate mean between vices of excess and deficiency.[37] But a truly virtuous politician, that is, a politician who has some capacity to check the volatility of political drives, will have a disposition that empowers her to do so. The virtuous politician, in other words, will have a critical awareness of her own drives and motivations. She will be inclined to think that these drives and motivations, from time to time, become excessive and will need to be checked. Reinhold Niebuhr's theological exploration of irony offers one approach to thinking about such a capacity for self-awareness in political life.

As the discussion above indicates, Niebuhr had little confidence that groups and their representatives would attend to interests beyond their own.

Many commentators have noted that Niebuhr's social philosophy, though it addresses the vicissitudes of group "egotism," does not adequately capture the complex dynamics of human association.[38] It is not clear, for example, what it means to suggest that a group per se exercises agency. It is also far from clear that human beings, when constituted in groups, necessarily pursue their own self-interest, disregarding the good of others.[39] When it comes to thinking theologically about political agency, Niebuhr's theological anthropology is far more helpful.

Niebuhr explores human agency at its limits. For Niebuhr, the limits of human agency are defined both by finitude and sin. Human beings find themselves in a peculiar situation. On the one hand, they are limited in a number of ways. Human lives have limited duration. Human beings have limited power, both to bring about new states of affairs and to change already existing states of affairs that condition their action. Human beings, furthermore, have limited capacities for moral discernment, being unable in some situations to weigh competing goods or to know just what the consequences of their actions will be.

On the other hand, human beings are drawn beyond their own finitude, in that they have a limited capacity for self-transcendence. Because of this capacity, humans know, first, that they are finite in the ways described above. They are able, moreover, to separate themselves from their own needs and desires. That separation creates critical distance; human beings can stand apart from themselves and critically evaluate their drives and motives. Self-transcendence accounts for the human capacity to love others unselfishly, to attend to the good of others even if that means sacrificing one's own good. Self-transcendence is therefore the necessary condition of moral agency. It is also the condition of the freedom, however limited, that human beings experience.

Human beings are thus in the paradoxical situation of being both finite and free, both tied to the creaturely conditions of their experience and also able to transcend them. Finitude distinguishes human beings from God; their freedom, however, pulls human beings in a Godward direction. In this paradoxical space, Niebuhr argues, human beings experience anxiety, "the inevitable concomitant of the paradox of freedom and finiteness in which man [sic] is involved."[40]

Anxiety is also the precondition of sin, which, in its basic form, is "rebellion against God, [the] effort to usurp the place of God."[41] Human beings recognize their own "weakness," as Niebuhr says, "the basic insecurity of their existence." They know death is imminent. In response to anxiety, humans attempt to secure themselves against the vicissitudes of finite existence. Exercising a "will-to-power," the human being, in the face of the "basic insecurity of human existence," aspires "to make himself doubly secure and by the insignificance of his place in the total scheme of life to prove his significance."[42] The exercise of the will-to-power in this way is what Christian traditions have called the sin of pride, "sin in its quintessential form."[43] Pride in its social dimension is "collective egotism," which takes the form of "lust-for-power," "contempt toward the other," "hypocrisy," and "the claim of moral autonomy by which the self-deification of the social group is made explicit by its presentation of itself as the source and end of existence."[44]

Human beings cannot escape their position in the paradoxical tension between freedom and finitude. They are beset by the anxiety that this paradoxical location generates. Anxiety is not itself sin, but it constitutes the ground of temptation to sin. To be genuinely human is to hold this paradoxical space, despite the dual temptations to pride, the false claim of unconditioned freedom, and to sensuality, the false abandonment of self-transcendence.

The dynamic between finitude and freedom creates the conditions of three characteristically human experiences: pathos, tragedy, and irony. The pathetic describes experiences in which human beings suffer hardship, or even meet their demise, for reasons that are beyond their control. Pathetic situations elicit pity, the empathetic response to the misfortune of others that is free from judgment.[45] The tragic sensibility, by contrast, describes those experiences in which human beings consciously assert a strength or virtue of some kind in the attempt to shape their destiny but are somehow undone in doing so. In "pure tragedy," Niebuhr writes, "suffering is self-inflicted. The hero does not transmute what happens to him but initiates the suffering by his own act."[46]

Irony, finally, recognizes that human beings assert agency in ways that reveal a "hidden vanity or pretension," which goes unrecognized by the agent. Both tragedy and irony are distinguished from the pathetic. Both the ironic and the tragic entail responsibility on the part of the actor, whereas the pathetic does not. Both tragedy and irony involve the assertion of one's agency to claim control over one's destiny, and both entail that assertion coming to ruin in some way. In the tragic situation, however, the assertion of agency is a conscious decision; in the ironic situation, it is an unconscious decision. The unrecognized or unconscious assertion of agency in ironic situations amounts to the agent's "unconscious weakness." Irony also has a comedic dimension. Like comedy, irony "consists of apparently fortuitous incongruities in life which are discovered, upon closer examination, to be not merely fortuitous."[47] Incongruities that emerge in ironic situations are not "merely fortuitous" since they involve the unrecognized assertion of agency. Thus, ironic situations "elicit not merely laughter," the mark of comedic situations, "but a knowing smile," the recognition on the part of an observer that another's unrecognized weakness has caused things to go afoul.

Pathos, tragedy, and irony are all motifs that describe situations in which the tension between freedom and finitude collapses, albeit for different reasons. Pathos relates most directly to human finitude; it is elicited when human beings, through no fault of their own, run up against the limits of human agency in ways that cause misfortune: "Suffering caused by purely natural evil," Niebuhr writes, "is the clearest instance of the purely pathetic."[48] In pathetic situations, human freedom is obviated when finitude comes to its logical, though sudden and unexpected, conclusion. Whereas pathos relates primarily to finitude, tragedy and irony relate primarily to freedom. Both involve sin as the unwarranted assertion of agency in ways that transgress the horizon of human freedom. Both tragedy and irony relate to the paradigmatic sin of pride. Both become possibilities when human beings put themselves in God's place and attempt to exercise godlike sovereignty over their own destinies. In tragedy, the assertion of freedom, which brings finitude to fruition, is conscious and unwarranted. In irony, the assertion of freedom, which brings finitude to fruition, is unconscious and unwarranted. Strength often hampers human efforts in the tragic situation; foible or weakness often hampers human efforts in the ironic one.

For Christians, Niebuhr argues, human history does not ultimately have a tragic quality. The tragic motif assumes that human destructiveness is inevitable, the logical result of the assertion of human virtue. But, Niebuhr writes, "there is always the ideal possibility that man [sic] will break and transcend the simple harmonies and necessities of nature, and yet not be destructive."[49] Human beings are both creatures and creators; the tragic motif embraces the latter but forgets the former. Thus, the tragic motif not only fails to "observe the limits of [human] freedom"; it effectively regards such limits with disdain.[50]

The proper view of human destructiveness in history is the ironic one. Irony is the attitude with which God judges the prideful assertion of human agency. God regards human history as the "divine judge who laughs at human pretensions without being hostile to human aspirations."[51] In tragic situations, human beings have lost sight of their own finitude. God, however, is always aware of the pretensions to godlikeness that are obscured in the human enthusiasm to achieve the superhuman. Since irony entails an observer's awareness of a condition that cripples a naïve other, God's perspective on human history is ironic. Therefore, Niebuhr argues, "the Christian faith tends to make the ironic view of human evil in history the normative one."[52]

Niebuhr does not present pathos, irony, and tragedy as virtues. They are instead motifs that describe the human experience in relationship to the ways in which human beings assert agency. But Niebuhr's own work in *The Irony of American History* suggests the possibility of an ironic disposition, the critical awareness that unrecognized motives likely inform one's motivations, passions, and drives. An ironic disposition induces an interrogation of one's own framing of value. Niebuhr assesses the unrecognized "pretensions" that inform American judgments about its motives for acting in the world. He analyzes the ways in which the American narrative, which emphasizes freedom, innocence, mastery over fate, prosperity, and the like, masks materialistic and imperialistic impulses that go unrecognized in public rhetoric. The American presence on the global scene is marked by ironic contradictions between its pretentious self-understanding and its latent motivations.

The ironic disposition, then, is the habit of second-guessing one's motivations and moral commitments.[53] It is an awareness of the distance between normative frameworks (of how the world ought to be) and reality on the ground (how the world really is). The ironic disposition also includes an awareness of the existence of implicit normative frameworks (what one really thinks) that may work at cross-purposes with explicit normative framings (what one says publicly that one thinks).

Normative frameworks in political life are often cast in stories, and skillful politicians are good storytellers. They construct narratives about their experiences and values that intersect with similar narratives constituents tell about themselves.[54] Indeed, as Niebuhr recognizes, there are narrative-driven myths about American life—myths of America as a "chosen nation," a "Christian nation," an "innocent nation," and so on. Political narratives often intersect with these myths, making them intelligible to public audiences. A politician with an ironic disposition would be careful about the way that myths and narratives construct value, and would question how these stories conceal ulterior motives that shape political action. Had Andrew Cuomo, in that relatively benign example, cultivated an ironic disposition, he might have seen the irony in naming so many of his achievements as exceptional and have been more judicious about his use of that label.

The ironic disposition is a political virtue in a theology of political vocation because it holds distance between the public self that politics requires and one's authentic sense of self. That space is necessary because the latter, the authentic self, is the one most likely to stay in tune with the greater purposes of political work. In a theology of political vocation, those greater purposes are cast in terms of the project of political vocation, God's unfolding project to reconcile creature and Creator.

The ironic disposition responds to the volatility of the political virtues that aim to preserve and expand power. They are virtues of self-assertion, which value, as Machiavelli writes, "greatness of spirit, strength of body, and all other things capable of making men very strong." The danger with self-assertion, Niebuhr recognizes, is that it ventures down a slippery slope toward pride and hubris. Self-assertion values freedom but threatens to turn a blind eye to finitude, ignoring the tension between them. It is therefore one condition of the tragic in political experience.

The ironic disposition both recognizes that the virtues of self-assertion are necessary to politics and also prevents them from confusing the purposes of the self with the greater purposes of political life. Politicians will need to dissimulate, to treat rivals as opponents and to fight hard (and dirty sometimes) to beat them, to assert their fundamental commitments as correct and their opponents' commitments as wrong, to compromise sometimes with the latter, and to experience violations of ordinary morality with a degree of toughness.[55] Irony reminds the politician that the public show that these behaviors often require is just a show that serves an instrumental purpose, not reality itself. It also reminds politicians to critically consider where the line between political instrumentality and outright moral evil is drawn.

A danger in recommending the ironic disposition as a political virtue is that irony can itself become a vice. Using the Aristotelian paradigm, one can imagine that irony exists on a continuum between naïveté (the vice of deficiency) and cynicism (the vice of excess). Irony helpfully guards against naïveté in political life, the vice of deficient attention to the difference between the political and private selves. Cynicism, by contrast, is creating excessive distance between the public and genuine selves, so much so that the public self can no longer translate the best aspirations of the genuine self into political agency. The cynic believes that politics is a sham, not worth the slings and arrows that political life inevitably brings. Irony's response to cynicism is that politics is not a sham, though it is an irreducibly human activity. It is fundamentally fragile and therefore requires irony's careful and constant attention.

8

GOOD POLITICAL COMPETITION

The last several chapters have argued that the idea of political vocation values the normative structure of political norms and practices as they exist in political institutions, because, as a "calling in" place, vocation affirms creation as a context in which God's project of redemption unfolds. But vocation also seeks to transform institutional structures in relationship to God's redeeming work. Vocation, in other words, pulls political life in the direction of God's redemptive purposes, orienting human work in the direction of God's work.

Vocation therefore inspires virtues and dispositions that critically respond to political dynamics. Another way of saying this is that vocational dispositions ensure that the political virtues remain virtues. Thus, discernment challenges allegiances to particular goods and constituencies by orienting political judgment to the common good. The ironic disposition, moreover, prevents the drive and desire for glory from degenerating into a destructive pridefulness. In orienting political work to the divine project of redemption, vocation makes secular political work as good as it can be. This final chapter explores the way vocation orients political agency in the form of competition.

CHALLENGE AND RESPECT

The practice of politics is fundamentally competitive. Politics is about winning and losing; thus, it is about winners and losers. Sometimes political competition generates decisive victory or defeat. More often, politics results in partial victories and losses. Whether victory or defeat is complete or partial, political competition requires thoughtful calculation. One can, for example, attempt to work with one's opponents to create a state of affairs in which everyone wins, or, more modestly, to compromise so that all parties secure some of what each wants at the cost of complete victory. In other situations, one may take a stand on a deeply held commitment, even if it means defeat. One might calculate that short-term defeat might invite long-term gain, or one might decide that some situations demand a stand even if defeat is total and devastating.

A sufficient understanding of political agency—questions about what one can and should do in a political vocation—can be answered only by considering the nature of political competition. Theologians have largely neglected this question. One reason for this is that in the past two decades, theologians have been mostly concerned about the way ordinary citizens, rather than political officials, should participate in political life. For ordinary citizens, theologians have argued, democratic politics is a public space in which informed citizens articulate arguments about political policies in light of their view of the good life. In democratic public spaces—in the "public square" in the metaphorical rendering—citizens of all kinds are obliged to provide rationales for their arguments so that other citizens can both understand and respond to them. Such an obligation is supposed to be problematic for citizens who rely on theological rationales for their public arguments, since theological rationales invoke faith commitments, resisting rational argumentation in public space. The question of how religious citizens are supposed to participate in democratic deliberation consumed much attention from theologians and political theorists alike in the 1990s and the first decade of the twenty-first century.

The residue of this debate still frames the way many theologians think about political agency. Theologians still imagine that democratic politics is much like an academic seminar, in which "conversation partners" make arguments about issues for others to consider. Conversation partners should offer responses and counterproposals to public arguments, and they are to do so in ways that reflect theological commitments to humility and civility.[1] They are encouraged to treat public conversation as a "playful" activity, in which participants are aware of their necessarily incomplete and contingent view of the good.[2] In playful public conversation, conversation partners should be aware of the opportunity to learn from others who have different fundamental commitments and thus differing proposals for law and policy. They should therefore be willing to abandon their views when colleagues show them more adequate ways of thinking about issues.

Politicians are well advised to follow some of the prescriptions theologians and other theorists offer to ordinary citizens who participate in the democratic public sphere. There is nothing wrong with reminding politicians that they, too, have an obligation to participate civilly in public debate in which important decisions are made about law and policy. But, in key respects, the political space that politicians and other political officials inhabit is not the democratic public sphere in which ordinary citizens participate. Politicians not only identify good ideas about law and policy and good arguments to back them up; they must ultimately use political power to put these ideas into practice. The putting of ideas into practice raises the stakes in politics for obvious reasons: communities have to live by and with the decisions politicians make.

In a democracy, political competition is supposed to be a civil practice. Absent functioning political structures, rival constituencies would likely resolve differences through violence. Democratic constitutions create structures in which citizens and their representatives first deliberate and then decide on laws and policies that govern the political community. Both deliberative and decisional processes are supposed to be open to the participation of all citizens or their duly elected representatives. The openness of political spaces in democratic polities lends legitimacy to the competitive moments of political life. In absolute terms, one might expect political competition to be anomic rather than unifying, since it undermines the coherence of political communities. No constituency, after all, wants to be denied its aspirations for political life. But, since citizens get to participate in a political process they fundamentally endorse, all will tolerate, at least to some extent, decisions generated in that process, even when decisions go against the will of some constituencies in favor of others. On a basic level, then, political competition is civil when political processes ensure the persistence of the political community (rather than its dissolution into violence), despite disagreements that only competition can resolve.

Keeping the political community going, however, is a low bar for civil political competition, and it is far from capturing what many would imagine good political competition to look like. At the moment, however, it often appears that the simple persistence of the political community (and the avoidance of political violence) is the only marker of political civility in the U.S. context. Politicians, particularly at the federal level, seem to be unwilling to participate in political processes that one might think demonstrate civil competition. The current and recent U.S. Congresses are infamously polarized. Republicans and Democrats in Congress are evidently resistant to compromise, preferring to spend time and effort undermining one another's

political aims. American politicians are skilled at the practice of campaigning, requiring a capacity to draw stark, even artificial, contrasts between
their opponents and themselves. But skillful governing, unlike skillful campaigning, requires a different approach to political competition, one that
values compromise, flexibility, and teamwork, rather than their opposites.
American politicians have apparently confused the competition involved in
good governing for the competition involved in good campaigning.[3]

If the simple persistence of the political community and the avoidance
of violence mark a low bar, it is difficult to know what might constitute
more robust criteria for good political competition. Political competition
is a curious phenomenon: it is apparently anomic, a force of social dissolution, but it is also intended to forestall social anomie. For political competition to be good, it must strike a delicate balance: it must challenge or oppose
political adversaries, aiming for victory, but it must do so without disrespect-
ing opponents. An adequate conception of good political competition will
therefore hold challenge and respect in tension, showing how one can both
oppose and still affirm another in the practice of politics.

In ordinary social contexts (i.e., in nonpolitical spaces), challenge and
opposition are sometimes construed or experienced as forms of disrespect.
Disagreement with a neighbor's opinion, for example, can be construed,
often falsely, as a negative judgment on the neighbor's character. In political
life, however, competition can be understood as a modality of respect. To
compete with another is to acknowledge that the other is indeed a competitor, an agent worthy of competition. Fair political competition, in other
words, confers political status; it affirms that competitors are fully empowered political agents whose passions and interests must be recognized and
considered, if not finally affirmed.[4] When done well, competition is a way
that citizens recognize and affirm one another as political agents.

THE LIMITS OF POLITICAL PASSION

If part of what makes political competition good is that it is a status-
conferring practice, one can ask what is going on when one confers status
on another by recognizing the other as a political competitor. The discussion of Bonhoeffer's ethics of responsibility above provided a theological
treatment of the relationship between the vocation of politics, political
responsibility, and political representation. For Bonhoeffer, vocation is participating in the ground of reality, Christ's taking form in the world. Ethics
as formation in Christ entails the work of taking responsibility for the dignity and flourishing of others. Bonhoeffer's theological rationale describes
the moral and theological shape of political work. Political work is one form

of responsibility. Political officials take responsibility for the constituencies they represent. Politicians seek to operationalize their fundamental commitments not just for themselves but for the good of their constituents, for whose political welfare they are responsible. One way of describing the status that political agents confer upon one another in good political competition, then, is in terms of the capacity agents exercise to represent political communities responsibly. In good political competition, therefore, competitors honor one another as responsible political agents who pursue fundamental commitments to enhance the welfare of the communities they represent.

The problem is that political competition itself militates against this; it invites competitors to blur the lines between good competition and disrespect, between adversaries and enemies. A political adversary in a democratic context, Chantal Mouffe argues, is an "opponent with whom we share a common allegiance to the democratic principles of 'liberty and equality for all,' while disagreeing about their interpretation."[5] What makes adversaries different from enemies is that adversaries do not take each other to be fundamentally wicked. Enemies are despised because they do not share, and are even hostile toward, the fundamental commitments that make citizenship in a particular political body intelligible.[6] Adversaries, by contrast, endorse the same fundamental commitments but disagree about how these commitments inform particular political judgments.

Competition can encourage a zero-sum logic of winners and losers, fostering habits of mind and practice that cast opponents as those who deserve to lose because they are unworthy of respect. Said another way, there is nothing about competition per se that prevents competitors from mistaking adversaries for enemies. Moreover, it is far easier to compete against enemies than against adversaries. It is easier to compete when competitors imagine that opposition comes from a place of fundamental and hostile disagreement, when it ordinarily does not. Enemies, after all, do not deserve political respect and, therefore, do not deserve the hard work that political respect requires. Enemies must be defeated, perhaps at any cost.

Competition both requires and inspires passion, and passion is a critically important political emotion. Political passion, in turn, sustains competition. Max Weber describes political passion as "matter-of-factness," a "passionate devotion to a cause, to the god or demon who is its overlord." He contrasts political passion to passion as an "inner bearing" of "sterile excitation." Political passion for Weber is more like devotion and less like excitation, in that passion requires an object toward which one's efforts are dedicated, a "cause."[7] And yet political passion is still passionate in the ordinary sense of the term. Passion is liable to get carried away, to become, as

Michael Walzer argues, "impetuous, unmediated, all-or-nothing."[8] Passion is a necessary condition of political competition, and it also infuses competition with emotional volatility.[9] The challenge is to endorse passion as an aspect of political competition but to constrain the impulses in competition that threaten to undermine political respect. The argument here is that a particular account of the *imago Dei* provides a theological rationale for good political competition.

It is easy to appeal to the *imago Dei* as a center of value, a "spark of the divine" conferring irreducible moral worth on each person. From a theological perspective, the argument might go, political competition is good when it does not distort the image of God in others and indeed honors and enhances human lives. In this approach, the *imago Dei* constitutes a stable moral criterion, which both sets a threshold requirement for the minimum conditions of human flourishing while also generating an imperative to promote human flourishing to the fullest extent possible.

This argument has promise, but there are problems with it. One problem has to do with the way in which the *imago Dei* confers value upon the human creation. The argument above holds that human beings are like God in that they are ontologically similar to God. Human beings possess faculties like reason and will that distinguish them from other animals. The ontological similarity that the *imago Dei* confers reflects God's being and therefore constitutes the basis of irreducible moral worth. This view, however, ignores insights from theological sources that emphasize "covenantal relationship," rather than "ontological identity," as the locus of human dignity in the image of God.[10] In God's trinitarian being, God is God-in-relationship. Thus, the ontology of the *imago Dei* is not merely reflected in the human capacity for reason and will; rather, it is more fundamentally reflected in the human capacity for relationship with God, other human beings, and the nonhuman world.

The relational character of the divine being, however, is in tension with competition in human affairs. Owing to the conditions of human finitude—of time, space, and causality—human beings always exist in potentially competitive relationships with one another. Even when human beings seek to work cooperatively with one another on shared projects, the condition of finitude creates opportunities for competition.[11] God, by contrast, exists on a "plane of being and activity" unconstrained by the conditions of finitude. The divine persons, therefore, do not exist in competitive relationships with one another or with creation. The problem, then, is this: How can the *imago Dei*, which grounds human dignity in the noncompetitive character of God's relational being, serve as a moral guide for political competition in a fundamentally competitive world?

At the root of this problem lies the distance between the different "planes of being and activity" on which human beings and God exist. The conditions that make competition possible on the human plane, but are absent on the divine plane, constitute one way of describing the intractable distance between the two. There are, of course, many theological accounts of how this distance is traversed, in God's graceful movement into history through the life, death, and resurrection of Jesus Christ; in the exercise of human agency in ways that close the distance between creature and Creator; or in combinations of both.

Reinhold Niebuhr, the discussion in the chapters above showed, offers a clear account of the distance between the divine and human planes. Niebuhr's analysis of group egotism is powerful in the elegance of its explanation of political dynamics. When one looks around the world, after all, one sees in political life many examples of human groups—political parties, lobbying organizations, nations, among others—working to pursue their self-interest in ways that demonstrate little regard for the interests of others. In Niebuhr's account, the capacity for limited self-transcendence, that which makes human beings human and also relates human beings to the divine being, is lost in the aggregating of individuals into groups. The quantitative combination of individuals into groups effectively measures the qualitative distance between the divine and human planes. Groups are, in effect, more animal than human. The work of politics amounts to constraining group egotism through the use of political power.

An advantage of Niebuhr's approach is that it preserves the distance between the plane of human finitude, in which competition is a condition, and the plane of divine action, in which it is not. But Niebuhr's view is not sufficiently fine grained to account for the complex workings of political agency. Commentators, for example, have argued that it simply is not the case that groups inevitably pursue base self-interest when they enter the political sphere.[12] Beyond that, if groups lose the defining human capacity, it is hard to make sense of political respect in Niebuhr's account, since respect is respect of humans qua humans. There is a line somewhere demarcating the forest of group egotism from the trees of individual political agency.

A theology of political vocation must account for some form of other-regarding virtue to make sense of good political competition. The ironic disposition described in the previous chapter empowers one to *step outside* oneself to appraise one's own interests critically. Similarly, for political agents to recognize and appreciate, if not fully to affirm and endorse, the interests of competitors, they need to *step inside* the perspectives of others, at least to some extent. Such a capacity makes political compromise possible, while also chastening competition so that it is not motivated by disrespect.

RELATIONALITY, RECOGNITION, AND COMPETITION

An understanding of the *imago Dei* as a "spark of the divine," an ontological feature of human being that reflects the divine image, threatens to obscure God's Trinitarian identity. Relationality is at the heart of the divine identity. To be made in the image of God is to exist in relationship with others; just as the identities of the Trinitarian persons are only intelligible in the relationships between them.

In his earlier work *Creation and Fall*, Bonhoeffer argues that at the heart of the idea of the image of God is the notion that human beings are created to be free for the other.[13] Relationality is similarly at the heart of the "Christological realism" Bonhoeffer articulates in his *Ethics*.[14] For Bonhoeffer, Jesus Christ is both ontologically and ethically primary: Christ is both the locus of the real and the "pattern for right action." To act responsibly is to be formed in the being of Christ by exercising "deputyship," as William Schweiker calls it, acting "for and on behalf of others just as Christ acted." To be formed in Christ as Christ's deputy is to inhabit an ontological space in which being in relationship with others is constitutive of identity: by "defining responsibility in terms of 'deputyship,'" Bonhoeffer also claims that the *moral identity* of any agent is constituted in his or her relation to the concrete other person."[15] What is most real about human being, that place where persons are formed in Christ, is irreducibly relational; human beings are what they are only in relationship to others. What shows that human beings exist in the divine image is that they are formed in Christ by virtue of deputyship.

There is, then, a close link in Bonhoeffer's work between creation in the divine image in which freedom means being for the neighbor and formation in Christ in which human beings take responsibility for the neighbor. Both ideas establish the divine identity in the human experience through relationality and service. Both, in other words, show the intersection of the divine and creaturely planes of existence at the point of relationality oriented to responsible action.

For Bonhoeffer, the ongoing presence of God in human experience implies a task, not simply a feature of human identity. The task is acting for and on behalf of others for their good. John Calvin had a similar understanding. Sanctification in Calvin's understanding is a process, a pilgrim's journey through the world, in which the image of God is gradually, though always incompletely, "renewed and restored" in the elect. As the image of God is restored, the capacity to recognize and respond in love to the image of God in others is enhanced. Calvin argues that the elect who discern the image of God in others have no reason not to respond in love to them. "Say, 'He is a stranger'; but the Lord has given him a mark that ought to be familiar to you, by virtue of the fact that he forbids you to despise your own flesh."[16] Just as it is gradually restored in each person, the image of God gradually elicits and empowers regard for the other.[17]

Political competition at its best, it has been argued, is a status-conferring practice in which competitors, in the very act of competition, bestow respect. Political respect means recognition of the competitor as one whose political agency is legitimate and whose passions and interests are worthy. In the theological framing developed here, political recognition is a capacity to see the image of God in the competitor. The divine image, however, is not simply a Godlike feature of the competitor's identity. It is, rather, the other's identity constituted in relationship to her neighbors (in political space, her constituents) that entails the task of taking responsibility for advancing their good. From a theological perspective, then, good political competition exists when competitors respect one another by virtue of recognizing the other's efforts to take responsibility for the good of the neighbor.

SEEING FROM THE OTHER'S POINT OF VIEW: THE INTEGRITY OF POLITICAL COMPETITION

So far, the argument has urged that a theological understanding of recognition and respect accounts for the meaning of good political competition. The next step is to specify the virtue of good political competition that generates recognition and respect—that disposition or quality of character, in other words, that makes political officials capable of competing well with others. The problem here is to describe a disposition that allows for recognition as a genuine appreciation for the competitor as a dedicated representative of a constituency but that falls short of a demand to embrace all of what the competitor values. In the theological framing developed above, recognition is a form of relationality, an affirmation of the relational character of the image of God—but what that means exactly also needs to be clarified.

The chapter above argued that persons who pursue a vocation in politics will cultivate the virtue of solidarity, the capacity both to imagine and passionately to pursue the common good, defined here in relationship to God's commitment to the flourishing of creation. As a virtue, solidarity tends to think big: it imagines the most expansive contexts in which created things (human and nonhuman alike) flourish in relationship to one another. The demands of political loyalty, however, are in tension with the demands of solidarity. Political loyalty, the chapter above suggested, demands that politicians will not always orient themselves to the goods of the most expansive communities. Common goods, of course, can be achieved on a number of associational levels: one can imagine common goods from the position of, and in relationship to, different community locations and scales (e.g., local, national, and global communities). Political loyalties, it might be said, encourage political agents to imagine common goods in more local scales and contexts, while solidarity pulls considerations of common goods in more expansive directions, across geographical, cultural, and experiential distances. While those who would pursue a political vocation will cultivate the virtue of solidarity, they will also negotiate the legitimate claims of political loyalty. The tension between competing loyalties creates the condition of political competition.

To be adversaries and not enemies, competitors need to recognize that they share commitments to fundamental political norms, to values like liberty, equality, fair opportunity, and the like. Agreement on fundamental norms makes competition intelligible. Were it not for some agreement on fundamental issues, disagreement would amount to unintelligible moral gibberish. In that sense, good political competition requires a degree of solidarity. But competitors are not required to share all of one another's interests, values, or goals in any robust way. In good competition, competitors remember that they recognize and affirm fundamental normative commitments, but they disagree about how these fundamental commitments inform judgments on specific issues shaping law and policy.

A degree of solidarity makes political competition intelligible. Similarly, a degree of toleration makes political competition possible. Toleration is a characteristic liberal virtue.[18] It is the habit of accommodation that allows persons to pursue whatever understanding of the good life they want as long as that pursuit does not interfere with the ability of others to do the same. Toleration does not require that persons engage difference in any meaningful way but only that they accommodate difference.[19] For example, compromise as a form of competition requires that competitors accept, even if they do not endorse, undesired outcomes that the other wants as a condition of securing desired outcomes. Toleration alone, however, is not enough to sustain good political competition.

In the theological framing developed above, political respect requires that political competitors affirm one another as representatives of the good of the constituencies they represent. Respect of this sort demands that competitors understand, in the most generous way possible, why it is that the other cares about what she cares about, even if competitors ultimately cannot affirm one another's interests, values, and goals. Competitors, in other words, need to step outside their own perspective to view the task of responsibility from the perspective of the other. Otherwise, competitors cannot genuinely understand what it means for the other to represent the good of a constituency. In some situations, toleration can generate a solution to a political impasse in the form of compromise. But toleration falls short of a robust form of mutual understanding. It does not challenge competitors, in other words, to step inside the other's perspective to appreciate the other's interests, values, and goals.

While solidarity and toleration are both important, the more urgent dispositions for political competition are integrity and collegiality. Integrity is "rightly relating the complexity of natural, social, and reflective goods through a commitment to respect and enhance life before God."[20] For any political agent to do her work with integrity, she needs to consider carefully how political goods can best be arranged to respect and enhance life before God. The problem, of course, is that political agents do not do this work unilaterally; they must work with others (cooperatively or competitively) to determine what constitutes political goods, how they should relate to other political goods, and how they should be rightly distributed. Political competition with integrity means the difficult, often tension- and conflict-filled work of determining, by working with others, how political goods should be arranged to respect and enhance the lives of communities that competitors represent.

Collegiality is the disposition to honor the integrity of the competitor. In the end, competitors may not be able to cooperate; political competition will sometimes end in compromise or even in a one-sided victory. A commitment to collegiality, to honoring integrity, however, means that competitors endeavor to understand in a generous way why each endorses the interests, values, and goals that she does. Generous understanding entails an imaginative stepping outside one's own commitments to view the political landscape from the competitor's point of view. It might be that such attempts at understanding clarify each competitor's position vis-à-vis the other and also vis-à-vis the self. They might also open opportunities for cooperative and imaginative solutions to difficult political problems. The burden of integrity—of determining how the ordering of political goods best respects and enhances life before God—can be sufficiently met only if competitors carefully consider conflicting points of view.

By engaging one another seriously in a collegial way, competitors meet the burden of recognition. Competition, in its very nature, militates against deep relationality. When one or more parties prevail over another (or others) in political competition, the result is likely to strain the relationships between them. But genuine disagreement also recognizes what is good in the other's point of view. Competitors who genuinely disagree affirm at least some of the underlying values of the other, even if they do not endorse the way the other views the implications of these values for specific proposals about law and policy. Otherwise, disagreement would itself be unintelligible. Democrats, for example, can appreciate the Republican emphasis on personal responsibility and freedom from coercion; all citizens of democratic republics appreciate these values to some extent—even if they do not finally endorse the ways in which these values are fleshed out in developing public policy.

Integrity and collegiality in political competition require seeing (but not necessarily endorsing) political possibilities from the other's perspective. That requirement affirms the relational identity of persons before God. The step into the perspective of the competitor in an attempt to better understand the other's point of view as well as one's own is, from the theological perspective developed here, an attempt to understand how the other takes the form of Christ in the world, how the other experiences the place of responsibility. That relational, imaginative leap provides the ground of recognition and respect in the midst of political competition.

THE LIMITS OF POLITICAL COMPROMISE

Political competition takes many forms. In general, competitors want to advance their agenda to the fullest extent possible. That might mean defeating opponents outright. More often, however, it will mean agreeing to compromise in various configurations, such that all parties get some, but not all, of what they want. This raises the question of what makes for good political compromise. How do one's fundamental commitments inform decisions about when compromise, in whatever configuration, is appropriate, and when no compromise will be possible? At the limit of compromise is the stand. When judgments threaten to undermine one's political commitments, one will need to take a stand, doing everything possible to prevent one's opponents from crossing that line.[21]

In the Winter 2013 edition of *Emory Magazine*, the quarterly periodical of Emory University in Atlanta, Georgia, President James Wagner extolls the Three-Fifths Compromise as a good example of the practice of political compromise. A measure to secure support for the U.S. Constitution among the slave states, the Three-Fifths Compromise proposed to count three-fifths of Southern slaves for the purposes of political representation and taxation.

Southern states would increase their representation in the House of Representatives by counting slaves not as citizens but as electorally quantifiable chattel. In effect, the Three-Fifths Compromise reinforced the contention that slaves are less than human, appropriate to be used to advance the interests of their slave masters.

Wagner points out that the Three-Fifths Compromise was not an appeal to the "lowest common denominator." Instead, he writes, "Both sides found a way to temper ideology and continue working toward the highest aspiration they both shared—the aspiration to form a more perfect union. They set their sights higher, not lower, in order to identify their common goal and keep moving toward it."[22] Wagner goes on to call the Three-Fifths Compromise a "great achievement," one that "facilitated the achievement of what both sides of the debate really aspired to—a new nation."[23]

Wagner's comments immediately courted the ire of detractors. Faculty in Emory's departments of history and African American studies responded with an open letter in which they pointed out that the fifty-five white male delegates to the Constitutional Convention in 1787 contrived a "more perfect union" at the expense of some seven hundred thousand enslaved Africans. The letter insisted that the Three-Fifths Compromise is not a good example of political compromise and that the Great Compromise (the compromise that lead to the bicameral legislature) is a better one: "Some compromises don't hold; others shouldn't hold. Surely," they wrote, "if the goal is to make Emory, and our nation, a 'more perfect union' that is inclusive instead of exclusive, and if compromise is a possible model, there are more admirable choices than the Three-Fifths Compromise."[24]

Commentators have often noted that national political life in the U.S. context has of late been averse to compromise. One wonders whether President Wagner's comments demonstrate a deeper problem: it may be that Americans are not only unwilling to compromise but that they are so unpracticed at it that they are unable to see clearly what compromise is. The Three-Fifths Compromise might be an example of how, as Wagner puts it, "pragmatic half-victories kept in view the higher aspiration of drawing the country more closely together."[25] But the content of that particular compromise further degraded the humanity of persons already subjected to the cruelties of slavery. Surely, no compromise that degrades humanity, even as it advances common goals, can be good.

That much is obvious. Less obvious is what makes for good compromise in politics. Compromise is "an agreement in which all sides sacrifice something in order to improve on the status quo from their perspective, and in which the sacrifices are at least partly determined by the other sides' will." Compromise requires a willingness to treat one's own principles prudentially—to determine, that is, the extent to which one's principles can accommodate a degree of sacrifice to advance the status quo. It also entails a respect for those with whom one disagrees.[26]

The most straightforward way of understanding good compromise is in instrumental terms: the best compromise is the one that maximizes desired goods and minimizes the sacrifice of them to undesired goods. There is, in other words, always a calculating element in compromise: one would rather not compromise at all, but, to the extent that one must, one would prefer to get as much of what is wanted and to give up as little as possible. Good compromise also has a relational dimension. The willingness to compromise is born of a capacity to recognize in the competitor the pursuit of some good or goods that is a worthy human pursuit, even if it is not a pursuit that others think is best. Compromise in the best sense, in other words, entails a recognition of human striving in the competitor, a striving that is worthy because it exists within a human (as opposed to a nonhuman) horizon. Such a recognition conduces to respect, and it validates the project of compromise.

The discussion above indicated the ways in which human limitations—the boundaries that sin and finitude draw around the human experience—"show up" in a particular way in political life. Human beings neither know nor will the good perfectly. They cannot control the circumstances of their judgment and action, nor can they determine with perfect accuracy what the outcomes of their action will be. "Nothing straight can be constructed from such warped wood as that man is made of," Immanuel Kant writes.[27] No one, unified moral vision can be constructed from such warped wood. Whether one believes a real moral order exists independently of the human experience of it, there is a kind of moral pluralism-in-fact. Moral pluralism-in-fact means that human beings recognize a variety of aims, values, and goods that do not in every respect mutually cohere. Moral pluralism-in-fact also means that human beings have a capacity to recognize aims, values, and goods as genuinely *human*, as falling within a human horizon and therefore within the boundaries of moral intelligibility.[28] But such recognition is different from affirmation: human beings can recognize that others pursue human goods but not affirm in every respect how others interpret these goods for social and political life. Political respect, therefore, means validating that the competitor's understanding of values is a genuinely human possibility, one, however, that other competitors cannot affirm.

In the theological framing developed above, respect is generated in the recognition of the competitor as bearing the relationship of responsibility toward a particular constituency. It involves the virtue of collegiality, the disposition to validate the competitor's integrity as a political agent committed to and responsible for the good of the communities the competitor represents. Colleagues validate the divine image in one another not only as a feature of the other's being but as a feature of the other's relationship to the constituents he or she represents. That validation constitutes the grounds of political respect.

Compromise involves a similar validation. It recognizes in the competitor the pursuit of aims, goals, and values intended to advance the good of the persons and communities the competitor represents. Compromise, in addition to being a strategic calculation aimed at generating the most good amid competition, is a recognition of the competitor as one who pursues genuinely human good on behalf of others. Compromise, then, is a particular kind of relationship to the competitor, one that validates the competitor's status as a responsible representative without affirming the competitor's understanding of value. Good compromise in this framing honors the relational character of the *imago Dei*.

Compromise is often appropriate, but not always. Not all competitors represent positions that merit respect. Sometimes, political agents should both disagree with and disrespect the views of their adversaries. In such situations, political agents should avoid compromise at all costs and do the best they can to defeat their adversaries in zero-sum political competition. There is something about tyrannical figures—Hitler, Stalin, Pol Pot—that makes compromise with them intolerable (if not unimaginable, since some leaders did in fact compromise with the likes of these). Just as compromise is good to the extent that it respects the competitor, it is impermissible in cases in which the compromise would threaten to diminish the image of God in persons affected by laws and policies resulting from compromise.

Israeli political theorist Avishai Margalit's notion of rotten compromise is helpful here. Margalit distinguishes between what he calls "anemic compromise," "sanguine compromise," and "rotten compromise." Anemic compromise is simply an agreement to cooperate. Sanguine compromise adds to cooperation an element of recognition. It is "an agreement (co-promise) that involves painful recognition of the other side, the giving up of dreams, making mutual concessions that express recognition of the other's point of view, and that is not based on coercion of one side by the other."[29] Sanguine compromise develops in such a way that the strife is reduced and the other is humanized in the process.[30] Rotten compromise, by contrast, is "an agreement that establishes or maintains an inhuman political order based on systematic cruelty and humiliation as its permanent features." Humiliation is about dehumanization, "treating humans as nonhumans," and cruelty is "a pattern of behavior that causes pain and distress."[31] Any compromise that leads to the dehumanization of persons whom the compromise affects should be opposed "at all costs."[32] The paradigm example of rotten compromise Margalit has in mind is the compromises various Allied powers made with the Third Reich, effectively abetting its genocidal program.

Humanization, then, distinguishes sanguine compromise from anemic compromise, and dehumanization distinguishes rotten compromise from both. At their best, not only do compromises get a job done; they make the other familiar in ways that require the exercise of empathy, the ability to put oneself in the place of the other to experience more fully the other's concerns.[33] Rotten compromises, by contrast, entail the dehumanization of persons whose lives are shaped by the compromise. They not only fail to advance human flourishing; they actively undermine it.

Seen from the perspective of the *imago Dei*, sanguine compromises are those in which competitors cooperate not only for mutual advantage but with a commitment to the collegiality and respect that come with recognition of the competitor as a legitimate and dedicated representative of the good of a constituency. Another way of saying this is that sanguine compromise is possible when competitors attribute the virtue of integrity, the commitment to respect and enhance the good of the constituents they represent, to one another. As a sign of collegiality and respect, sanguine compromises will, as Margalit recognizes, often require that competitors make difficult decisions to sacrifice goods they very much want.

The *imago Dei*, it has been argued, is more fundamentally a task than a feature of a person's identity. In that framing, Margalit's notion of sanguine compromise could be said to represent the difficult task of validating the other's vocational calling. That is, of course, a tough proposition. To reach sanguine compromise with the other is to affirm the other as a worker dedicated to God's redemptive project, even as one rejects, or partially rejects, the way the other is trying to accomplish this work. Compromise of this sort, then, is really about validating the other as a certain kind of self, one who defines herself in relationship to the center of value that is God's work. Viewed in this theological perspective, compromise is not ultimately about the work; it is about the worker's commitment to God's work and about the kind of self the worker becomes in her commitment to the project of political vocation. To be disposed collegially to the competitor is to imagine that she is pursuing a vocational project, with all the implications the vocational framing of political work carries. Such an orientation generates its own humanizing energies and sustains good political work even in the midst of disagreement and competition.

Anemic compromises entail cooperation but without the collegial commitment to validating the integrity of the other. Sanguine compromises go to the relationship between competitors. They trade on an affirmation of the relationship between competitors and of the competitors' status as representatives worthy of recognition and respect. Rotten compromises relate not only to the relationship between competitors but also to the relationship between constituents and the political community. That is, they not only undermine an affirmation of the competitor's status as a representative who has integrity, one committed to enhancing the good of constituents. Rotten compromises also undermine or cut off completely the relationship of constituents to the larger political community. They treat affected constituents as unworthy of full status and participation in the political community, thus robbing them of their identity as citizens. By undermining the relational connection between citizens and their state, cutting off or restricting access to political goods, rotten compromises degrade their capacity to flourish.

Of course, it is not always easy to recognize a rotten compromise. At minimum, it has the characteristic of severing some constituency from the political community, either by undermining the status of persons as citizens or by undermining the status of noncitizens who nonetheless make important contributions to social, economic, and political life. Rotten compromises will also undermine a citizen's access to the basic goods of political life—the goods of defense, education, health care, and the like—goods required for persons to flourish as participants in a political order.

This chapter has argued that the relational structure of the *imago Dei* suggests virtues that encourage good competition and delineates the limits of compromise as a mode of political competition. The relational demands that the *imago Dei* imposes—in particular, the collegial disposition to recognize the integrity of the competitor—pulls political competition in the direction of the divine "plane" on which there is no competition. Competition will, of course, always be a condition of political life in secular time. But the human connection to the divine can make it as good as it can be.

Conclusion

THE POSSIBILITY OF POLITICAL VOCATION

The Ways of Paradox

This book has proposed that the idea of vocation holds in tension the paradoxical way in which God responds to fallen creation. To say that God redeems creation is to say that God has chosen to heal the fractured relationship between creature and Creator despite the enduring effects of sin in the world. God redeems in two paradoxically related ways. First, God brings creation to culmination and wholeness in its eschatological destiny, which not only stands at the end of history but also is present in and makes claims on history at the same time. God redeems creation, in other words, by changing it, by re-creating it in some profound, fundamental, and ultimate way. Second, in the person and work of Jesus Christ, God redeems creation by being present with it amid its brokenness. In Jesus Christ, God enters fully into the complexity of human experience, transfiguring the wounds of body, mind, and soul, which Christ himself bears, into places where God is working to heal and restore. God also redeems by not altering creation at all but by showing that where human beings are most human is where God is most God.

To say that God's redemptive work has a paradoxical quality—that God redeems creation both by changing it and by not changing it—is not to suggest that God's redemptive purposes are ultimately incoherent. It might be that this paradox reflects the limitations on the human capacity to know who God is, what God is doing, and how God is doing it. Or it might be that indeed a sovereign God, a God who can do whatever God wants, has chosen to redeem creation in two logically incoherent ways, as only such a God could do. At any rate, it is hard to know just what the paradox means; it is mysterious. But it is also the canvas on which all theo-ethical reflection must paint. All theological reflection on the moral life must in some way account for how God relates to a fractured created order.

Contemporary Augustinian thinkers, the arguments above suggested, emphasize the created order's relationship to the eschatological one. The "really real" is the eschatological city of God; the penultimate time known as "the world" is a mere simulacrum of the real. Some Augustinian thinkers use this distinction to suggest that the secular moment is a corrupted one. The church stands against the world, witnessing to the "really real" polity that is the eschatological city of God. Other Augustinians push the world to yearn for the real, to pattern worldly practices and institutions on ulti-mate reality. Thus, for thinkers like Kristen Deede Johnson and Charles Mathewes, public engagement across lines of difference is most real when it engages the unity that characterizes the city of God.[1] Agonistic compe-tition in political life is merely epiphenomenal; genuine political engage-ment acknowledges peace, rather than strife, as the ultimate condition of the eschatological city.[2] In Augustinian framings, in short, the earthly city, penultimate time, always pales in comparison to its heavenly counterpart. The secular moment is always ontologically deficient; it is only theologically significant to the extent that eschatological time reaches into the earthly city and claims its traditions, institutions, practices, identities, norms, politics, and so on.

The turn to Bonhoeffer represents a turn from time in place to per-son in space as the basis of the real. For Bonhoeffer, Jesus Christ is the real. Christ is where the world meets God, where the penultimate and the ultimate intersect, each defining the other in terms of itself. In Christ, the "really real" is neither simply the ultimate (as it is in Augustinian framings) nor simply the penultimate; it is always fully both at the same time. Thus, to the extent that Christ is fully present in them, the vicissitudes of the penulti-mate are not simply deficient simulacra of eschatological time; they are real-ity. Bonhoeffer's approach, it was argued, opens up space to take seriously the moral complexity of political life in penultimate time, since Christ's presence in the moral complexity of the world just is reality. For Bonhoeffer, anywhere in "the world" is a site of the real, not simply a shadow of the real.

Vocation as a "calling in" signals that work happens in a particular space. For Bonhoeffer, that place is where Christ takes form, and thus it is a place of authentic reality. But vocation is also a "calling to" work of a kind, which the argument here has defined in terms of a particular understanding of the common good. The common good is finally God's work to redeem creation, God's work to create the conditions of the flourishing of creation, a process that unfolds in the secular moment and culminates in eschatological time. God's redemptive project, as it has been explored here, is a description of the eschaton, the time that sits outside history but that also reaches into history and lays claim to the meaning of the good life in human experience. As a "calling in," the idea of vocation does not simply dismiss as deficient the moral complexities of work as it is conditioned in particular places. But, as a "calling to," vocation also pulls work in the direction of the redemptive work that God does, which has been termed the "project" of political vocation. A theological understanding of vocation therefore works in the paradoxical tension between the "calling in" and the "calling to" of vocational work.

Vocation, it has been argued, is not just about the kind of work persons are called to do, nor is it simply about *how* such work should be done. It is also about workers. The idea of vocation implies a process of self-formation; it is about the kind of selves workers become by virtue of participating in vocational work. The idea of vocation holds that in the doing of vocational work, persons become the kind of selves God intends them to be. The problem is that the process of self-formation in any vocational space, especially political space, is not a straightforward trajectory from some understanding of incomplete toward complete self-development. The places of vocation condition how selves are formed in them. Political institutions, therefore, condition how persons become political agents. But these conditions are morally ambiguous, neither obviously good nor obviously evil. Political spaces, to reiterate Reinhold Niebuhr's insight, always partially obscure the hands and feet of the devil. That moral ambiguity works its way into the political self as one works in political spaces. The moral ambiguity of political space was described in terms of five conditions, related, respectively, to five aspects of ethical reflection: (1) the moral ambiguity of political virtues (related to political agents), (2) the moral ambiguity of political power (related to political agency), (3) the moral ambiguity of political logic (related to political action), (4) the moral ambiguity of competing goods and loyalties (related to the ends of political action), and (5) the moral ambiguity of money in politics (related to external pressures).

The argument of the first part of the book, then, unfolded in this way: (1) from Bonhoeffer, Christ's taking form in the world constitutes places of authentic reality; (2) those places are not therefore mere simulacra of a more real eschaton; rather, they have their own theological integrity; (3) the places in which vocational work happens condition both worker and work in morally complex and ambiguous ways; and (4) therefore, a careful description of these conditions must be provided to better understand what it means to understand them as places of authentic reality.

The second part of the book posed this question: How does the project of political vocation pull political work in the direction of God's redemptive purposes, that is, toward the project of political vocation? The idea of vocation pulls the self- and group interest in the direction of the common good, albeit without denying the validity of more local interests. To understand political work as a vocation is to practice openness to the common good. It is to pursue, as best as one can, the interests of the most expansive human communities that political agents have the power to address, to care for the flourishing of human persons and communities on the broadest possible levels. The idea of vocation affirms that the institutional structures that condition work participate in God's redemptive project. In democratic societies, political structures, for good reasons, require that political agents attend to the needs of the local communities they represent. Political agents are not always in the position, therefore, to address the common good as it pertains to the most expansive human communities who might be affected by a political agent's work. Still, agents who regard their work in the framing of vocation will strive to seek the common good—to participate more fully in the project of political vocation—in and through their work. The virtues of discernment, solidarity, repentance, irony, and collegiality empower political agents to orient their work to the project of political vocation. Such virtues are necessary if political agents are to stand both in and, at the same time, above the fray of political life.

The argument above has at various points stressed that a theological understanding of vocation both affirms (as a "calling in" a place of work) and also creates tension with (as a "calling to" the vocational project) the institutional spaces in which politics happens. Vocational work, in other words, is both conditioned by and conditions the institutional spaces in which it is situated. At various points throughout, the discussion has also pointed to the many ways in which money has compromised—even corrupted—American politics. That is to say that politics in American life may no longer have integrity as institutional space; politics may simply be another region of a globalized market system. Indeed, it might even be the case that democracy in America has transitioned into full-blown oligarchy. Some version of this argument is probably true, though a determination of the extent to which it is true is a task for another book, many of which have already been written.

It is important, in any case, that political institutions in American life not be the only determinants of good political work. Vocation is a powerful category in this regard because it acknowledges that good work is only intelligible in the context of the institutions that give it shape. But, in its commitment to a project that transcends the claims of any particular institution, vocation has the moral resources to transform the contexts in which work happens.

A SPIRITUALITY OF POLITICAL VOCATION

Vocation is a pilgrimage, a journey that moves along the rough terrain between the calling to work in a place and the calling to work toward the project of political vocation. The life and work of vocation is, however, not a linear journey, not an uninterrupted ascent toward a place of perfection. The discussion above suggested that the pilgrimage of political vocation, because it is in part a journey of self-becoming, should be understood as a sanctifying process. Sanctification, in the Calvinist framing, implies a transformation of the self, a gradual recovery of the distorted image of God. Sanctification in the context of political vocation implies the development of virtues like discernment, solidarity, repentance, irony, and collegiality that empower persons to work with one another for the common good of all created things.

But sanctification happens only under the weight of the cross. The morally complex claims of the world continually challenge the sanctified pilgrim; they never go away. Thus, political agents must always reckon with the moral ambiguity of political virtues, power, and logics; of competing goods and loyalties; and of money in politics. There are no straightforward theologically resonant strategies for addressing these conditions of political place.

The Protestant idea of vocation is problematic because it requires that persons hold in their experience of sanctification a tension that may be ultimately unsustainable. Charles Taylor argues that in opening up access to the experience of holiness to all persons in any vocational setting (not only the "renunciative vocations"), the Reformers restructured the experience of vocation such that all persons participate in it. This restructuring took three forms. All persons, first, were required to live a "disciplined personal life," according to high moral standards (as with their monastic predecessors). The observance of high moral standards was particularly relevant in rejecting an undue enjoyment of worldly goods, lest the enjoyment of worldly goods lead to idolatry. Second, in addition to raising the standards of personal morality, the Reformers thought it necessary to reinforce holiness through formal and informal social structures, to control the "vices of the whole society, lest the vicious infect the others."[3] Finally, Christians needed to develop a "correct" "inner attitude" about their experience of sanctification through secular work. The correct inner attitude has a paradoxical quality. On the one hand, Taylor argues, Christians needed to develop an internalized sense of their own powerlessness over sin and depravity. Only God's grace can empower a Christian to progress in the journey of sanctification. On the other hand, Christians needed to avoid feeling so powerless that they had no agency to combat the temptations of sin.

These three "levels of order" that the Protestant understanding of vocation enjoined, Taylor argues, ultimately backfired. Although the disciplines of sanctification were to attune Christians to the sovereignty of God, they had the effect of preparing a sense of individual agency. That is, as Christians exercised order over their own lives, they experienced themselves as autonomous agents capable of exercising order. "As an order is built into conduct," Taylor writes, the "possibility is opened to slide *de facto* . . . into a confidence that we have these things under control, we can pull it off."[4] The Reformation aspired to create selves capable of holding a tension between experiencing God as the primary moral agent in their lives and experiencing themselves as autonomous agents, capable of providing order to themselves. The tension ultimately broke in favor of the latter conception, initiating a process leading to the "exclusive humanism" that marks the "secular age" we now inhabit.

The warning here is that any theological understanding of vocation, at least those that represent the distinctive commitments of the Protestant tradition, run the risk of proposing a way of being in the world that is unsustainable. Protestant understandings of vocation paradoxically require persons at once to deny and affirm their capacity for autonomous agency, all in service to what Max Weber calls "worldly asceticism."[5] If Taylor is right, this orientation to the world is unstable and will likely devolve into the modernist model of autonomous human agency.

The virtues that a theology of political vocation recommends—discernment, solidarity, repentance, irony, and collegiality—all demand that political agents step outside their perspective, both to evaluate critically their own motives and aspirations and to inhabit the perspective of others, capacities that make possible the orientation of political work to the common good. These virtues are intended not to replace but to create tension with the Machiavellian political virtues, "vigor, fortitude in adversity, public achievement, order, discipline, happiness, strength, justice, above all assertion of one's proper claims and the knowledge and power needed to secure their satisfaction."[6] To do their work well, political agents must passionately pursue, with vigor, strength, and fortitude, the purposes that they think make life good. But those who regard their work as a vocation must ensure that the passionate pursuit of political ends does not devolve into base egotism, as it so often seems to do in political life. In the framing of political vocation, political work is not ultimately about oneself; it is about God and God's work.

To pursue a political vocation is to inhabit a tenuous, tension-filled space in which agents work to align the self's drives and desires with God's. History teaches that the holding of vocational space is not easy; indeed, if Taylor is right, the holding of vocational space is a largely unsustainable endeavor. The virtues of political vocation the preceding chapters explored together point to a spirituality of political vocation. A spirituality of political vocation is just the holding in tension the pull of politics toward the local, and to some extent legitimate, purposes of self and community on the one hand, and the universal purposes of God on the other. The spiritual disciplines of the vocational virtues empower political agents to step outside themselves and toward the redemptive project into which God invites all persons to participate. Ultimately, for political work to be done well, politicians must constantly and actively attend to the relationship of local political goods to the ultimate good. A theology of political vocation offers the hope that this delicate work is possible, both for the greater glory of God and for the flourishing of all creation.

NOTES

ACKNOWLEDGMENTS

1   Alasdair MacIntyre, *After Virtue* (New York: Bloomsbury Academic, 2011), 27.

INTRODUCTION

1   David Edmonds and Nigel Warburton, "Quentin Skinner on Machiavelli's *The Prince*," *Philosophy Bites*, podcast audio, last modified July 27, 2008, http://philosophybites.com/2008/07/quentin-skinner.html.

2   I take this definition of politics from John Dunn's *The Cunning of Unreason: Making Sense of Politics* (New York: Basic Books, 2000), 133.

3   Isaiah Berlin, *The Crooked Timber of Humanity*, ed. Henry Hardy (Princeton: Princeton University Press, 1998), 12.

4   Here I follow Andrew Sabl's definition of "office": "a social or political position that embodies ethical value: a position, devoted to a characteristic kind of action, whose existence is judged to serve worthy purposes, and whose grounding in those purposes give rise to particular duties and privileges that derive from the position." Sabl, *Ruling Passions: Political Offices and Democratic Ethics* (Princeton: Princeton University Press, 2002), 1.

5   One of the peculiar characteristics of political power and political agency, which will be explored in detail in the chapters below, is that it bears an ambiguous relationship to accountability. On the one hand, the exercise of political power is instrumental in creating structures and institutions that themselves constitute patters of accountability and that are used in turn to hold the exercise of political power accountable. But political power, as the architect of these structures and institutions, is in an absolute sense positioned outside of mechanisms of accountability. Thus, Carl Schmitt famously argues, the political sovereign, like the sovereign God, is "he who decides the exception" rather than the rule. See Carl Schmitt, *Political Theology: Four Chapters on the Concept of Sovereignty*, trans. George Schwab (Chicago: University of Chicago Press, 1985), 5.

6   For Weber, the modern state should be defined in terms of the distinctive way in which political power is configured in it. The state, he argues, is the political organization that "claims a monopoly on the legitimate use of force within a given territory." See Max Weber, "Politics as a Vocation," in *From Max Weber: Essays in Sociology*, ed. H. H. Gerth and C. Wright Mills (New York: Oxford University Press, 1998), 78.

7   Oliver O'Donovan observes, "the most distinctive feature of political judgment is its universal and categorically binding character" (52). When persons freely choose to inhabit roles in institutional settings, they voluntarily limit their freedom in order to exercise powers and responsibilities and enjoy entitlements that come with these roles. Persons, in other words, limit their absolute freedom in order to enjoy other freedoms. Political judgment evidences a similar dialectic. But unlike personal freedom, political judgment does not entail self-limitation. "Political authority," O'Donovan writes, "realizes goods that never were the ends of our action, and political authority is not itself a means to realize anyone's end" (53). Thus, O'Donovan concludes, "the judgments of political authority, then, have a radically *other-binding* character: they bind those who have not bound themselves" (53–54). O'Donovan proposes that obedience is one way of viewing one's response to political judgment. But it might also be viewed as solidarity. "More precisely, solidarity is a way of *suffering* together, rather than acting together, since the corporate character of what we do in response to legitimate authority consists essentially in allowing ourselves to be restricted in our own freedom of action by others' necessities. In community we may deny ourselves for the sake of achieving something together" (54). The binding character of political judgment is different from coercion, because political communities receive and enjoy freedoms by virtue of allowing themselves to be bound via political judgment. See O'Donovan, *The Ways of Judgment* (Grand Rapids: Eerdmans, 2005), emphases in original.

8   Carl von Clausewitz famously argued that war is itself always a political act. Indeed, war is not merely a political act but a "real political instrument," the "continuation of political commerce . . . by other means." Clausewitz, *On War*, ed. Anatol Rapoport (New York: Penguin, 1982), 119.

9   For a helpful discussion of the traditions of and distinctions between political, public, and liberation theologies, see Gaspar Martinez, *Confronting the Mystery of God: Political, Liberation, and Public Theologies* (New York: Continuum, 2001). For recent developments in public theology, see Elaine Graham, *Between a Rock and a Hard Place: Public Theology in a Post-Secular Age* (London: SCM Press, 2013), 69–105. See also Michael Jon Kessler, ed., *Political Theology for a Plural Age* (New York: Oxford University Press, 2013).

I stress that I do not view the current volume as an exercise in public theology or political theology, as these terms are conventionally understood. "Public theology," Graham argues, "is the study of the public relevance of religious thought and practice" (70). It is often concerned to illumine the proper orientation of Christian citizens to the secular public sphere, both in terms of the form that the participation of Christian citizens in the public sphere should take and the substance of their contribution in that space. Political theology is similar. Peter Scott and William T. Cavanaugh define political theology as "the analysis and criticism of political arrangements (including cultural-psychological, social and economic aspects) from the perspective of differing interpretations of God's way with the world." Cavanaugh and Scott, introduction to *The Blackwell Companion to Political Theology*, ed. Peter Scott and William T. Cavanaugh (Malden, Mass.: Blackwell, 2004), 1. Recent political theology has emphasized the divergences between the practices and traditions of "the Church" and those of secular political life, opening space for the former to bring critique to bear on the latter.

The current project, by contrast, might best be described as "theological political theory." Here I follow Nicholas Wolterstorff, who has argued, "contrary to what the term suggests, political theology is not theology. It is not discourse about God with a political cast. That's what a freestanding account of the nature and grounds of God's authority would be: discourse about God with a political cast. The subject of political theology is not God but the state. It is not a branch of theology but a species of political theory. Theology is the modifier, political theory the substantive. The task of political theology is to develop a theological account of the state and of its relation to various other realities." See Wolterstorff, *The Mighty and the Almighty: An Essay in Political Theology* (New York: Cambridge University Press, 2012), 112. The church is not the relevant institutional location in this discussion; it is rather the secular polity. But I am also not developing a "theological account of the state," as is the ordinary subject matter of political theology. I am ultimately interested in political work rather than political institutions—that is, what a particular construction of the Christian theological tradition has to say about the work of statecraft rather than the meaning and destiny of worldly political institutions.

10 Desiderius Erasmus, *The Education of a Christian Prince*, ed. Lisa Jardine (New York: Cambridge University Press, 1997), 14.

11 Erasmus, *Education of a Christian Prince*, 38, 22.

12 Erasmus, *Education of a Christian Prince*, 23.

13 Erasmus, *Education of a Christian Prince*, 103.

14 Erasmus, *Education of a Christian Prince*, 52.

15 Machiavelli's *The Prince* was composed in 1513 and published in 1532. Erasmus' *The Education of a Christian Prince* was published in 1516.

16 For a discussion of Machiavelli's understanding of *montanere lo stato*, see Quentin Skinner, *Machiavelli: A Very Short Introduction* (New York: Oxford University Press, 2001), 29.

17 Niccolò Machiavelli, *The Prince*, 2nd ed., ed. and trans. Harvey Mansfield (Chicago: University of Chicago Press, 1998), 70-71.

18 Erasmus, *Education of a Christian Prince*, 51.

19 Machiavelli, *The Prince*, 61.

20 Niccolò Machiavelli, *Discourses on Livy*, ed. and trans. Harvey C. Mansfield and Nathan Tarcov (Chicago: University of Chicago Press, 1996), 131.

21 Glory, it should be noted, does draw moral boundaries in Machiavelli's account. Princes who exercise power brutally for no good reason, and thereby do not achieve glory, are vicious. Thus, Agathocles, the king of Syracuse, who had the wealthy citizens of Syracuse murdered to cement his hold on power, acquired, Machiavelli argues, "empire but not glory." Machiavelli, *The Prince*, 35.

22 Michael Ignatieff observes that "while a painter's medium is paint, a politician's medium is time: he must adapt, ceaselessly, to its sudden, unexpected and brutal changes. An intellectual may be interested in ideas and policies for their own sake, but a politician's interest is exclusively in the question of whether an idea's time has come. When we call politics the art of the possible, we mean the art of knowing what is possible *here* and *now*." Ignatieff, *Fire and Ashes: Success and Failure in Politics* (Cambridge, Mass.: Harvard University Press, 2013), 34, emphasis in original.

23 I follow here an insight gleaned from the Union theologian John C. Bennett. Bennett, in turn following an innovation that he credits to the ecumenist J. H. Oldham, prescribes a form of public speech that he calls the "middle axiom." John C. Bennett, *The Christian as Citizen* (New York: Association Press, 1955), 38. The middle axiom offers a Christian response to social policy that is "more definite than a universal ethical principle, and less specific than a program that includes legislation and political strategy." Bennett, *Christian Ethics and Social Policy* (New York: Scribner's, 1946), 77. Middle axioms set "goals which represent the purpose of God for our time" (76). They translate the most general Christian ethical principles into broad formulations that direct the aims of social policy. But middle axioms stop short of making recommendations about the minutiae of public policy—an area of expertise about which Christian ethics has nothing to say. In this way, Bennett thinks, Christians can contribute to public discussions about policy issues without presuming the expertise needed to craft policy on the level of technical particulars.

I do not mean that the theological reflections offered in this book are axiomatic in a formal sense. Rather, the idea of the middle axiom is a helpful way of describing what work theological reflection can do. In part because of the institutional complexity of modern societies described in detail below, theological reflection is not equipped to enter conversations about technique in any area of human endeavor outside of ecclesiastical settings, except as moral questions bear upon them. Theological reflection can, however, offer insights about how and why human endeavors are meaningful. These insights, in turn, provide a sense of the shape particular practices should take.

24 Frank Newport, "Congress Job Approval Drops to All-Time Low for 2013," *Gallup.com*, last modified December 10, 2013, http://www.gallup.com/poll/166196/congress-job -approval-drops-time-low-2013.aspx. It probably does not help matters that Pew rated the 113th Congress, the current Congress at the time of this writing, as the least productive in recent history. See Drew DeSilver, "Congress Ends Least-Productive Year in Recent History," *Pew Research Center*, last modified December 13, 2013, http://www.pewresearch .org/fact-tank/2013/12/23/congress-ends-least-productive-year-in-recent-history/.

25 Frank Newport, "Congress Retains Low Honesty Rating," *Gallup.com*, last modified December 3, 2012, http://www.gallup.com/poll/159035/congress-retains-low-honesty -rating.aspx.

26 Art Swift, "Honesty and Ethics Rating of Clergy Slides to New Low," *Gallup.com*, last modified December 16, 2013, http://www.gallup.com/poll/166298/honesty-ethics -rating-clergy-slides-new-low.aspx.

27 See Larry M. Bartels, *Unequal Democracy: The Political Economy of the New Gilded Age* (Princeton: Princeton University Press, 2008). Bartels further argues that the policies of Republican administrations in particular have created the conditions for unprecedented economic inequality in the U.S. context.

28 Martin Gilens shows that the preferences of affluent Americans are more often reflected in policy outcomes than are the preferences of middle-class or lower-income Americans. See Martin Gilens, *Affluence and Influence: Economic Inequality and Political Power in America* (Princeton: Princeton University Press, 2012).

29 Bartels, *Unequal Democracy*, 2.

30 John Calvin, *The Institutes of the Christian Religion*, ed. John T. McNeill (Philadelphia: Westminster, 1960), 4.20.4, 1490.

31 James M. Gustafson, "Professions as 'Callings,'" in *Moral Discernment in the Christian Life: Essays in Theological Ethics*, ed. Theo A. Boer and Paul E. Capetz (Louisville, Ky.: Westminster John Knox, 2007), 127. Jacques Ellul argues that modern capitalism, which "reduces work to nothing more than a commodity" and asserts the dominance of technique over craftsmanship, undermines the meaningfulness of work in the modern age. The "theological rapport between vocation and work," he argues, "has been broken." Ellul, "Work and Calling," *Katallagete* 4 (1972): 11.

32 Charles Mathewes uses the phrase "during the world" to signal that the idea of the secular in Christian theological traditions captures a time more than a place, a penultimate time before the eschatological moment. Reading Augustine, Mathewes locates the "proper form of public life" in eschatological time; secular political institutions are always a simulacrum of this proper form. Mathewes, *A Theology of Public Life* (New York: Cambridge University Press, 2007), 181.

33 Reinhold Niebuhr, *The Nature and Destiny of Man: A Christian Interpretation*, vol. 2, *Human Destiny* (New York: Scribner's, 1964), 81.

34 Niebuhr, *Nature and Destiny of Man*, 2:76-90.

35 Niebuhr, *Nature and Destiny of Man*, 2:243.

36 See Reinhold Niebuhr, "We Are Men and Not God," in *Essays in Applied Christianity*, ed. D. B. Robertson (New York: Living Age Books, 1959), 172.

37 James Davison Hunter, *To Change the World: The Irony, Tragedy, and Possibility of Christianity in the Late Modern World* (New York: Oxford University Press, 2010), 102, 188.

38 Jennifer M. McBride, *The Church for the World: A Theology of Public Witness* (New York: Oxford University Press, 2012), 5, 23-54.

39 See Charles Mathewes' critique of apocalypticism in his *Theology of Public Life*, 37-42. "Apocalypticism," he writes, "is fundamentally an epistemological attitude, a claim already to know. The Greek word *apokalyptō* means 'to unveil' or 'to disclose'; it suggests a mindset that basically looks to the future as an already determined and knowable reality" (39).

CHAPTER 1

1 Paul Marshall notes that the idea of a calling as it is developed in Hebrew and Christian scriptures does not capture the meaning of calling to "one's social position, occupation, or indeed anything external" as it would later be developed by Protestant Reformers. "This means that the Bible does not contain a notion of vocation or calling in one of the senses in which these terms were used in Reformation theology." Marshall, *A Kind of Life Imposed on Man: Vocation and Social Order from Tyndale to Locke* (Toronto: University of Toronto Press, 1996), 14.

2 Joseph L. Allen distinguishes between the "outer" and "inner" dimensions of a calling, both of which distinguish callings from other framings of work. The outer dimension of calling relates to offices in the context of which persons serve the common good, "the well-being of the whole community, not only of individuals within it." The inner dimension, Allen argues, has to do with the "motivation with which one pursues it": "inwardly, then, one has a calling when she understands that God has called her to this position." See Allen, "Politics as a Calling," occasional paper for the Cary M. Maguire Center for Ethics and Public Responsibility, Southern Methodist University, 1998, http://www.smu.edu/~/media/Site/Provost/Ethics/pdfs/99214%20AllenTextFA.ashx?la=en.

3   Here I follow the authors of *Habits of the Heart*, who distinguish among job, career, and calling: "In the sense of a 'job,' work is a way of making money and making a living. It supports a self defined by economic success, security, and all that money can buy. In the sense of a 'career,' work traces one's progress through life by achievement and advancement in an occupation. It yields a self defined by a broader sort of success, which takes in social standing and prestige, and by a sense of expanding power and competency that renders work itself a source of self-esteem. In the strongest sense of a 'calling,' work constitutes a practical ideal of activity and character that makes a person's work morally inseparable from his or her life. It subsumes the self into a community of disciplined practice and sound judgment whose activity has meaning and value in itself, not just in the output or profit that results from it. But a calling not only links a person to his or her fellow workers. A calling links a person to the larger community, a whole in which the calling of each is a contribution to the good of all." Robert N. Bellah et al., *Habits of the Heart: Individualism and Commitment in American Life* (Berkeley: University of California Press, 1985), 66.

4   I draw here on the moral and theological framings of work that emerge in the Protestant Reformation. The historian Richard M. Douglas argues that humanist theologians and philosophers like Erasmus and Protestant Reformers like John Calvin had markedly different conceptions of work, and these two conceptions illustrate conceptual divergences between two adjacent chapters in the history of Western thought—the Renaissance and the Reformation. For Erasmus and other Renaissance humanists, the term *genus vitae* described an "inborn aptitude" that was to guide an "individual's life-style," including his or her occupation. Work, in other words, was for the humanists one way in which people realize an innate identity. For Calvin and other Protestant Reformers, by contrast, the term *vocatio* describes participation in work that God ordains and directs for purposes that include and also transcend an individual's project of self-realization. A calling to vocational work mirrors the process of election that determines the ultimate fate of creation. See Douglas, "Talent and Vocation in Humanist and Protestant Thought," in *Action and Conviction in Early Modern Europe: Essays in Memory of E. H. Harbison*, ed. Theodore K. Rabb and Jerrold E. Seigel (Princeton: Princeton University Press, 1969), 261-98.

5   Here I have in mind James M. Gustafson's distinction between the "outward" and "inward" significance of vocation. The outward significance of vocation relates to "the larger context within which any person's contributions can be seen to have significance." The outward significance of vocation is what relates work to a "common good." The "inward" significance of vocation relates to the "dignity to one's work that can be affirmed, and thus a dignity to the worker; and there is a sense of fulfillment and meaning that can come from being of service to others and to the common good." James M. Gustafson, "Professions as 'Callings,' " 129.

6   Marshall, *Kind of Life Imposed on Man*, 18-22.

7   The Protestant Reformers radically broadened the medieval concept of vocation, understood as formal service to the church, to include secular careers. Renaissance humanists, developing one strand of classical thinking about work, stressed the human capacity to discern the calling that is most appropriate to one's innate aptitudes. A life's work, in other words, is the product of human agency in the form of self-knowledge and conscious choice. The Reformers, however, emphasized in the concept of vocation divine agency: God calls human beings to the work for which they are intended. See Richard

M. Douglas, "*Genus Vitae* and *Vocatio*: Ideas of Work and Vocation in Humanist and Protestant Usage," in *Action and Conviction in Early Modern Europe: Essays in Memory of E. H. Harbison*, ed. Theodore K. Rabb and Jerrold E. Seigel (Princeton: Princeton University Press, 1969).

8   Thus, Luther writes in "Freedom of a Christian," "The Word of God cannot be received and cherished by any works whatever but only by faith." *Martin Luther: Selections from His Writings*, ed. John Dillenberger (St. Louis: Concordia, 1962), 55.

9   Martin Luther, *Luther's Works*, ed. Jaroslav Pelikan, Hilton C. Oswald, and Helmut T. Lehmann (St. Louis: Concordia, 1955), 295. Luther argues that the commitments that all Christians make at baptism sufficiently determine the nature of Christian work; monastic vows obscure baptismal vows by suggesting that monastic work is somehow more special than the work any baptized Christian does. Of St. Francis, Luther writes, "Francis must have been under an illusion when he taught his followers (if ever he did) to vow a second time which both they and everybody else had vowed in baptism, namely, that which we hold most in common, the gospel" (256).

10   In *Kirchenpostille 1522*, Luther writes, "What if I am not called? What should I do? Answer: How can it be that you are not called? You are certainly in a station, you are either a husband or wife, son or daughter, male or female servant." Cited in Miroslav Volf, *Work in the Spirit: Toward a Theology of Work* (Eugene, Ore.: Wipf & Stock, 2001), 106.

11   Vocation for Calvin, and for the Reformed tradition generally, Alister McGrath argues, is oriented to the glorification of God and to the promotion of the common good: "All human work, however lowly, is capable of glorifying God. Work is, quite simply, an act of praise—a potentially productive act of praise. Work glorifies God, it serves the common good, and it is something through which human creativity can express itself." McGrath, "Calvin and the Christian Calling," *First Things* 94 (1999), 31–35.

12   Calvin, *Institutes*, 3.1.1, 538.

13   Calvin, *Institutes*, 3.25.3, 991.

14   Calvin continuously refers to earthly existence as a pilgrimage. See, e.g., *Institutes* 2.16.14, 523; 3.1.3, 540; 3.7.3, 693 (also n. 7); 3.10.1, 719; 3.16.2, 799, passim.

15   Calvin, *Institutes*, 3.9.4, 716.

16   "Indeed, this life, however crammed with infinite miseries it may be, is still rightly to be counted among those blessings of God which are not to be spurned." Calvin, *Institutes*, 3.9.3, 714. Calvin also counsels against an unnecessarily ascetical relationship to earthly goods. He writes, "Let this then be our principles: that the use of God's gifts is not wrongly directed when it is referred to that end to which the Author himself created and destined them for us, since he created them for our good, not for our ruin" (3.10.2, 720).

17   Calvin, *Institutes*, 3.9.3, 715.

18   Calvin succinctly describes the movement of regeneration in his 1539 response to Cardinal Jacopo Sadoleto. He writes, "Christ regenerates to a blessed life those whom He justifies, and after rescuing them from the dominion of sin, hands them over to the dominion of righteousness, transforms them into the image of God, and so trains them by His Spirit into obedience to His will." John Calvin and Jacopo Sadoleto, *A Reformation Debate: Sadoleto's Letter to the Genevans and Calvin's Reply*, ed. John C. Olin (Grand Rapids: Baker, 1976), 68.

19   Calvin, *Institutes*, 3.3.6, 598.

20   Calvin, *Institutes*, 3.7.1, 702.

21 Calvin, *Institutes*, 3.8.1.

22 Calvin, *Institutes*, 3.9.1, 712–13.

23 Calvin, *Institutes*, 3.10.

24 Calvin, *Institutes*, 3.11.6, 724. William J. Bouwsma in his biography of Calvin makes much of Calvin's existential anxiety and its relationship to Calvin's preoccupation with order and disorder. See William J. Bouwsma, *John Calvin: A Sixteenth-Century Portrait* (New York: Oxford University Press, 1988). For Bouwsma's understanding of the larger intellectual tensions around issues of order and disorder that are addressed in Renaissance thought, see Bouwsma, *A Usable Past: Essays in European Cultural History* (Berkeley: University of California Press, 1990), 19–73. A number of other scholars have challenged Bouwsma's psychological portrait of Calvin in this regard. See, e.g., Richard A. Muller, *The Unaccommodated Calvin: Studies in the Foundation of a Theological Tradition*, Oxford Studies in Historical Theology (New York: Oxford University Press, 2000), 79–98.

25 Calvin, *Institutes*, 3.10.6, 724–25.

26 Calvin, *Institutes*, 3.7.5, 695. Richard Baxter, the Puritan leader and theologian, later wrote, "The callings most useful to the public good are the magistrates, the pastors, and teachers of the church, the schoolmasters, physicians, lawyers, etc., husbandman (ploughmen, graziers, and shepherds); and next to them are mariners, clothiers, booksellers, tailors, and such others that are employed about matters most necessary to mankind." Quoted in Joan M. Martin, "Between Vocation and Work: A Womanist Notion of a Work Ethic," in *Feminist and Womanist Essays in Reformed Dogmatics*, ed. Amy Plantinga Pauw and Serene Jones (Louisville, Ky.: Westminster John Knox, 2006), 183.

27 For an analysis of Calvinist understandings of social justice, see Douglas Ottati, "What Reformed Theology in a Calvinist Key Brings to Conversations about Justice," *Political Theology* 10, no. 3 (2009), 447–69.

28 Calvin writes, "For the purpose of encouraging him to fight such a fight courageously, he calls it *good*; that is successful, and therefore not to be shunned; for if earthly soldiers do not hesitate to fight, when the result is doubtful, and when there is a risk of being killed, how much more bravely ought we to do battle under the guidance and banner of Christ, when we are certain of victory?" He continues, "Because men would run at random, and to no purpose, if they had not God as the director of their course, for the purpose of promoting their cheerful activity, [St. Paul] mentions also the *calling*; for there is nothing that ought to animate us with greater courage than to learn that we have been 'called' by God; for we conclude from this, that our labor, which God directs, and in which he stretches out his hand to us, will not be fruitless." John Calvin, *Commentaries on the Epistles to Timothy, Titus, and Philemon*, trans. William Pringle (Grand Rapids: Baker, 1948), 162–63; emphasis in original.

29 Ernst Troeltsch argues that for Luther and the Lutheran legacy, the vocational structure of human work is fixed. Once God calls a person to a vocation, one cannot leave or disturb the vocational setting but can only serve God in the context of one's work (*in vocatione*). The Reformed legacy, in contrast, posits a fallen world in which social structures are never perfectly organized and are thus always in need of reformation. Not only is one's place in the vocational order subject to change, but the order itself is mutable as well. In the Reformed Christian imaginary, one serves God not only in but also through one's work (*per vocationem*). Thus, according to Troeltsch, then, both Lutheran and Reformed Christians understand vocation to be integral to service to the common

good. But only in the Reformed conception does vocation also include a socially trans-formative dimension. See Troeltsch, *The Social Teaching of the Christian Churches*, vol. 2, trans. Olive Wyon (Louisville, Ky.: Westminster John Knox, 1992), 609. See also Nicho-las Wolterstorff, *Until Justice and Peace Embrace* (Grand Rapids: Eerdmans, 1983), 15–17; and Douglas A. Hicks, *Money Enough: Everyday Practices for Living Faithfully in the Global Economy* (San Francisco: Jossey-Bass, 2010), 90–95. A useful study of the development of the concept of vocation in Christian ethical thought is Robert C. Trawick, "Ordering the Earthly Kingdom: Vocation, Providence, and Social Ethics" (Ph.D. diss., Emory University, 1997).

30 Here I follow insights about the relationship between identity and moral commitment that Charles Taylor explores in his work. In his early article "What Is Human Agency?," Taylor argues that human beings make "strong evaluations," qualitative distinctions among desires, inclinations, and motivations. Among strong evaluations, some are "fundamental evaluations" that prioritize and give meaning to all other evaluations that human beings make. Our commitment to fundamental evaluations, in turn, deter-mines our identity: "Our identity is therefore defined by certain evaluations which are inseparable from ourselves as agents. Shorn of these we would cease to be ourselves, by which we do not mean trivially that we would be different in the sense of having some properties other than those we now have—which would indeed be the case after any change, however minor—but that shorn of these we would lose the very possibility of being an agent who evaluates; that our existence as persons, and hence our ability to adhere as persons to certain evaluations, would be impossible outside the horizon of these essential evaluations, that we would break down as persons, be incapable of being persons in the full sense." Charles Taylor, "What Is Human Agency?," in *Philosophical Papers 1: Human Agency and Language* (New York: Cambridge University Press, 1985), 34.

In his later book *Sources of the Self*, Taylor argues that human beings all operate within a set of normative presuppositions that determine fundamental moral commitments. Taylor calls these presuppositions a "framework," that which "we presuppose when we judge that a certain form of life is truly worthwhile, or place our dignity in a certain achievement of status, or define our moral obligations in a certain manner." In Taylor, *Sources of the Self: The Making of Modern Identity* (Cambridge, Mass.: Harvard University Press, 1989), 26. For Taylor, we cannot do without frameworks (27). He goes on to show the necessary connection between frameworks and identity: "To know who I am is a species of knowing where I stand. My identity is defined by the commitments and identifications which provide the frame or horizon within which I can try to determine from case to case what is good, or valuable, or what ought to be done, or what I endorse or oppose. In other words, it is the horizon within which I am capable of taking a stand" (270). Frameworks create a kind of "moral space" in which identity is situated: "to know who you are is to be oriented in moral space, a space in which questions arise about what is good or bad, what is worth doing and what not, what has meaning and importance for you and what is trivial and secondary" (28).

31 Douglas J. Schuurman, e.g., summarizes the social and cultural pressures that have transformed the traditional understanding of vocation: "Add to these already powerful economic and social influences the cultural forces involving systematic exclusion of Christianity from public education, a pervasive moral individualism in the service of self-expression, the dominance of a 'scientific' view of nature and a managerial view of social relations—and the religious value of life as vocation becomes exceedingly difficult

to sustain." Schuurman, *Vocation: Discerning Our Callings in Life* (Grand Rapids: Eerdmans, 2004), 11.

32 The most notable account of secularism recently offered is Charles Taylor's *A Secular Age* (Cambridge, Mass.: Belknap Press, 2007), discussed in the conclusion to this book.

33 Sociologist W. Richard Scott develops a definition of institutions encompassing "regulative," "normative," and "cultural-cognitive" "pillars." The regulative pillar relates to the ways institutions are formed in formal and explicit structures, especially in law. The normative pillar relates to the dimension of institutional life that shapes the moral awareness of persons, especially in terms of expectations and obligations. The cultural-cognitive pillar, finally, relates to the way that institutions socialize persons with meaning-making resources (concepts and categories) by means of which they interpret their experience. Scott's definition of institutions is as follows: "institutions comprise regulative, normative, and cultural-cognitive elements that, together with associated activities and resources, provide stability and meaning to social life." Scott, *Institutions and Organizations: Ideas, Interests, and Identities* (London: Sage, 2013), 56.

34 See Robert Bellah et al., *The Good Society* (New York: Vintage, 1992), 10. Bellah and his colleagues write, "Institutions may be such simple customs as the confirming handshake in a social situation, where the refusal to respond to an outstretched hand might cause embarrassment and some need for an explanation; or they might be highly formal institutions such as taxation upon which social services depend, where refusal to pay may be punished by fines and imprisonment. Institutions always have a moral element."

35 Amy Gutmann and Dennis Thompson distinguish between the norms and practices of campaigning and those of governing, and argue that American politics has mistaken the former for the latter. See their book *The Spirit of Compromise: Why Governing Demands It and Campaigning Undermines It* (Princeton: Princeton University Press, 2012).

36 Roger Friedland and Robert Alford provide a classic definition of institutional logic as "a central logic—a set of material practices and symbolic constructions—which constitutes its organizing principles and which is available to organizations and individuals to elaborate." Friedland and Alford, "Bringing Society Back In: Symbols, Practices, and Institutional Contradictions," in *The New Institutionalism in Organizational Analysis*, ed. Walter W. Powell and Paul J. DiMaggio (Chicago: University of Chicago Press, 1991), 248.

   Patricia H. Thornton emphasizes that institutional logics orient meaning making, practice, and identity construction: "Conceptualized as a theoretical model, each institutional order of the interinstitutional system distinguishes unique organizing principles, practices, and symbols that influence individual and organizational behavior. Institutional logics represent frame of reference that condition actors' choices for sensemaking, the vocabulary they use to motivate action, and their sense of self and identity. The principles, practices, and symbols of each institutional order differentially shape how reasoning takes place and how rationality is perceived and experienced." Thornton et al., *The Institutional Logics Perspective: A New Approach to Culture, Structure, and Process* (Oxford: Oxford University Press, 2012), 2.

37 Steven Tipton argues that different "ethical styles" are characteristically found in particular institutional locations. A "consequential" style, emphasizing cost-benefit calculation, is found in institutional spaces in which actors must determine what they want and how they will go about getting it. Consequential logics can be found in the market and corporate economies, as well as in "group-interest politics." Negotiation is a form of consequentialism; it is a calculus by which persons achieve desired ends. Religious

communities, by contrast, are typically marked by authoritative and regular styles, those emphasizing the commands of law and love, virtue, and principled behavior. See Steven Tipton, "Social Differentiation and Moral Pluralism," in *Meaning and Modernity: Religion, Polity, and Self*, ed. Richard Madsen et al. (Berkeley: University of California Press, 2002), 15-40.

38   See Mary Douglas, *How Institutions Think* (Syracuse, N.Y.: Syracuse University Press, 1986), 55-67.

39   Institutional theorists have long debated how persons are formed in institutions. Some hold that persons are socialized in the norms and values of institutions, a process marked by conscious commitment. Others hold that formation happens as a "cognitive process" in which persons grasp and rehearse "taken-for-granted scripts, rules, and classifications." Still others hold that formation happens in nondiscursive practices that form habits. See Paul J. DiMaggio and Walter W. Powell, introduction to *The New Institutionalism in Organizational Analysis*, ed. Paul J. DiMaggio and Walter W. Powell (Chicago: University of Chicago Press, 1991) 14-15. See also Antti Gronow, "Not By Rules or Choice Alone: A Pragmatist Critique of Institution Theories in Economics and Sociology," *Journal of Institutional Economics* 4, no. 3 (2008), 351-73, and a response to Gronow in Scott, *Institutions and Organizations*, 70.

40   Here I draw on Steven M. Tipton's argument that modern societies are marked both by social differentiation and moral pluralism. "Social differentiation" means that modern societies are divided into many different institutional settings in which persons live their lives. "Moral pluralism" means that different institutional settings have different moral logics and languages, different "styles" of meaning making. Modern selves must learn to negotiate multiple institutional contexts and the pluralism of moral languages they require. Tipton, "Social Differentiation and Moral Pluralism," 15-40.

41   Michael Walzer and Michael Sandel both point to the problematic ways in which the moral logic of the marketplace spills over into other areas of social life. See Walzer, *Spheres of Justice: A Defense of Pluralism and Equality* (New York: Basic Books, 1983), 95-128; and Sandel, *What Money Can't Buy: The Moral Limits of Markets* (New York: Farrar, Straus & Giroux, 2012).

42   William E. Connolly argues that pluralism is a fundamental condition not only of human relations but of the universe itself, a view he calls "multidimensional pluralism": "Multidimensional pluralism I call it, arguing that the expansion of diversity in one domain ventilates life in others as well. We then consider the radical contention that not only human culture but the nonhuman world contains an unruly element of pluralism within it." Connolly, *Pluralism* (Durham, N.C.: Duke University Press, 2005), 6.

43   Kristen Deede Johnson develops an Augustinian framing of pluralism according to which the ultimate unity of truth that exists in the eschatological moment creates the conditions under which genuine engagement with difference is possible. Kristen Deede Johnson, *Theology, Political Theory, and Pluralism: Beyond Tolerance and Difference* (New York: Cambridge University Press, 2007).

44   William T. Cavanaugh argues that, contrary to a dominant narrative in contemporary social and political theory, moral and theological pluralisms were not the primary causes of the Wars of Religion in the sixteenth and seventeen centuries. Rather, European princes exploited weakening church authority to advance their own self-interest. See Cavanaugh, "A Fire Strong Enough to Consume the House: The Wars of Religion and the Rise of the State," *Modern Theology* 11, no. 4 (1995): 397-420.

45 This historical setting of Weber's "Politics as a Vocation" is illuminating. The year 1919 dawned on a season of social and political turmoil in Germany. Germany's devastating defeat at Allied hands left a political vacuum, and liberal leftist, anarchist, and pacifist factions competed to fill it. The collapse of the German war effort culminated in sailor's mutinies in Wilhelmshaven and Kiel, igniting a revolution. Leftist workers and soldiers seized power, formed local governing councils in cities and towns all over Germany, and pushed the revolution toward Berlin. Kaiser Wilhelm II abdicated on November 9, a republic was proclaimed, and an armistice with Allied forces followed two days later. From November 1918 until January 1919, various social democratic and communist factions struggled for power, while a Council of People's Commissioners clumsily administered the new republic. A worker's uprising in Berlin in early January 1919 was put down on January 15, its ending punctuated by the murders of socialist leaders Karl Liebknecht and Rosa Luxemburg. Germany, the late historian John Patrick Diggins writes, "had not only lost a war but seemed to have lost its head as well." See Diggins, *Max Weber: Politics and the Spirit of Tragedy* (New York: Basic Books, 1996), 249.

46 Weber writes, "Hence it is of course utterly ridiculous for such people to condemn *morally* the 'politicians of violence' of the old regime for using precisely the same means as they are prepared to use no matter how justified they may be in rejecting the *aims* of the other side." Weber, "Politics as a Vocation," in *From Max Weber*, 122, emphasis in original.

47 "An official's honor," Weber writes, "consists in being able to carry out [the leader's] instruction, on the *responsibility* of the man issuing it, conscientiously and precisely in the same way as if it corresponded to his own convictions." Weber, "Politics as a Vocation," in *From Max Weber*, 95, emphasis in original.

48 Weber writes, "Precisely those who are officials by nature and who, in this regard, are of high moral stature, are bad and, particularly in the political meaning of the word, irresponsible politicians, and thus of low moral stature in this sense—men of the kind we Germans, to our cost have had in positions of leadership time after time." Weber, "Politics as a Vocation," in *From Max Weber*, 331.

49 Weber contrasted political officers who live "from" politics and those who live "for" politics. A politician who lives "from" politics engages in political life in order to generate income. A politician who lives "for" politics, in contrast, " 'makes this his life' in an *inward* sense, either by enjoying the naked possession of the power he exercises or by feeling his inner balance and self-esteem from the sense that he is giving his life *meaning* and *purpose* by devoting it to a 'cause.' " Weber, "Politics as a Vocation," in *From Max Weber*, 84, emphasis in original.

50 Weber, "Politics as a Vocation," in *From Max Weber*, 348.

51 Weber scholars have varied views of Weber's own political sensibilities. Wolfgang Mommsen, Fritz Ringer explains, emphasizes Weber's nationalism. See Mommsen, *Max Weber and German Politics, 1890–1920* (Chicago: University of Chicago Press, 1985). Fritz Ringer's Weber, however, is sympathetic to liberal pluralism. See Ringer, "Max Weber's Liberalism," *Central European History* 35, no. 3 (2002). Interestingly, Weber's relationship to socialism was complicated. He was often critical, but in some episodes he appeared demonstrably sympathetic to at least some stripes of German socialism. See, e.g., J. J. R. Thomas, "Weber and Direct Democracy," *British Journal of Sociology* 35, no. 2 (1984): 216–40.

52 Weber, "Politics as a Vocation," in *From Max Weber*, 78.

53 Weber, "Politics as a Vocation," in *From Max Weber*, 127.
54 Weber, "Politics as a Vocation," in *From Max Weber*.

CHAPTER 2

1 Weber, "Politics as a Vocation," in *From Max Weber*, 126.
2 Weber, "Politics as a Vocation," in *From Max Weber*.
3 Weber, "Politics as a Vocation," in *From Max Weber*, 127.
4 That is not to say that the political vocation is the only form of human development; there are other trajectories as well.
5 For more on the market system as an institutional setting and its distinctive moral logics, see Charles Edward Lindblom, *The Market System: What It Is, How It Works, and What to Make of It* (New Haven: Yale University Press, 2001).
6 For analyses of recent work on responsibility ethics, see William Schweiker, "Responsibility and Moral Realities," *Studies in Christian Ethics* 22, no. 4 (2009): 472–95; idem, "Disputes and Trajectories in Responsibility Ethics," *Religious Studies Review* 27, no. 1 (2001): 18–24.
7 See, among other works, John Milbank, *Theology and Social Theory: Beyond Secular Reason* (Malden, Mass.: Blackwell, 1990); William Cavanaugh, *Migrations of the Holy: God, State, and the Political Meaning of the Church* (Grand Rapids: Eerdmans, 2011); Stanley Hauerwas, "A Haunting Possibility: Christianity and Radical Democracy," in *Christianity, Democracy, and the Radical Ordinary: Conversations between a Radical Democrat and a Christian*, ed. Stanley Hauerwas and Romand Coles (Eugene, Ore.: Cascade Books, 2008), 17–30; Charles Mathewes, *Theology of Public Life*; idem, *The Republic of Grace: Augustinian Thoughts for Dark Times* (Grand Rapids: Eerdmans, 2010); Kristen Deede Johnson, *Theology, Political Theory, and Pluralism*; Luke Bretherton, *Christianity and Contemporary Politics* (Malden, Mass.: Wiley-Blackwell, 2010); Robert Dodaro, *Christ and the Just Society in the Thought of Augustine* (New York: Cambridge University Press, 2008); Eric Gregory, *Politics and the Order of Love: An Augustinian Ethics of Democratic Citizenship* (Chicago: University of Chicago Press, 2010); and James Wetzel, "Splendid Vices and Secular Virtues: Variations on Milbank's Augustine," *Journal of Religious Ethics* 32, no. 2 (2004), 271–300; and idem, *Augustine and the Limits of Virtue* (New York: Cambridge University Press, 2008).
8 I use the term "secular" here in Augustine's sense, i.e., as the penultimate time between the fall and the resurrection of the dead.
9 Augustine, *The City of God against the Pagans*, ed. R. W. Dyson (New York: Cambridge University Press, 1998), 632, 634.
10 Bretherton, *Christianity and Contemporary Politics*, 3. Bretherton emphasizes the division of humanity in the Augustinian scheme between "wheat and tares," "sheep and goats," "godly and wicked," Babylon and Jerusalem. These divisions have implications in the way Augustinian frameworks interpret theological anthropology, a point developed in the discussions below.
11 Augustine, *City of God*, 945–47.
12 In his "Sermon 13: On the Words of Psalm 2.10," Augustine writes, "But now let us address those who judge the earth in the everyday physical understanding of the phrase. Kings, leaders, rulers, judges, they judge the earth; each one of them judges the earth in accordance with the office he has been given on earth." Augustine, *Political Writings*, ed. E. M. Atkins (New York: Cambridge University Press, 2001), 124.

13 Augustine, *City of God*, 927.

14 Augustine, *City of God*, 927–28.

15 Augustine, *City of God*, 927.

16 Augustine admonishes judges to carefully consider whether they are exercising their authority justly, lest they risk imperiling their soul: "If, then, you don't want to exercise your authority unjustly, all you human beings who wish to have authority over human beings, well, *be instructed*, so that you avoid judging corruptly, and perishing in your soul before you manage to destroy anyone else in the flesh." The judge should examine his own conscience first before judging others: "But first, for your own sake, act as judge on yourself. Judge yourself first, and then you'll be able to leave the inner cell of your conscience in security and go out to someone else." Augustine, *Political Writings*, 124, emphasis in original.

17 In his "Sermon 302: On the Feast of St. Laurence," Augustine warns the people to avoid mob justice: "But leave the judges to account for [persons who are bad]. Why do you want the difficult task of accounting for someone else's death? The burden of authority isn't yours to carry. God has given you the freedom of not being a judge." Augustine, *Political Writings*, 115.

18 Following other scholars, James Wetzel notes that Augustine uses the term *civitas terrena* (the earthly city) in two different ways in *City of God*. At times, the earthly city is synonymous with all that is sinful, so that all earthly loves are wicked. At other times, Augustine uses *civitas terrena* to mean the human community in the time between the fall and the second coming of Christ (i.e., secular time), during which the city of God and the city of the damned are mixed and so also their loves are mixed. Wetzel argues that the "confused concept" would be clarified if Augustine had kept the idea of a mixed city and "removed the absoluteness of the opposition between the secular city and the City of God." He goes on to say: "Augustine speaks of two cities being on pilgrimage, *civitas terrena* and *civitas Dei*, and he pits the love that characterizes the one against the love that characterizes the other. To be consistent, he would have to say that there is only one city on pilgrimage, the secular city, and that its love is unresolved." See James Wetzel, "Splendid Vices and Secular Virtues," 275.

19 Mathewes, *Theology of Public Life*, 122.

20 Rowan Williams writes, "So we arrive at the paradox that the only reliable political leader, the only ruler who can be guaranteed to safeguard authentically *political* values (order, equity, and the nurture of souls in these things) is the man who is, at the end of the day, indifferent to their survival in the relative shapes of the existing order." Williams, "Politics and the Soul: A Reading of the *City of God*," *Milltown Studies* 55 (1987): 67, emphasis in original.

21 Mathewes, *Republic of Grace*, 116.

22 Williams, "Politics and the Soul," 58, emphasis in original.

23 See Niebuhr's essay "Augustine's Political Realism" in *Christian Realism and Political Problems* (New York: Scribner's, 1953), 119–46.

24 Martin Luther writes in *On Secular Authority*: "All those who are not Christians belong to the kingdom of the world or [in other words] are under the law. There are few who believe, and even fewer who behave like Christians and refrain from doing evil [themselves], let alone not resisting evil [done to them]. And for the rest God has established another government, outside the Christian estate and the kingdom of God, and has cast them into subjection to the Sword. So that, however much they would like to do

evil, they are unable to act in accordance with their inclinations, or, if they do, they cannot do so without fear, or enjoy peace and good fortune. In the same way, a wicked, fierce animal is chained and bound so that it cannot bite or tear, as its nature would prompt it to do, however much it wants to; whereas a tame, gentle animal needs nothing like chains or bonds and is harmless even without them. If there were [no law and government], then seeing that all the world is evil and that scarcely one human being in a thousand is a true Christian, people would devour each other and no one would be able to support his wife and children, feed himself and serve God. The world [Welt] would become a desert. And so God has ordained the two governments, the spiritual [government] which fashions true Christians and just persons through the Holy Spirit under Christ, and the secular [weltlich] government which holds the Unchristian and wicked in check and forces them to keep the peace outwardly and be still, like it or not." Luther and John Calvin, *Luther and Calvin on Secular Authority*, ed. Harro Höpfl (New York: Cambridge University Press, 1991), 10.

25   Emil Brunner, *The Divine Imperative* (Philadelphia: Westminster, 1947), 445.

26   Brunner, *Divine Imperative*, 461.

27   Reinhold Niebuhr, *Moral Man and Immoral Society: A Study in Ethics and Politics* (Louisville, Ky.: Westminster John Knox, 2001), 26.

28   Niebuhr, *Moral Man and Immoral Society*, 27.

29   Niebuhr writes, "Men will never be wholly reasonable, and the proportion of reason to impulse becomes increasingly negative when we proceed from the life of individuals to that of social groups, among whom a common mind and purpose is always more or less inchoate and transitory, and who depend therefore upon a common impulse to bind them together." Niebuhr, *Moral Man and Immoral Society*, 35.

30   Niebuhr, *Moral Man and Immoral Society*, 83.

31   Niebuhr, *Moral Man and Immoral Society*, 173.

32   Reinhold Niebuhr, *Love and Justice: Selections from the Shorter Writings of Reinhold Niebuhr*, ed. D. B. Robertson (Gloucester, Mass.: P. Smith, 1976). See also idem, *The Nature and Destiny of Man*, vol. 2, *Human Destiny*, 56-57.

33   Niebuhr writes, "Valuable as this kind of perfectionism is, it certainly offers no basis for a social ethic that deals responsibly with a growing society. Those of us who believe in the complete reorganization of modern society are not wrong in using the ideal of Jesus as a vantage point from which to condemn the present social order, but I think we are in error when we try to draw from the teachings of Jesus any warrant for social policies which we find necessary to attain to any modicum of justice." Niebuhr, *Love and Justice*, 33.

34   Niebuhr writes, "One contribution which Christianity certainly ought to make to the problem of political justice is to set all propositions of justice under the law of love, resolving the fruitless debate between pragmatists and legalists and creating the freedom and maneuverability necessary to achieve a tolerable accord between men and nations in ever more complex human relations." Niebuhr, *Christian Realism and Political Problems*, 110.

35   Reinhold Niebuhr, *Christianity and Power Politics* (Hamden, Conn.: Archon Books, 1969), 26. Niebuhr writes, "Justice is basically dependent upon a balance of power. Whenever an individual or a group or a nation possesses undue power, and whenever this power is not checked by the possibility of criticizing and resisting it, it grows inordinate." He goes on to say, "A balance of power is different from, and inferior to, the harmony of love. It is a basic condition of justice, given the sinfulness of man. Such a

balance of power does not exclude love. In fact, without love the frictions and tensions of a balance of power would become intolerable. But without the balance of power even the most loving relations may degenerate into unjust relations, and love may become the screen which hides the injustice" (26-27).

36 Niebuhr, *Christianity and Power Politics*, 116. Niebuhr writes, "The final victory over man's disorder is God's and not ours; but we do have responsibility for proximate victories. Christian life without a high sense for the responsibility for the health of our communities, our nations and our cultures degenerates into an intolerable other-worldliness. We can neither renounce this earthly home of ours nor yet claim that its victories and defeats give the final meaning to our existence."

37 Early Christians understood, Weber notes, that "he who lets himself in for politics, that is, for power and force as means, contracts with diabolical powers and for his action it is *not* true that good can follow only from good and evil only from evil, but that often the opposite is true. Anyone who fails to see this is, indeed, a political infant." Weber, "Politics as a Vocation," in *From Max Weber*, 122-23. Emphasis in original.

38 Dietrich Bonhoeffer, *Ethics*, ed. Clifford J. Green (Minneapolis: Fortress, 2005), 244.

39 Bonhoeffer's participation in a plot to assassinate Hitler led to his arrest, imprisonment, and execution just weeks before the German surrender in 1945. Interestingly, Bonhoeffer framed his response to the Nazi threat as a "terrible alternative," a decision between relative evils. The American theologian Reinhold Niebuhr recounted Bonhoeffer's explanation for leaving New York and a job Niebuhr had secured for him there in 1939 to return to Germany and participate in the resistance to the Nazi regime. According to Niebuhr, Bonhoeffer explained, "I must live through this difficult period of our national history with the Christian people of Germany. . . . Christians in Germany are going to face the terrible alternative of either willing the defeat of their nation in order that Christian civilization may survive, or willing the victory of their nation and thereby destroying our civilization. I know which of these alternatives I must choose." Quoted in Elizabeth Sifton and Fritz Stern, "The Tragedy of Dietrich Bonhoeffer and Hans von Dohnanyi," *New York Review of Books*, October 25, 2012, http://www.nybooks.com/articles/archives/2012/oct/25/tragedy -dietrich-bonhoeffer-and-hans-von-dohnanyi/?pagination=false.

40 Bonhoeffer writes, "There are not two realities, but only one reality, and that is God's reality revealed in Christ in the reality of the world. Partaking in Christ, we stand at the same time in the reality of God and in the reality of the world. The reality of Christ embraces the reality of the world in itself. The world has no reality of its own independent of God's revelation in Christ." Bonhoeffer, *Ethics*, 55.

41 Bonhoeffer argues against a framing of ethics that would prescribe "universally valid" laws of human behavior. Such an ethic, Bonhoeffer argues, aspires ultimately to control God. See his arguments in *Ethics* ("The 'Ethical' and the 'Christian' as a Topic") and in his early lecture on ethics, "Basic Questions of a Christian Ethic," in *Barcelona, Berlin, and New York: 1928-1931*, ed. Clifford J. Green (Minneapolis: Fortress, 2009), 359-78.

42 Bonhoeffer, *Ethics*, 53.

43 Bonhoeffer, *Ethics*, 267.

44 Bonhoeffer emphasizes that the Christian life entails engagement with the world: "Christ has died for the world, and Christ is Christ only in the midst of the world. It is nothing but unbelief to give the world . . . less than Christ. It means not taking seriously

the incarnation, the crucifixion, and the bodily resurrection. It means denying the body of Christ." Bonhoeffer, *Ethics*, 67.

45 Bonhoeffer elaborates the relationship between the "ultimate" and the "penultimate" in the section of *Ethics* entitled "Ultimate and Penultimate Things." Bonhoeffer, *Ethics*, 146-70.

46 With many commentators, Larry Rasmussen notes the etymological link in German between the idea of responsibility (*Verantwortung*, containing *Antwort*, an answer) and the idea of answering God's call. There is then, etymologically in German, a close link between the idea of vocation as calling and responsibility as an answer to God's call. See Rasmussen, "The Ethics of Responsible Action," in *The Cambridge Companion to Dietrich Bonhoeffer*, ed. John W. de Gruchy (New York: Cambridge University Press, 1999), 206-25.

47 Bonhoeffer, *Ethics*, 224.

48 Bonhoeffer, *Ethics*, 226.

49 Bonhoeffer, *Ethics*, 221-22.

50 Bonhoeffer, *Ethics*, 257.

51 Dietrich Bonhoeffer, *Sanctorum Communio: A Theological Study of the Sociology of the Church*, ed. Clifford J. Green (Minneapolis: Fortress, 1998), 155-56. Bonhoeffer emphasizes in *Sanctorum Communio* that vicarious representative action "*is not an ethical possibility or standard, but solely the reality of the divine love for the church-community; it is not an ethical, but a theological concept*" (156; emphasis in original).

52 "Responsible action is vicarious representative action." Bonhoeffer, *Ethics*, 232.

53 By "integrity," William Schweiker means "rightly relating the complexity of natural, social, and reflective goods through a commitment to respect and enhance life before God." Schweiker, *Power, Value, and Conviction* (Cleveland, Ohio: Pilgrim Press, 1998), 7, 13.

54 Bonhoeffer, *Ethics*, 259.

55 Bonhoeffer, *Ethics*, 232.

56 Bonhoeffer, *Ethics*, 241.

57 Bonhoeffer, *Ethics*, 233.

58 Bonhoeffer writes in a letter from July 18, 1944, "It is not the religious act that makes the Christian, but participation in the sufferings of God in the secular life. That is *metanoia*; not in the first place thinking about one's own needs, problems, sins, and fears, but allowing oneself to be caught up in the way of Jesus Christ, into the messianic event, thus fulfilling Isa. 53." Bonhoeffer, *Letters and Papers from Prison*, ed. Eberhard Bethge (New York: Collier Books, 1971), 363.

59 Bonhoeffer, *Ethics*, 234.

60 Bonhoeffer elaborates this understanding of Christ's humility in his 1933 lectures on Christology. See Bonhoeffer, *Christ the Center*, trans. Edwin H. Robertson (New York: HarperOne, 1978), 108-13.

61 Bonhoeffer, *Ethics*, 284.

62 Bonhoeffer, *Ethics*.

63 "There are no acts that are bad in and of themselves; even murder can be sanctified," Bonhoeffer writes. He goes on to say, "All we can do is examine the concrete situation of decision and point out one of the possibilities for decision that emerges there." Bonhoeffer, "Basic Questions of a Christian Ethic," in *Barcelona, Berlin, and New York*, 367, 369.

64 Bonhoeffer is unclear about what exactly it means to incur guilt on behalf of others and how a person can incur guilt if she is responding to a divine command. For discussions of Bonhoeffer on guilt, see Christine Schliesser, "Accepting Guilt for the Sake of Germany: An Analysis of Bonhoeffer's Concept of Accepting Guilt and Its Implications for Bonhoeffer's Political Resistance," *Union Seminary Quarterly Review* 60, nos. 1–2 (2006): 56–68. See also Schliesser, *Everyone Who Acts Responsibly Becomes Guilty: Bonhoeffer's Concept of Accepting Guilt* (Louisville, Ky.: Westminster John Knox, 2008), 175–205.

65 Bonhoeffer, *Ethics*, 299, 291.

66 Bonhoeffer, *Ethics*, 268–69.

67 Another condition that shapes responsibility is what Bonhoeffer calls the "divine mandates," the social and institutional settings of work, marriage, government, and the church. In his early writing, Bonhoeffer was concerned to respond to Emil Brunner's notion of the "orders of creation." Brunner took the orders of creation to be natural configurations of human life that inhere in God's creation. Bonhoeffer viewed institutions not as natural features of the created order but as God's response to a fallen creation in need, in Bonhoeffer's term, of "preservation" against its own destructive tendencies. The orders of preservation secure human life against the deleterious effects of sin so that human beings can participate fully in the redemption of creation, effected in Christ: "All orders of our fallen world are God's orders of preservation that uphold and preserve us for Christ. They are not orders of creation but orders of preservation. They have no value in themselves; instead they find their end and meaning only through Christ. God's new action with humankind is to uphold and preserve humankind in its fallen world, in its fallen orders, for death—for the resurrection, for the new creation, for Christ." Dietrich Bonhoeffer, *Creation and Fall: A Theological Exposition of Genesis 1–3*, ed. John W. de Gruchy (Minneapolis: Fortress, 1997), 140. Bonhoeffer's orders of preservation became what he later called "divine mandates."

For Bonhoeffer, the mandates work together to build up "the whole human being," to enhance human capacities and experiences in their lives before God (*Ethics*, 73). The mandates provide structures and patterns for human social experience, changing and evolving to suit human needs. A vocation lived out in the context of a mandate, then, will generally respond to the moral norms the mandate places on responsible action (though, of course, God is free to command responses that contravene such norms). Bonhoeffer's understanding of the divine mandates is explored in more detail below.

68 Bonhoeffer, *Ethics*, 284.

CHAPTER 3

1 The marketplace exercises a profound formative process on persons. Harvey Cox argues that the marketplace has a religious quality, forming selves in a "vast catechetical network" that "[conveys] teachings to those who require enlightenment." See Cox, "Mammon and the Culture of the Market: A Socio-Theological Critique," in *Meaning and Modernity: Religion, Polity, and Self*, ed. Richard Madsen (Berkeley: University of California Press, 2001), 126. A similar argument is in Daniel Bell, *The Economy of Desire: Christianity and Capitalism in a Postmodern World* (Grand Rapids: Baker, 2012), 93–122.

2 For an overview of recent theoretical approaches to the relationship between institutional logics and moral formation, see Royston Greenwood et al., *The Sage Handbook of Organizational Institutionalism* (London: Sage, 2008), 111–12.

3 The concept of political office is a close relative to political space. See the note in the introduction regarding Andrew Sabl's definition of political office. The idea of political space draws attention to the relationship between the institutional settings of politics and political agency. Office, in Sabl's definition, is a position or role that confers authority to do certain kinds of work. Political space emphasizes the formative power that institutional settings exert on political agents. An agent, that is, does not simply exercise a "characteristic kind of action"; in political space, that self at the same time becomes a political agent of a particular kind by virtue of exercising the "duties and privileges" of the office.

4 Political theorist Sheldon Wolin makes the intriguing suggestion that American political life requires what he calls a "multiple civic self." The multiple civic self, he writes, is one "who is required to act the citizen in diverse settings: national, state, city or town, neighborhood, and voluntary association." Wolin calls the multiple civic self "perhaps the most complex conception of citizenship ever devised," and yet, he writes, "we have no coherent conception of it." Wolin, *The Presence of the Past: Essays on the State and the Constitution* (Baltimore: Johns Hopkins University Press, 1989), 190.

For Wolin, the U.S. Constitution posits a conception of the citizen sharply divided from the practices of citizenship in the early Republic. Following the legacy of Alexander Hamilton, the Constitution contemplates both a strong national government, wielding the powers of war, taxation, trade and monetary regulation, and interpretation of the Constitution itself, and a weak conception of the citizen, connected to a distant national government only through periodic elections. But a vibrant, local democratic culture, reflected in the sensibilities of Thomas Jefferson and James Madison, also informs the framing of citizenship in the Constitution. Citizens, in this view, are empowered, efficacious, and consistent participants in the political life of town, city, and state. Wolin argues that these two competing visions of citizenship ill equips the American political tradition to negotiate what he calls "the challenge of modern power." Wolin, *Presence of the Past*, 190.

5 *Success and Failure in Politics* is the subtitle of Ignatieff's recent book, in which he reflects on his experience in Canadian political life. See Ignatieff, *Fire and Ashes*.

6 Ignatieff, *Fire and Ashes*, 133.

7 Ignatieff, *Fire and Ashes*, 80.

8 Ignatieff, *Fire and Ashes*, 54.

9 Jim Galloway, "Sadie Fields Retires from the Georgia Christian Alliance," *Political Insider* (blog), *Atlanta Journal Constitution*, May 22, 2010, http://blogs.ajc.com/political-insider-jim-galloway/2010/05/22/sadie-fields-retires%20the-georgia-christian-alliance/.

10 Michelle Hiskey, "The Convictions of Sadie Fields," *Nieman Storyboard*, October 24, 2006, http://www.niemanstoryboard.org/2006/10/24/the-convictions-of-sadie-fields/.

11 Hiskey, "Convictions of Sadie Fields."

12 Hiskey, "Convictions of Sadie Fields." Hiskey notes that, in canvassing Georgia to build support for the Christian Coalition, Fields would "brake for antique stores, looking for Queen Anne and French furniture that suited the traditional decor in Sadie's home. She remains the quintessential steel magnolia, raised by a mother who wore gloves to get the mail. She enjoys valet parking and expects men to open doors. She even wears a fragrance called Magnolia and has decorated empty fireplaces with the big white blooms."

Fields herself cultivated a public face of the Christian Coalition that conservative Georgians could recognize as their own.

13 Hiskey, "Convictions of Sadie Fields."

14 Alexis de Tocqueville, *Democracy in America*, trans. Harvey Mansfield and Delba Winthrop (Chicago: University of Chicago Press, 2012), 501.

15 For a discussion of the one-to-one relational meeting, the tool organizers use to build public relationships, see Edward T. Chambers, *Roots for Radicals: Organizing for Power, Action, and Justice* (New York: Bloomsbury Academic, 2003), 44-52. See also Jeffrey Stout, *Blessed Are the Organized: Grassroots Democracy in America* (Princeton: Princeton University Press, 2010), 148-64.

16 Jeffrey Stout notes, "Anger is one of the most important traits [organizers] look for in potential leaders. Someone who professes love of justice, but is not angered by its violation is unlikely to stay with the struggle for justice through thick and thin, to display the passions that will motivate others to join in, or to have enough courage to stand up to the powers that be." Stout, *Blessed Are the Organized*, 64.

17 Stout describes how a "public being" emerges in a house meeting: "Ideally, something is already happening to the people participating. It might be that Carmen, by engaging in the sort of discussion for the first time, begins to have a sense of herself as a public being, not merely identified with her roles as daughter, mother, and wife. When she speaks, others listen. They are moved by what she says. She is moved by what they say. Someone tells her that she speaks powerfully and wisely. Someone else tells her that she is courageous when she stands up for her family. She has told a story from her own experience, and exposed her concerns and emotions to them. Now she is receiving an image of herself back from them. Over time, people outside her circle of family members and personal friends not only defer to for her judgment, but explain to her what, in their eyes, her story and identity are." Stout, *Blessed Are the Organized*, 155.

18 Stout, *Blessed Are the Organized*, 120.

19 Political theorist Romand Coles argues that broad-based community organizing trains ordinary citizens in three "practices of receptivity," "listening," "traveling," and "tabling." Citizens learn how to attend carefully to one another's concerns and discern shared interests (listening), become familiar with the political geographies of their cities (traveling), and build relationships with diverse and ever-changing constituencies and conversation partners (tabling). It is through these practices, Coles argues, that ordinary citizens form political habits and virtues needed to sustain democracy. See Coles, *Beyond Gated Politics: Reflections for the Possibility of Democracy* (Minneapolis: University of Minnesota Press, 2005), 213-37.

20 Mark R. Warren discusses the IAF approach to developing citizen leadership in Warren, *Dry Bones Rattling: Community Building to Revitalize American Democracy* (Princeton: Princeton University Press, 2001), 211-38.

21 Chantal Mouffe describes the political adversary as "the opponent with whom we share a common allegiance to the democratic principles of 'liberty and equality for all,' while disagreeing about their interpretation." See Mouffe, "For an Agonistic Public Sphere," in *Radical Democracy: Politics Between Abundance and Lack*, ed. Lars Tonder and Lasse Thomassen (New York: Palgrave, 2005), 123-32.

22 See John Rawls' discussion of comprehensive doctrines in his *Political Liberalism* (New York: Columbia University Press, 1996), 36-40.

23 See, e.g., Rawls' notion of public reason. Rawls, *Political Liberalism*, 212-54.

24 See, e.g., Seyla Benhabib's "deliberative model of democracy" in her essay "Toward a Deliberative Model of Democratic Legitimacy," in *Democracy and Difference: Contesting the Boundaries of the Political*, ed. Seyla Benhabib (Princeton: Princeton University Press, 1996), 67–94.

25 Amy Gutmann and Dennis F. Thompson, *Democracy and Disagreement* (Cambridge, Mass.: Belknap Press, 1996), 40–41.

26 Participants in these debates are well known. See, e.g. (among many others), Richard Rorty, "Religion as a Conversation-Stopper," in *Philosophy and Social Hope* (New York: Penguin, 1999), 148–67; idem, "Religion in the Public Square: A Reconsideration," *Journal of Religious Ethics* 31, no. 1 (2003), 141–49; Rawls, *Political Liberalism*; Jürgen Habermas, "Reconciliation through the Public Use of Reason," in *The Inclusion of the Other*, ed. Ciaran Cronin and Pablo De Greiff (Cambridge, Mass.: MIT Press, 1999); idem, "Transcendence from Within, Transcendence in this World," in *Religion and Rationality: Essays on Reason, God and Modernity*, ed. Eduardo Mendieta (Cambridge, Mass.: MIT Press, 2002), 67–94; Robert Audi, "The State, the Church, and the Citizen," in *Religion and Contemporary Liberalism*, ed. Paul J. Weithman (Notre Dame, Ind.: University of Notre Dame Press, 1997), 38–75; Nicholas Wolterstorff, "Why We Should Reject What Liberalism Tells Us about Speaking and Acting in Public for Religious Reasons," in *Religion and Contemporary Liberalism*, ed. Paul J. Weithman (Notre Dame, Ind.: University of Notre Dame Press, 1997), 162–81; idem, "An Engagement with Rorty," *Journal of Religious Ethics* 31, no. 1 (2003): 129–39; Ronald F. Thiemann, *Religion in Public Life: A Dilemma for Democracy* (Washington, D.C.: Georgetown University Press, 1996); Jeffrey Stout, *Democracy and Tradition* (Princeton: Princeton University Press, 2004), chap. 3.

27 See Elaine Graham, *Between a Rock and a Hard Place*, 69–105.

28 Thus, e.g., theologian Franklin L. Gamwell has proposed that Christians understand that there is a "common Christian vocation" to participation in democratic political life. For Gamwell, this is "a Christian calling that does not distinguish some Christians from others by commission to specialized responsibilities within the Christian community or to a certain kind of secular work as one's principal occupation." Gamwell, *Politics as a Christian Vocation: Faith and Democracy Today* (New York: Cambridge University Press, 2005), 3. Gamwell's concern, unlike the focus of this book, is about what political vocation means for ordinary citizens. For Gamwell, democratic politics requires "full and free political discussion and debate or politics by the way of reason" (4). Christians have often resisted subjecting their fundamental moral commitments to the democratic process of "public discussion and debate" because, Christians believe, these fundamental commitments are affirmed by revelation. On the contrary, Gamwell argues that the "moral principles implied by Christian faith prescribe democracy . . . as a form of political rule." Since Christian moral principles imply democratic rule, ordinary citizenship in democratic polities is therefore a "general form of Christian witness" (4). Gamwell goes on to argue that if Christian faith is true, its fundamental assumptions and commitments can be validated in public argument (76). Gamwell later writes, "The God in whom Christians believe is necessarily present to all humans, calling them to love God without reservation. Hence, Christian belief can be assessed through reasons authorized by common human experience, and Christian faith prescribes the humanistic commitment" (79). Christians should feel obligated to participate in conversation and deliberation in the public sphere. They should also feel confident that their fundamental moral commitments will find validation in those conversations. Gamwell's view is

one among many Christian theological approaches to political life that takes the public forum to be a dominant form of political space.

A second, Augustinian view understands that an eschatological reality not only constitutes the destiny of creation; it also reaches into creation and claims it in the penultimate moment known as "the world." God is the proper object of love. All loves ought to be ordered to God. In the eschaton, the eternal, beatific communion with God, all loves are ordered properly to God. The eschaton does not sit idly at the end of creation. Instead, the love of God lays claim to creation in secular time. All human experience is therefore eccentric in a literal sense: the source of human meaning, value, and ultimate desire resides outside of human beings, in God. Because of sin, human beings have an incomplete view of love's proper order and are unable to order their loves perfectly to God. Human viewpoints on ultimate values are inevitably plural, though the unity of the good in God, not pluralism, is the ultimate condition of creaturely experience. Public discourse acknowledges the inevitability of moral pluralism as a symptom of sin and finitude. It frees conversation partners to explore one another's perspectives as expressions of an inevitably incomplete ordering of value in relationship to the ultimate source of value. Public conversation should therefore invite constructive feedback and may also occasion the revision of one's own views. See Mathewes, *Theology of Public Life*; Kristen Johnson, *Theology, Political Theory, and Pluralism*; Luke Bretherton, *Christianity and Contemporary Politics*.

Robin W. Lovin articulates a still different view. In his recent book *Christian Realism and the New Realities* (2008), he argues that modern societies are marked by a pluralism of institutional "contexts," such as the market, church, and polity, in which human goods are created and maintained. Each context has a particular discursive space, which he calls a "forum." In the context of forums, discussions about goods are conducted in terms of moral logics and languages characteristic to each forum. As God has ordained a plurality of institutional contexts in the ordering of human social life, Lovin argues, so all citizens are called to engage these "discussions" without flattening the moral complexity of contextual pluralism. For Lovin, discussions within and across forums are inevitably conflictual, but conflict marks the integrity of a pluralistic society.

Politics for Lovin is the site in which competing moral claims are negotiated through public discourse: "Politics is made up of discussion of goods within contexts and the negotiation and renegotiation of claims between contexts. The differentiation of a variety of interdependent contexts that shape important areas of life makes that inevitable" (139). Negotiation of goods across contexts happens in what Lovin calls the "public forum." The public forum is not a separate entity from particular forums, as though public discussions about goods could abstract from the meanings and logics that different contexts attach to them. Rather, "the public forum is located within each of the forums that contexts create, not in some one place separate and apart from them" (137). See Lovin, *Christian Realism and the New Realities* (New York: Cambridge University Press, 2008).

29   "Deliberation contributes to the legitimacy of decisions made under conditions of scarcity," Amy Gutmann and Dennis Thompson write. "Even with regard to political decisions with which they disagree, citizens are likely to take a different attitude towards those that are adopted after careful consideration of the relevant conflicting moral claims and those that are adopted only after calculation of the relative strength of the competing political interests. Moral justifications do not of course make up for

the material resources that citizens fail to receive. But they help sustain the political legitimacy that makes possible collective efforts to secure more of those resources in the future, and to live with one another civilly in the meantime." Gutmann and Thompson, *Democracy and Disagreement*, 41–42.

30 Jeffrey Stout writes that "the democratic practice of giving and asking for reasons" is "where the life of democracy principally resides." "Democracy isn't all talk," Stout explains. There is marching, protesting, organizing, voting, and the like. But all of these practices involve discursive acts, that is, speech acts made in public spaces in which persons make public and politically relevant claims. "Protestors rarely just march," Stout writes. "They also carry signs that say something. They chant slogans that mean something. They sing songs that convey a message. And they march to or from a place where speeches are given." Stout, *Democracy and Tradition*, 6.

Mika LaVaque-Manty in his *Arguments and Fists* argues that constitutive of the liberal framing of political agency is the claim that political agency necessarily involves communicative acts in which political agents raise claims about the legitimacy of authority. LaVaque-Manty, *Arguments and Fists: Political Agency and Justification in Liberal Theory* (New York: Routledge, 2002).

31 See Benhabib, *Democracy and Difference*.

32 Kant famously writes, "*Enlightenment is man's* [sic] *emergence from the self-incurred immaturity. Immaturity is the ability to use one's own understanding without the guidance of another.*" *Kant: Political Writings*, ed. Hans Reiss (New York: Cambridge University Press, 1991), 54; emphasis in original.

33 Kant puts it this way: "by the public use of one's own reason, I mean that use which anyone may make of it *as a man of learning* addressing the entire *reading public.*" *Kant: Political Writings*, 55; emphasis in original.

34 Kant's conception of public reason reflects broader social, political, economic, and cultural transformations that gave rise to the democratic public sphere in the early modern period. See especially Jürgen Habermas, *The Structural Transformation of the Public Sphere: An Inquiry into a Category of Bourgeois Society* (Cambridge, Mass.: MIT Press, 1991).

35 The private use of reason, by contrast, "is that which a person may make of it in a particular *civil post* or office with which he is entrusted." *Kant: Political Writings*, 55; emphasis in original. Persons use reason privately when they carry out the duties appropriate to the office or social role they occupy, as determined by whatever authority structure is germane to a particular office or social role. Thus, it is incumbent upon a citizen qua taxpayer to pay her taxes, using her faculties appropriately to fulfill that duty, just as it is incumbent upon a clergy person to use her rational faculties to espouse the doctrines of the church.

36 Theologian Ellen Ott Marshall explores the norms of love, moral ambiguity, and theological humility that structure responsible political speech and action, in part because of her commitment to the interrelated character of human being. See Marshall, *Christians in the Public Square: Faith That Transforms Politics* (Nashville: Abingdon, 2008).

37 Fair competition is different, however, from the unmitigated use of coercive power. The latter happens when one constituency acquires and consolidates political power, allows no competition for it, and then uses its power to enforce its will against the wishes of other political constituencies. Such is the case in political dictatorships that use political power violently to secure themselves against competitors. The unmitigated use of coercive political power would seem to have little meaningful moral standing.

38 Walzer, *Politics and Passion: Toward a More Egalitarian Liberalism* (New Haven: Yale University Press, 2006), 92.

39 Walzer, *Politics and Passion*, 101.

40 "There is, however, another way of recognizing others: not only as individuals who are rational in exactly the same way that we are but also as members of groups with beliefs and interests that mean as much to them as our beliefs and interests mean to us." Walzer, *Politics and Passion*, 104.

41 Walzer goes on to say that "the democratic way to win is to educate, organize, and mobilize more people than the other side does. 'More' is what makes the victory legitimate, and while legitimacy is strengthened if good arguments can be made about the substantive issues at stake, the victory is rarely won by making good arguments." Walzer, *Politics and Passion*, 103-4.

CHAPTER 4

1 Weber, "Politics as a Vocation," in *From Max Weber*, 123.

2 Augustine, *City of God*, V.12.

3 To be sure, politics builds up moral character in distinctive ways. But the moral ambiguity of political space also threatens to corrode character: "[Because] the stakes are so high," political theorist Michael Walzer writes, "participants in [economic and political competition] also learn to watch and distrust one another, to conceal their plans, to betray their friends." Competition for power and wealth in political and market systems, respectively, put persons under "great pressure" to win, even if winning means compromising moral standards. Just as there are constitutional restraints on the ways persons compete for and exercise power in political life, so too, Walzer argues, should constitutional provisions moderate the competition for wealth in capitalist market systems. Walzer, "Does the Free Market Corrode Moral Character? Of Course It Does." *John Templeton Foundation*, September 3, 2013, http://www.templeton.org/market/PDF/Walzer.pdf.

4 Robert Caro, "The Transition: Lyndon Johnson and the Events in Dallas," *New Yorker*, April 2, 2012, 43, http://www.newyorker.com/magazine/2012/04/02/the-transition.

5 Kennedy was, Caro notes, "a man so stunned by grief and shock that he hardly knew what he was saying, or even, to some extent, what he was hearing." Caro, "Transition," 44.

6 "If the desired assent by Bobby Kennedy to [the oath's] immediate administering was not obtained, at least he had been asked whether he objected to it, and had not replied, so it would be difficult for him to criticize it later." Caro, "Transition," 45.

7 Of the incompatibility of Christian and republican virtue, political theorist Isaiah Berlin wrote that "what [Machiavelli] institutes is something that cuts deeper still—a differentiation between two incompatible ideals of life, and therefore two moralities. One is the morality of the pagan world: its values are courage, vigor, fortitude in adversity, public achievement, order, discipline, happiness, strength, justice, above all assertion of one's proper claims and the knowledge and power needed to secure their satisfaction. . . . Against this moral universe . . . stands in the first and foremost place Christian morality. The ideals of Christianity are charity, mercy, sacrifice, love of God, forgiveness of enemies, contempt for the goods of this world, faith in the life hereafter, belief in the salvation of the individual soul as being of incomparable value—higher than, indeed wholly incommensurable with, any social or political or other terrestrial goal, any

economic or military or aesthetic consideration." For Berlin, Machiavelli's argument about the incompatibility of the Christian and republican virtues constitutes the earliest theory of moral pluralism in the West. Isaiah Berlin, *The Proper Study of Mankind: An Anthology of Essays*, ed. Henry Hardy and Roger Hausheer (New York: Farrar, Straus & Giroux, 2000), 289.

8   By "republican virtue," I mean the virtues of persons who lead republics, not the virtues of adherents to the Republican Party.

9   Machiavelli, *Discourses on Livy*, 131.

10 See Marshall, *Christians in the Public Square*.

11 Stanley Hauerwas, "Haunting Possibility," in *Christianity, Democracy, and the Radical Ordinary*, 25.

12 Hauerwas finds these virtues in figures like Ella Baker, Miles Horton, and Robert Moses. Hauerwas, "Haunting Possibility," in *Christianity, Democracy, and the Radical Ordinary*, 27.

13 Weber, "Politics as a Vocation," in *From Max Weber*.

14 Weber, "Politics as a Vocation," in *From Max Weber*, 364.

15 The politician, Weber writes, "is becoming involved, I repeat, with the diabolical powers that lurk in all violence." Weber, "Politics as a Vocation," in *From Max Weber*, 365.

16 It is important, John Dunn notes, to distinguish between power and authority in political life. Power is "in one useful sense, a relation between two or more human wills, in which one can for some purposes effectively control the other will or set of wills." Authority is "a relation between specifiable human values, particular human understandings, and the wills guided or determined by those understandings." Though power can be used to require persons to participate in arrangements that they may not want, it cannot be used to coerce attitudes of endorsement that confer authority. If power is not authorized, it is significantly weakened.

17 In a 2011 analysis, four University of North Carolina legal scholars argued that the amendment would prohibit the state from creating civil union or domestic partnership arrangements for same-sex couples, thus blocking access to legal protections these arrangements carry and would eliminate insurance benefits already provided to same-sex domestic partnerships in some North Carolina counties. Additionally, the authors speculated that "it is very possible, however, that courts would interpret the Amendment to bar the state from giving any protections to unmarried couples—straight or same-sex—based on their relationships." These include domestic violence, child custody and visitation, hospital visitation, and medical emergency protections, among others. See Maxine Eichner, Barbara Fedders, Holning Lau, and Rachel Blunk, "Potential Legal Impact of the Proposed Domestic Legal Union Amendment to the North Carolina Constitution," November 8, 2011, http://www.law.unc.edu/documents/faculty/marriageamendment/dlureportnov8.pdf.

18 North Carolina State Board of Elections, last modified June 13, 2012, http://results.enr.clarityelections.com/NC/36596/85942/en/vt.html.

19 Michael Gordon, "Federal Judge Overturns NC Same-Sex Marriage Ban," *Charlotte Observer*, October 10, 2014, http://www.charlotteobserver.com/2014/10/10/5232525/nc-gop-leaders-given-until-noon.html.

20 Specifically, Snowden was charged with theft of government property, unauthorized communication of national defense information, and willful communication of classified communications intelligence information to an unauthorized person. See "Edward

Snowden Unsealed Complaint," *Politico*, June 21, 2013, http://www.politico.com/story/2013/06/edward-snowden-complaint-unsealed-93181.html.

21 Obama said, "I guarantee you that in European capitals, there are people who are interested in, if not what I had for breakfast, at least what my talking points might be should I end up meeting with their leaders. . . . That is how intelligence services operate." See Tom Cohen and Michael Pearson, "All Nations Collect Intelligence, Obama Says," *CNN*, July 2, 2013, http://www.cnn.com/2013/07/01/world/europe/eu-nsa/index.html?iref=allsearch.

22 Philosopher Bernard Williams calls this "Truman's kitchen-heat principle": "a certain level of roughness is to be expected by anyone who understands the nature of the activity [of politics], and it is merely a misunderstanding to go on about it in a way which might be appropriate to more sheltered activities." Williams, "Politics and Moral Character," in *Public and Private Morality*, ed. Stuart Hampshire (New York: Cambridge University Press, 1978), 62.

23 Michael Walzer notes that what makes the so-called problem of dirty hands intelligible is that only relatively good persons capable of agonizing over their culpability can have dirty hands. Walzer famously argues that all politicians will emerge from politics with dirty hands because politics is an inevitably tragic undertaking. It sometimes involves choices in which politicians cannot help but do some evil. But good politicians will understand that tragic choice entails culpability—that they accept they have done something wrong and are therefore guilty—and will suffer personally under the weight of their culpability. Though the actions of politicians often go undisclosed, and should often go undisclosed, politicians will judge themselves. Good polities, he thinks, instill in all persons, including politicians, an awareness of culpability and a capacity for self-judgment, and constitute a public that critically interrogates political actions in light of a vigilantly maintained "moral code." We know "the moral politician," Walzer argues, "by his dirty hands": "if he [sic] were a moral man and nothing else, his hands would not be dirty; if he were a politician and nothing else, he would pretend that they were clean." Walzer, "Political Action: The Problem of Dirty Hands," *Philosophy and Public Affairs* 2, no. 2 (1973): 168.

24 Drawing on the work of Franz Neumann, theologian J. Philip Wogaman argues that political power has two dimensions. First, it involves the capacity to make things happen, to "control nature" in such a way that the world responds to the needs and desires of a political community. Political power might work, for example, to mobilize public resources, to build roads, schools, sanitation plants, or public utilities. But, more fundamentally, political power is the capacity to influence the human will so that persons or communities act in desired ways. Political power therefore always has an instrumental quality: it aims for the achievement of particular goals and ends. Thus, Wogaman concludes, "*every human interest or value having any influence over the will of any person is potentially a form of political power.*" Wogaman, *Christian Perspectives on Politics*, rev. ed. (Louisville, Ky.: Westminster John Knox, 2000), 25; emphasis in original. Here I speak of "modalities" of political power, by which I mean the different forms or configurations that political power takes in the practice of politics.

25 The heart of the AUMF is the following: "that the President is authorized to use all necessary and appropriate force against those nations, organizations, or persons he determines planned, authorized, committed, or aided the terrorist attacks that occurred on September 11, 2001, or harbored such organizations or persons, in order to prevent

any future acts of international terrorism against the United States by such nations, organizations or persons." See Authorization for the Use of Military Force, S.J. Res. 23, 107th Congress, http://thomas.loc.gov/cgi-bin/query/z?c107:S.J.RES.23.ENR, *Gov-Track.us,* https://www.govtrack.us/congress/bills/107/sjres23/text. These sixty words of the AUMF constitute the basis of the president's power to wage the War on Terror.

Some have argued that this short passage has too broadly expanded the president's power, resulting in an unbounded effort to fight terrorism. See Gregory D. Johnsen, "60 Words and a War without End: The Untold Story of the Most Dangerous Sentence in U.S. History," *BuzzFeed,* January 16, 2014, http://www.buzzfeed.com/gregorydjohns en/60-words-and-a-war-without-end-the-untold-story-of-the-most.

26   Authorization for Use of Military Force.

27   Lee's speech on the floor of the House is quoted in Johnsen, "60 Words and a War without End."

28   Johnsen recounts the prayer service at the National Cathedral in "60 Words and a War without End."

29   Johnsen, "60 Words and a War without End."

30   See Jane Mayer, "Schmooze or Lose," *New Yorker,* August 27, 2012, http://www.newyorker .com/magazine/2012/08/27/schmooze-or-lose.

31   In an interview with NPR's Terry Gross, Mayer commented, "Obama has had to make a terrible choice between his principles and politics, and the practicalities of the political landscape right now—and it's an impossible bind he is in." See Gross, "Jane Mayer: Obama in 'Impossible Bind' over Donors," *Fresh Air,* August 22, 2012, http://www.npr .org/2012/08/23/159768245/jane-mayer-obama-in-impossible-bind-over-donors.

32   David Axelrod, Obama's chief campaign strategist, described the dilemma: "we concluded we couldn't play touch football if they were playing tackle." Mayer, "Schmooze or Lose."

33   For this summary of *Shelby County v. Holder,* I rely on Ilya Shapiro's article "Supreme Court Recognizes Jim Crow's Demise, Restores Constitutional Order," *SCOTUSblog,* June 25, 2013, http://www.scotusblog.com/2013/06/supreme-cour-recognizes-jim-crows -demise-restores-constitutional-order/.

34   A *New York Times* editorial from June 20, 2013, notes that the Supreme Court's ruling does not prevent the Justice Department from invalidating discriminatory voting practices. The ruling also does not completely prevent the Justice Department from enforcing preclearance in local jurisdictions. But now the department "must show clear intent of racial discrimination, which is easy to hide. Congress should revise that section to allow coverage when a state makes a voting change with a disparate racial impact, not just discriminatory intent." "The Future of Voting Rights," *New York Times,* op-ed, June 29, 2013, http://www.nytimes.com/2013/06/30/opinion/sunday/ the-future-of-voting-rights.html.

35   See Adam Liptak and Charlie Savage, "U.S. Asks Court to Limit Texas on Ballot Rules," *New York Times,* July 25, 2013, http://www.nytimes.com/2013/07/26/us/holder-wants -texas-to-clear-voting-changes-with-the-us.html?hp.

36   Commentator Bill Barrow writes, "States like North Carolina and Virginia provide apt examples of the potential fallout. An influx of non-whites have turned those Republican strongholds into battlegrounds in the last two presidential elections, and minority voters helped President Barack Obama win both states in 2008 and Virginia again in 2012. Nationally, Republican Mitt Romney lost among African-Americans by about

85 percentage points and Latinos by about 44 percentage points, margins that virtually ensure a Democratic victory." Bill Barrow, "Voting Rights Act Decision Leaves GOP with Tough Choices," *Huffington Post*, September 3, 2013, http://www.huffingtonpost .com/2013/07/04/voting-rights-act-gop_n_3546796.html.

37 See, e.g., Karl Rove, "More White Votes Alone Won't Save the GOP," *Wall Street Journal*, June 26, 2013, http://online.wsj.com/article/SB10001424127887323873904578569480696746650.html.

38 These obligations may be competing, but they are not necessarily mutually exclusive. There are many ways the Justice Department might try to regulate state election policy without violating the Supreme Court's interpretation of *Shelby County v. Holder* and other relevant laws. The administration might not be successful in this pursuit, but it probably will not run into a zero-sum choice simply by trying. The administration might, in other words, be able to have its cake and eat it, too.

39 Hard decisions might instead be called dilemmas, and, indeed, many use the term "dilemma" informally to describe hard decisions. For the purposes of analytical clarity, however, I want here to reserve the term "dilemma" for a different kind of choice, a moral dilemma. A moral dilemma is, as theologian Timothy Jackson says, "a situation in which, through no antecedent fault of your own, you can't avoid real guilt." Timothy P. Jackson, *Love Disconsoled: Meditations on Christian Charity* (New York: Cambridge University Press, 1999), 202. Jackson continues, "Real guilt is, by definition, blameworthy; and being blameworthy ought to elicit remorse. In a dilemma, then, no possible knowledge or will-power or liberation would deliver you from appropriately feeling remorse. You would suffer significant moral loss, become vicious and blameworthy, no matter who you are, how you behave, or what you achieve. You would be faced with extreme moral tragedy, not just moral perplexity or frustration; at the limit, you would have to betray charity itself." Jackson goes on to argue that, as a matter of faith, his view of the priority of agapic love as the "preeminent virtue" for Christian ethics rules out the existence of genuine moral dilemmas of this sort (212).

A moral dilemma, in this somewhat idiosyncratic usage, is a decision made between two or more alternatives, any one of which will cause one to commit moral error (to sin, as Christians would say). In a moral dilemma, one cannot but emerge from the decision, judgment, and associated actions as genuinely guilty or culpable in some way.

40 This is certainly a hard decision, but it is probably not an example of a moral dilemma as defined in the note above. It is not a moral dilemma because there is likely a course of action that takes priority over political considerations. Surely, any meaningful moral framework will ensure the protection of citizens, especially historically disenfranchised persons, from communities that seek to oppress them. Such a decision may not be a politically tenable one for Republicans, but political considerations do not make a hard choice into a moral dilemma.

41 For more on moral problems associated with the imposition of money in politics and other settings of social life, see Sandel, *What Money Can't Buy*.

42 An excellent portrait of the role fund-raising plays in the everyday work of U.S. congressmen and women is "Take the Money and Run for Office" (episode 461), *This American Life*, http://www.thisamericanlife.org/radio-archives/episode/461/take-the -money-and-run-for-office.

43 Lawrence Lessig, *Republic, Lost: How Money Corrupts Congress—and a Plan to Stop It* (New York: Twelve, 2011), 138.

44 Ryan Grim and Sabrina Siddiqui, "Call Time for Congress Shows How Fundraising Dominates Bleak Work Life," *Huffington Post*, January 9, 2013, http://www.huffington post.com/2013/01/08/call-time-congressional-fundraising_n_2427291.html.

45 Lessig, *Republic, Lost*, 125–71.

46 Lessig, *Republic, Lost*, 107–24.

47 One attack ad criticized Snow's support of the 2009 Racial Justice Act, a North Carolina law that required a reduction of an offender's death sentence to life in prison if the offender could prove racial bias in his conviction, later repealed by the North Carolina General Assembly in 2013. The ad implied that Snow favored the unqualified release of child rapists and other heinous offenders. This and other ads portrayed Snow as soft on crime. In fact, Snow had been a strong supporter of the death penalty. See Jane Mayer, "State for Sale," *New Yorker*, October 10, 2011, http://www.newyorker.com/reporting/2011/10/10/111010fa_fact_mayer?mobify=0.

48 "The Multimillionaire Helping Republicans Win N.C.," *NPR*, October 6, 2011, http://www.npr.org/2011/10/06/141078608/the-multimillionaire-helping-republicans-win-n-c.

49 "The Decline of North Carolina," *New York Times*, July 9, 2013, http://www.nytimes.com/2013/07/10/opinion/the-decline-of-north-carolina.html.

50 Sean Sullivan, "What Is a 501(c)(4), Anyway?," *Washington Post*, May 13, 2013, http://www.washingtonpost.com/blogs/the-fix/wp/2013/05/13/what-is-a-501c4-anyway/.

51 Mayer, "State for Sale."

52 "Multimillionaire Helping Republicans Win N.C."

CHAPTER 5

1 Stanley Hauerwas is a prominent voice among theological critics who make this kind of argument. For Hauerwas, liberal democracy is the political system that creates space in which modernity's isolated, autonomous self allegedly has the freedom to create its own destiny. Such a system is needed in a political context in which there is no shared story and thus no shared conception of the good life. Political rights protect each person from others, creating space for each to pursue the version of the good life that she thinks is best. Hauerwas writes, "We have made 'freedom of the individual' an end in itself and have ignored the fact that most of us do not have the slightest idea of what we should do with our freedom." Hauerwas, *A Community of Character: Toward a Constructive Christian Social Ethic* (Notre Dame, Ind.: University of Notre Dame Press, 1981), 80.

Liberalism, Hauerwas argues, is not a coherent tradition of moral meaning and practice that forms people to live good lives. It is instead an impoverished, if not an empty, moral tradition: "The great self-deception," Hauerwas writes, "is in thinking that the tradition of liberalism gives us the means to recognize that it is indeed a tradition. Instead it continues to promise new tomorrows of infinite creation. And the more we are convinced we are free, the more determined we become." Hauerwas, *Community of Character*, 83.

The liberal political regime does nothing more than to ensure the survival of its citizens. As such, liberal political thought manifests a fear of death that is a fundamental concern of modern worldviews in which the autonomous self stands at the center. Hauerwas makes this point in *A Community of Character*: "Most of us live as if we assume our social order is secure and we are safe. We can do this because we assume death happens only to other people. We are sometimes vaguely comforted by reports of others' deaths, as such reports confirm our own presumption that we are protected by a magical invulnerability. Absorption into most societies is training in self-deception as we conspire with one another to keep death at bay" (18). And he reiterates it in *After Christendom*: "I hope we have learned from this foray into Augustinian thought that genuine politics is about the art of dying. That places the church at cross purposes with the politics of liberalism, built as it is on the denial of death and sacrifice." Hauerwas, *After Christendom? How the Church Is to Behave If Freedom, Justice, and a Christian Nation Are Bad Ideas* (Nashville: Abingdon, 1991), 43.

2 See Walter Rauschenbusch, *Christianizing the Social Order* (New York: Macmillan, 1913; repr., Waco, Tex.: Baylor University Press, 2010).

3 See Niebuhr, *Nature and Destiny of Man*; idem, *Moral Man and Immoral Society*.

4 John XXIII, *Mater et Magistra (Christianity and Social Progress)*, in *Catholic Social Thought: The Documentary Heritage*, ed. David J. O'Brien and Thomas A. Shannon (Maryknoll, N.Y.: Orbis Books, 2003), 94. For a discussion of the influence of the natural law tradition on CST, see Stephen J. Pope, "Natural Law in Catholic Social Teaching," in *Modern Catholic Social Teaching: Commentaries and Interpretations*, ed. Kenneth Himes (Washington, D.C.: Georgetown University Press, 2005), 41–71.

5 John Paul II defines solidarity as "a firm and persevering determination to commit oneself to the common good." John Paul II, *Sollicitudo Rei Socialis (On Social Concern)*, in O'Brien and Shannon, *Catholic Social Thought*, 421.

6 Pius XI formulates the principle of subsidiarity in this way: "As history abundantly proves, it is true that on account of changed conditions many things which were done by small associations in former times cannot be done now save by large associations. Still, that most weighty principle, which cannot be set aside or changed, remains fixed and unshaken in social philosophy: Just as it is gravely wrong to take from individuals what they can accomplish by their own initiative and industry and give it to the community, so also it is an injustice and at the same time a grave evil and disturbance of right order to assign to a greater and higher association what lesser and subordinate organizations can do. For every social activity ought of its very nature to furnish help to the members of the body social, and never destroy and absorb them." Pius XI, *Quadragesimo Anno*, Section 79, in O'Brien and Shannon, *Catholic Social Thought*, 60.

7 Pope John XXIII in *Mater et Magistra* describes the balance that CST wants to achieve in advancing the principles of subsidiarity and socialization: "Accordingly, as relationships multiply between men, binding them more closely together, commonwealths will more readily and appropriately order their affairs to the extent these two factors are kept in balance: (1) The freedom of individual citizens and groups of citizens to act autonomously, while cooperating with one another; (2) the activity of the State whereby the undertakings of private individuals and groups are suitably regulated and fostered." John XXIII, *Mater et Magistra*, in O'Brien and Shannon, *Catholic Social Thought*, 94–95.

8 Michael Hardt and Antonio Negri famously explore an emergent form of sovereignty they term "empire," a "network power" rather than a unilateral or multilateral one, which "includes as its primary elements, or nodes, the dominant nation-states along with supranational institutions, major capitalist corporations, and other powers." Hardt and Negri, *Multitude: War and Democracy in the Age of Empire* (New York: Penguin, 2004), xii. Globalization creates the conditions for the constellations of aristocratic and oligarchic power known as "empire." But it also creates the conditions for new

constellations of democratic power, which Hardt and Negri term "multitude." See also Hardt and Negri, *Empire* (Cambridge, Mass.: Harvard University Press, 2001).

9   For recent accounts of the eclipse of democratic political life, see Jeffrey Stout's discussion of plutocracy in American politics, Colin Crouch's discussion of "post-democracy," Garry Dorrien's discussion of "economic oligarchy," and Sheldon Wolin's discussion of "inverted totalitarianism." Stout, *Blessed Are the Organized*; Colin Crouch, *Post-Democracy* (Malden, Mass.: Polity, 2004); Sheldon S. Wolin, *Democracy Incorporated: Managed Democracy and the Specter of Inverted Totalitarianism* (Princeton: Princeton University Press, 2010); Gary Dorrien, *Economy, Difference, Empire: Social Ethics for Social Justice* (New York: Columbia University Press, 2010).

10 Using the framing of an Augustinian eschatology, Charles Mathewes argues that citizens should feel empowered to engage in the "play" of public conversation, since constructive public dialogue allows conversation partners to explore and revise their fundamental commitments. Similarly, Kristen Deede Johnson, drawing on Augustine, argues that an ultimate ontological unity resides in the eschaton, which, in worldly polities, makes possible "public conversations" that genuinely engage difference and diversity. Mathewes, *Theology of Public Life*; Johnson, *Theology, Political Theory, and Pluralism*.

11 See Mathewes, *Republic of Grace*, 147–80.

12 Catholic theologian William T. Cavanaugh has argued that the modern state is a political space developed to advance the interests of the powerful and that any attempt to rehabilitate the modern state on its own terms is facile. Catholic theologians following in the tradition John Courtney Murray, Cavanaugh argues, have promoted the church's role in policy advocacy to correct shortcomings in the state's public provision. Other theorists like Harry Boyte, rather than focusing on policy advocacy, promote civil society as a political space that holds the workings of the modern state in check. Cavanaugh thinks that both approaches are problematic because no part of the political space generated in the modern state, the public square, civil society, or otherwise, is ultimately real. The church, through its practices, especially the practice of the Eucharist, rehearses the city of God, which is the authentic political space. See William T. Cavanaugh, *Theopolitical Imagination: Christian Practices of Space and Time* (Edinburgh: T&T Clark, 2003), 9–95.

For Cavanaugh, Augustine's eschatological vision in the city of God upends the idea that church and state share one political space. Rather, the earthly city and the heavenly city share two political spaces that are utterly different. Cavanaugh writes, "For a more adequate construal of political space, I turn to Augustine, who speaks not of one city but two. For Augustine, there is no division of goods: both cities use the same finite goods, but use them for different ends. The two cities compete for the same goods; both are practices of binding, alternate practices of religio. At the same time that Augustine is more clear-eyed about the opposition of two alternate practices of religio, however, he also allows us to avoid simple dichotomies of church versus state. The two cities are not two institutions but two performances, two practices of space and time." Cavanaugh, *Migrations of the Holy*, 49.

13 Bonhoeffer, *Ethics*, 67.

14 Early on, Bonhoeffer was concerned to respond to Emil Brunner's notion of the "orders of creation." Brunner took the orders of creation to be natural configurations of human life that inhere in God's creation. Bonhoeffer viewed institutions not as natural features of the created order but as God's response to a fallen creation in need, in Bonhoeffer's

term, of "preservation" against its own destructive tendencies. Bonhoeffer writes, "All orders of our fallen world are God's orders of preservation that uphold and preserve us for Christ. They are not orders of creation but orders of preservation. They have no value in themselves; instead they find their end and meaning only through Christ. God's new action with humankind is to uphold and preserve humankind in its fallen world, in its fallen orders, for death—for the resurrection, for the new creation, for Christ." Bonhoeffer, *Creation and Fall*, 140. The orders of preservation secure human life against the deleterious effects of sin so that human beings can participate fully in the redemption of creation, effected in Christ. Bonhoeffer's orders of preservation in their last incarnation become what he later calls "divine mandates."

15 Bonhoeffer, *Ethics*, 389.

16 Bonhoeffer, *Ethics*, 68–69.

17 Bonhoeffer, unlike Emil Brunner, emphasizes that although God calls the mandates into being, an adequate understanding of the work of the mandates depends on their situation in particular historical moments. Theologian Robin Lovin writes, "The principal difference between Bonhoeffer's mandates and Brunner's orders is that Bonhoeffer incorporates into the mandates an element of theology and history that cannot be understood in purely natural terms. Brunner argues that the orders of creation are shaped by invariant requirements that apply in all ages. For Bonhoeffer, the requirements that govern labor, marriage, church, or state are not absolutes built into nature but limits that have evolved in history." Robin W. Lovin, *Christian Faith and Public Choices: The Social Ethics of Barth, Brunner, and Bonhoeffer* (Philadelphia: Fortress, 1984), 152.

18 Bonhoeffer, *Ethics*, 73.

19 Robin Lovin, "The Future of Political Theology: From Crisis to Pluralism," in *Political Theology for a Plural Age*, ed. Michael Jon Kessler (New York: Oxford University Press, 2013), 197. In his recent work, Lovin has explored the ways in which different institutional "contexts" create and maintain human goods differently and has considered how these differences should be negotiated in the "public forum." Like Bonhoeffer, Lovin does not focus on multiple moral formations in institutional "contexts" and how these are to be reconciled with one another. See Lovin, *Christian Realism and the New Realities*.

20 Calvin, *Institutes*, 3.24.2, 967.

21 Calvin, *Institutes*, 3.10.6, 724.

22 Calvin writes, "However, it is among members of the household of faith that this same image is more carefully to be noted [Gal 6:10], in so far as it has been renewed and restored through the Spirit of Christ. Therefore, whatever man you meet who needs your aid, you have no reason to refuse to help him. Say, 'He is a stranger'; but the Lord has given him a mark that ought to be familiar to you, by virtue of the fact that he forbids you to despise your own flesh [Isa 58:7, Vulg.]. Say, 'He is contemptible and worthless'; but the Lord shows him to be one to whom he has deigned to give the beauty of his image. Say that you owe nothing for any service of his; but God, as it were, has put him in his own place in order that you may recognize toward him the many and great benefits with which God has bound you to himself. Say that he does not deserve even your least effort for his sake; but the image of God, which recommends him to you, is worthy of your giving yourself and all your possessions." Calvin, *Institutes*, 3.7.6, 696.

At the heart of the journey of sanctification, Calvin argues, is self-denial, the "sum of the Christian life." Self-denial is not simply an ascetic rejection of the desires of the flesh—although it is in part that. More fundamentally, self-denial is the process whereby the elect recognize that "we are not our own"; rather, our ultimate belongingness is to God. Calvin, *Institutes*, 3.7.1.

23 Calvin, *Institutes*.

24 Bonhoeffer, *Ethics*, 284.

25 Michael Walzer, *Thick and Thin: Moral Argument at Home and Abroad* (South Bend, Ind.: University of Notre Dame Press, 1994), 98.

CHAPTER 6

1 See Bellah et al., *Good Society*, 3–18.

2 See Aristotle, *Nicomachean Ethics*, in *The Basic Works of Aristotle*, ed. Richard McKeon (New York: Random House, 1941), 1106a, 957–64.

3 Aristotle, *Nicomachean Ethics*, in McKeon, *Works*, 1107a, 959–64.

4 Drawing on Freud's notion of melancholia, David Kyuman Kim argues that modern agents are melancholic because they are unable to mourn and thus unable to put to rest the loss of goods, values, and identities that render the moral life ordered, coherent, and intelligible. He defines melancholy/melancholia as "a state or condition of the self and the soul in which we cannot let go of something that we love even if it has become lost to us through death or some kind of annulment, such as experiences of supercession, obsolescence, or nostalgia. In other words, melancholy/melancholia is a condition in which the self is unable to mourn." David Kyuman Kim, *Melancholic Freedom: Agency and the Spirit of Politics* (New York: Oxford University Press, 2007), 5. Modern agency, Kim urges, is achieved at a cost—the loss of enduring conceptions of the good—that comes with the sort of freedom that moderns take themselves to enjoy, "the freedom of individual choice or will, responsibility, and personal autonomy" (16). As modern agents engage in their own normative projects, they must constantly attend to this sense of loss.

    Interestingly, the melancholic in Freud's view seems hardly to be able to exercise any meaningful moral agency at all. Freud writes that "melancholia is mentally characterized by a profoundly painful depression, a loss of interest in the outside world, the loss of the ability to love, the inhibition of any kind of performance and a reduction in the sense of self, expressed in self-recrimination and self-directed insults, intensifying into the delusory expectation of punishment" (311). He goes on to suggest that melancholia, unlike mourning, is characterized by "an extraordinary reduction in self-esteem, a great impoverishment of the ego." The melancholic "really is as apathetic, as incapable of love and achievement, as he says he is. But that, as we know, is secondary; it is the consequence of the internal work, unknown to us and comparable to mourning, that is devouring his ego" (313). See Sigmund Freud, "Mourning and Melancholia," in *The Penguin Freud Reader*, ed. Adam Phillips (New York: Penguin, 2006). Kim recognizes that Freud "pathologizes melancholia as a kind of overbearing narcissism" and therefore turns to contemporary theorists to develop his own notion of melancholy/melancholia. These theorists include Judith Butler, Julia Kristeva, Wendy Brown, and Peter Homans, among others, whom Kim takes to appeal "to melancholy/melancholia for more constructive and critical purposes" (114), Kim never, in my estimation, deals adequately with the deeply problematic nature of moral agency in Freud's conception of melancholy. This is odd since Kim appropriates Freud's conception of melancholy for precisely the purpose of exploring moral agency in the modern milieu.

5 Cheryl Kirk-Duggan argues that the concept of the common good has not tradition-ally upheld genuine engagement with difference and has failed to respond adequately to systemic oppression. Kirk-Duggan argues that both of these criteria constitute stan-dards of building "true community." See Kirk-Duggan, "A Rose by Any Other Name: Deconstructing the Essence of Common," in In Search of the Common Good, ed. Dennis P. McCann and Patrick D. Miller (New York: Continuum, 2005), 190-210.

6 Niebuhr's insights about group egotism and balancing power, examined above, respond in one way to the moral ambiguity surrounding political loyalties. The egotistical preten-sions of dominant groups will not be diffused or moderated by appeals to the common good. Instead, the power that these groups assert in their pursuit of their own interests can be checked effectively only in opposition to countervailing powers and interests. Politicians, the discussion above showed, are often torn between their commitments to the constituencies that elected them and their commitments to broader publics. Niebuhr imagines that there is not really much of a conflict here: various constituencies and their representatives, at least those that hold power, are given to pursuing their own interests, often to the exclusion of the common good. Indeed, as one looks around the current political landscape, it is difficult to deny Niebuhr's insistence on the necessity of balancing power and interest in the incremental move toward justice in political life. See the discussion of Niebuhr's understanding of irony as he develops it in his Irony of American History in chap. 7 above.

Even if Niebuhr is fundamentally correct about the way group egotism operates among empowered groups in political life, his realist framing is not sufficiently fine grained to account for the agency of individual political actors. It is not as though individual political agents are inevitably given over to the egotistical aspirations of the groups they represent. There is a line somewhere, in other words, between group agency, which is often egotistical in the ways Niebuhr describes, and that of individual political agents, who might imagine their work in the framing of vocation and thus consider how their work both defines and advances the common good.

7 Calvin, Institutes, 2.2.13, 272.

8 Calvin, Institutes, 4.20.16, 1504.

9 Arnold Huijgen discusses Calvin's theological treatment of the concept of equity in his Divine Accommodation in John Calvin's Theology: Analysis and Assessment (Göttingen: Vandenhoeck & Ruprecht, 2011), 189-90.

10 Douglas Ottati describes the Reformed view of the natural awareness of justice as a "sen-sibility," a capacity to know the fundamental shape and form of justice and of injustice when we see it, even if persons cannot agree on elaborate schemes of justice. See Ottati, "What Reformed Theology in a Calvinist Key Brings to Conversations about Justice," 462-64.

11 Calvin, Institutes, 1.6.1, 70.

12 Calvin, Institutes, 4.20.9, 1486.

13 Calvin, Institutes, 4.20.2, 1487.

14 Ottati, "What Reformed Theology in a Calvinist Key Brings to Conversations about Justice," 460.

15 The Reformed tradition holds that discernment is a corporate and cooperative process. Community is the context in which the Holy Spirit is understood to be at work. The awareness of human finitude suggests that human beings produce more informed and more nuanced judgments when they work together to discern in community. Because

discernment is a corporate and cooperative practice, persons learn the virtue of discernment only in community contexts.

16 James M. Gustafson, *Ethics from a Theocentric Perspective*, vol. 1 (Chicago: University of Chicago Press, 1981), 338.

17 James M. Gustafson, "Moral Discernment in the Christian Life," in *Moral Discernment in the Christian Life: Essays in Theological Ethics*, ed. Theo A. Boer and Paul E. Capetz (Louisville, Ky.: Westminster John Knox, 2007), 37.

18 Scott F. Aikin and Robert B. Talisse, *Why We Argue (and How We Should)* (New York: Routledge, 2014), 11.

19 Aiken and Talisse, *Why We Argue*, 8.

20 Aiken and Talisse, *Why We Argue*, 29.

21 Also see the discussion of Kant's scholar in chapter 3 above. Contemporary political theories generally address in some way or other the problem of pluralism that emerges from Enlightenment conceptions of reason. Many of them assume with the Enlightenment model that rationality is the distinctive feature of human moral agency. Not all of them understand that persons using their reason together to make decisions about political life—public reason, in short—is central to an understanding of liberal democracy. Some theorists, such as Isaiah Berlin, argue that liberalism creates a modus vivendi that manages competing views of the good life such that all conceptions can coexist in political association with minimum interference on the part of the state. See Berlin's discussion of value pluralism in Berlin, *Crooked Timber of Humanity*, 1–47. Other theorists, such as John Rawls, argue that rational persons, operating from different conceptions of the good, will endorse a minimum conception of justice that can be used to structure political association. Still others understand some conception of public reason as the central legitimating feature of modern liberal polities. Gerald F. Gaus usefully discusses the ways in which different theories of liberalism treat this problem of pluralism. Gaus, *Contemporary Theories of Liberalism: Public Reason as a Post-Enlightenment Project* (Thousand Oaks, Calif.: Sage, 2003).

The question that this last set of theories wants to answer is, What is the proper functioning of public reason, and which principles will ensure that it does properly function? Not all deliberative theories are procedural theories, however. James Bohman, for example, finds procedural models of deliberative democracy to explain insufficiently why deliberation is a democratic process at all. He argues instead from a sociological perspective that public reason is better understood as a dialogical process rather than as a procedure that creates a social bond in its very enactment. He thinks that this approach better explains how public deliberation could effectively create political agency. "Rather than procedural, the account developed here is dialogical in that the exchange of public reasons in the give and take of dialogue makes speakers answerable and accountable to one another. In such a process, citizens may have the reasonable expectation that they may affect the outcome of deliberation or revise unacceptable outcomes in the future" (17). Bohman, *Public Deliberation: Pluralism, Complexity, and Democracy* (Cambridge, Mass.: MIT Press, 1996).

In the American context, political theorists like Amy Gutmann and Dennis Thompson theorize what they call "deliberative democracy," a conception of the liberal democratic polity that "asks citizens and officials to justify public policy by giving reasons that can be accepted by those who are bound by it." Gutmann and Thompson, along with other theorists of deliberative democracy, seek to address the problem of moral disagreement without resorting to a conception of politics that amounts either to modus vivendi or tyranny of the majority. They think that democratic institutions constructed and maintained on the basis of ongoing and productive deliberation better negotiate moral disagreement than either procedural or constitutional models of democracy.

Gutmann and Thompson argue for a conception of deliberative democracy over against both procedural and constitutional conceptions. The problem with the latter two alternatives, they argue, is that they fail to resolve the tension between majority rule (which procedural theories privilege) and the protection of individual rights (which constitutional theories privilege). These therefore cannot adequately address the problem of genuine moral disagreement, which the deliberative model seeks to remedy. In Gutmann and Thompson's version, deliberative democracy rests on three procedural principles—reciprocity, publicity, and accountability—and three constitutional principles—basic liberty, basic opportunity, and fair opportunity—that, when extended through public institutions, facilitate opportunities for productive deliberation that addresses itself to moral disagreement. Gutmann and Thompson, *Democracy and Disagreement*, 42.

In the German context, the philosopher and social theorist Jürgen Habermas has constructed a similar model based on his own work in communicative and discourse ethics. Habermas works out this model via his discourse ethical paradigm in *Between Facts and Norms*. Habermas, *Between Facts and Norms: Contributions to a Discourse Theory of Law and Democracy* (Cambridge, Mass.: MIT Press, 1996).

Models of deliberative democracy are not without criticism. See for example Walzer's critique in "Deliberation . . . and What Else?" from his *Politics and Passion*, discussed below. I am not interested in exploring the promise and problems of deliberative models of democracy here. I wish only to note that these theories, as opposed to other theories of liberalism, treat public reason as a foundational element of a theory of democracy.

Public reason plays a more generic role in many theories of liberal democratic politics, deliberative and otherwise. Most theorists of liberal democratic politics value some notion of an ongoing, public, and in some way disciplined deliberation about shared norms and values as a distinctive feature of political life in vibrant democratic polities. In both deliberative theory, in which public reason plays a central role, and in other theories of liberalism, in which public reason is not central, the scope of public reason— questions regarding the matters to which it ought to apply—is a matter of some debate. Some theorists limit the scope of public reason to deliberations about formal law, particularly constitutional law. Other theorists mean for the scope of public reason to apply to *any* formal or informal public discourse about shared norms and values that might affect the development of policies. Richard Rorty's influential essay "Religion as a Conversation-Stopper" (1994) is an example in this regard. Rorty tends to think in terms of conversations about "public policy" in general. Rorty, *Philosophy and Social Hope*, 168-74. Rorty revises his position, taking a more reconciliatory tone toward religious citizens, in his later essay "Religion in the Public Square: A Reconsideration." Public reason in this approach forms the basis of a general political ethic.

22 Eddie S. Glaude, defending John Dewey's tragic sensibility, writes, "Tragedy, then, is a part of the moral exigencies of life. It involves principally the moral choices we make between competing and irreconcilable goods, and it entails the consequences we must endure, if we live, and the responsibility we must embrace without yielding to despair." The political vocation is tragic in Glaude's sense because it deals in the currency of

"competing and irreconcilable goods." Glaude, *In a Shade of Blue: Pragmatism and the Politics of Black America* (Chicago: University of Chicago Press, 2007), 20.

23 Pope John Paul II, *Sollicitudo Rei Socialis* in O'Brien and Shannon, *Catholic Social Thought*, 421; emphasis in original.

24 It is often imagined that, as Jean Porter writes, "modern Catholic social thought is grounded more or less directly in Aquinas' political theory," and thus the idea of the common good, central to CST, is also central to the thought of Thomas Aquinas. But, Porter argues, Aquinas does not offer a "substantive account" of the common good. See Porter, "The Common Good in Thomas Aquinas," in Miller and McCann, *In Search of the Common Good*, 94–120.

25 Pope Paul VI, *Gaudium et Spes*, in O'Brien and Shannon, *Catholic Social Thought*, 181. CST, beginning with Leo XIII's *Rerum Novarum* (1891), explores the idea of the common good in a number of historically situated and responsive framings. For an analysis of the idea of the common good in CST, see Dennis P. McCann, "The Common Good in Catholic Social Teaching: A Case Study in Modernization," in Miller and McCann, *In Search of the Common Good*, 121–46.

26 David Hollenbach, S.J., provides a summary discussion of the ways in which Catholic traditions view different forms of justice, their complementary arrangement, and the contribution each makes to the common good. See Hollenbach, *The Common Good and Christian Ethics* (New York: Cambridge University Press, 2002), 173–211.

27 Meghan J. Clark argues that in the tradition of Catholic social teaching, solidarity is a "social virtue" that "requires the participation of both the 'agent' and those with whom the 'agent' seeks to be in solidarity." Clark, *The Vision of Catholic Social Thought: The Virtue of Solidarity and the Praxis of Human Rights* (Minneapolis: Fortress, 2014), 113.

28 Solidarity, Rebecca Todd Peters argues, implies praxis rather than a vague sense of fellow feeling or empathy. That is, solidarity requires that participants develop "a new model for working across chasms of difference toward a common goal." Peters, *Solidarity Ethics: Transformation in a Globalized World* (Minneapolis: Fortress, 2014), 51.

29 Jennifer McBride helpfully emphasizes that Bonhoeffer's perspective on repentance entails acknowledgment of guilt and taking responsibility for "social sin." McBride develops a theology of public witness "aimed" primarily at "white Protestants who benefit in countless recognized and unrecognized ways from being part of the dominant culture" (9). She understands that the work of responsibility in response to social sin will look different in dominant and marginalized communities. All political officials enjoy the privilege of political power by virtue of their office, though, of course, some will come from dominant and others from marginalized contexts. The argument here is that the privilege of political power, if it is to participate fully in God's redemptive project, requires taking responsibility for past social sin, which Bonhoeffer's understanding of repentance illumines. See McBride, *The Church for the World : A Theology of Public Witness* (New York: Oxford University Press, 2012).

30 Bonhoeffer, *Ethics*, 146.

31 Bonhoeffer, *Ethics*, 146.

32 Bonhoeffer, *Ethics*, 148.

33 Bonhoeffer, *Ethics*, 160.

34 Bonhoeffer, *Ethics*, 160.

35 Bonhoeffer, *Ethics*, 164.

36 Bonhoeffer, *Ethics*, 162–63.

37   Bonhoeffer, *Ethics*, 162.
38   Bonhoeffer, *Ethics*, 164.
39   Bonhoeffer, *Ethics*, 165.
40   Bonhoeffer, *Ethics*, 165.
41   Calvin similarly foregrounds repentance as the initial movement toward participation in the life of Christ. In the mortification of the flesh and the vivification of the Spirit, "the Spirit of God so imbues our souls, steeped in his holiness, with both new thoughts and feelings, that they can rightly be considered new." Repentance for Calvin leads to regeneration, the conforming of the self to Jesus Christ in the vivifying work of the Spirit.

CHAPTER 7

1   Thomas Kaplan, "Cuomo Says He Makes History, Then Repeats It," *New York Times*, April 27, 2012, http://www.nytimes.com/2012/04/28/nyregion/cuomo-says-he-makes -history-then-repeats-it.html.
2   Susanne Craig, William K. Rashbaum, and Thomas Kaplan, "Cuomo's Office Hobbled Ethics Inquiries by Moreland Commission," *New York Times*, July 24, 2014, http://www .nytimes.com/2014/07/23/nyregion/governor-andrew-cuomo-and-te-short-life-of -the-moreland-commission.html.
3   Aristotle, *Ethics*, in McKeon, *Works*, 1107a, 959–64.
4   See Isaiah Berlin, "The Originality of Machiavelli," in Hardy, *Proper Study of Mankind*, 269–325. See also Stuart Hampshire, "Morality in Machiavelli," in *Innocence and Experience* (Cambridge, Mass.: Harvard University Press, 1989), 161–89; and Harvey Mansfield, *Machiavelli's Virtue* (Chicago: University of Chicago Press, 1998), 6–52.
5   Machiavelli, *Discourses on Livy*, 289.
6   Machiavelli, *Discourses on Livy*. Montesquieu, a later exponent of the republican tradition, argues that republican virtue is "love of homeland" and "love of equality." Republican virtue is different from "moral virtue" and "Christian virtue." Thus, Montesquieu suggests, the "Christian good man" is distinguished from "the political good man." Charles-Louis de Secondat, Baron de la Brède et de Montesquieu, *The Spirit of the Laws*, ed. Anne M. Cohler, Basia C. Miller, and Harold S. Stone (New York: Cambridge University Press, 1989), xli.
7   The American founders, following ancient republican forebears, were preoccupied with the possibility of corruption understood as an attenuation of civic virtue leading to the malformation not only of individual politicians but of the whole body politic. Republics could only be sustained through the cultivation and maintenance of civic virtue. The American Constitution is striking in its rigorous treatment of corruption. Indeed, the early American republic was thought to be more rigorous in its legal response to corruption than its European counterparts. See Zephyr Teachout, *Corruption in America: From Benjamin Franklin's Snuff Box to Citizens United* (Cambridge, Mass.: Harvard University Press, 2014).
8   Cicero, "On the State," in *On Government*, trans. Michael Grant (New York: Penguin, 1993), 190–91.
9   Augustine, *City of God*, 213–14.
10   The apostles, Augustine writes, "referred [the great glory that followed them] to the glory of God, by whose grace they were what they were." Augustine, *City of God*, 214. For an analysis of Augustine's understanding of glory as a reflection of God's glory, see

Hauerwas, "Haunting Possibility," in *Christianity, Democracy, and the Radical Ordinary*, 17–30.

11 Augustine, *City of God*, 225.

12 Augustine, *City of God*, 215.

13 For a discussion on the differences among glory, honor, and fame in both ancient and modern understandings, and on the devotion of the American founders to fame, see Douglas Adair, "Fame and the Founding Fathers," in *Fame and the Founding Fathers: Essays by Douglas Adair*, ed. Trevor Colbourn (New York: Norton, 1974), 3–26.

14 Cicero, "On the State," in Grant, *On Government*, 190.

15 Adair, "Fame and the Founding Fathers," 12.

16 Here I am indebted to Andrew Sabl's discussion of "democratic constancy" that undergirds his theory of political office. See Sabl, *Ruling Passions: Political Offices and Democratic Ethics* (Princeton: Princeton University Press, 2002), 55–95.

17 Alexander Hamilton, *Federalist* No. 72 in Alexander Hamilton, James Madison, and John Jay, *The Federalist Papers, with Letters of "Brutus,"* ed. Terence Ball (New York: Cambridge University Press, 2003), 353

18 Augustine, *City of God*, 218.

19 Augustine recognizes that the desire for humanly glory and the lust for mastery differ from one another, "although he who delights excessively in human glory will also be much inclined ardently to desire mastery." Augustine, *City of God*, 223–24. Augustine also claims that while the desire for glory is a vice, it is a virtue to the extent that it restrains "greater vices" (212–15).

20 Augustine writes, "For we do not say that certain Christian emperors were happy because they ruled for a longer time, or because they died in peace and left behind sons to rule as emperors, or because they subdued the enemies of the commonwealth, or because they were able to avoid and suppress uprisings against them by hostile citizens." Augustine, *City of God*, 231.

21 Augustine's lengthy description of the happy Christian emperor is thus: "Rather, we say that they are happy if they rule justly; if they are not lifted up by the talk of those who accord them sublime honors or pay their respects with an excessive humility, but remember that they are only men; if they make their power the handmaid of His majesty by using it to spread His worship to the greatest possible extent; if they fear, love and worship God; if they love that Kingdom which they are not afraid to share with others more than their own; if they are slow to punish and swift to pardon; if they resort to punishment only when it is necessary to the government and defense of the commonwealth, and never to gratify their own enmity; if they grant pardon, not so that unjust men may enjoy impunity, but in the hope of bringing about their correction; if they compensate for whatever severe measures they may be forced to decree with the gentleness of mercy and the generosity of benevolence; if their own self-indulgence is as much restrained as it might have been unchecked; if they prefer to govern wicked desires more than any people whatsoever; if they do all these things not out of craving for empty glory, but from love of eternal felicity; and if, for their sins, they do not neglect to offer to their true God the sacrifices of humility and contrition and prayer." Augustine, *City of God*, 232.

22 Republican thinkers emphasize that the statesman is motivated to build lasting political institutions by his desire for fame or glory. See Cicero, "On the State," in Grant, *On Government*, 190–91.

Machiavelli writes in *The Prince*: "For one sees that in the things that lead men to the end that each has before him, that is, glories and riches." Machiavelli, *The Prince*, 99. For an analysis of Machiavelli's understanding of glory, see Russell Price, "The Theme of *Gloria* in Machiavelli," *Renaissance Quarterly* 30, no. 4 (1977): 588-631.

23 New rulers, Machiavelli argues, have an opportunity to secure "the double glory of having made the beginning of a new principality, of having adorned it and consolidated it with good laws, good arms, good friends, and good examples, just as he has a double shame, who, having been born prince, has lost it through his lack of prudence." Machiavelli, *The Prince*, 96.

24 Mansfield argues that, unlike the Aristotelian conception of virtue, Machiavelli's *virtù* "replaces the confidence in the kindness of nature or God with a more secure base in necessity. It is necessary for humans to trust in necessity; necessity is the only trust that fully reflects one's inability to trust. Necessity means the necessity to acquire; so men cognizant of necessity must devote themselves to acquisition." Mansfield goes on to argue that Machiavelli's *virtù* is parasitic on a traditional understanding of virtue. The ruler sometimes needs to discipline a population with vicious sanctions and then seems to possess traditional virtue when those sanctions are lifted or moderated. Mansfield, *Machiavelli's Virtue*, 14, 19.

25 Mark Philp argues that Machiavelli's concept of *virtù* departs from classical conceptions of virtue in these three ways. See Philp, *Political Conduct* (Cambridge, Mass.: Harvard University Press, 2007), 40-41. For Machiavelli, virtue need not be a cultivated feature of the prince's character, an argument that departs from the classical understanding of virtue. Machiavelli is well known for his argument in *The Prince* that the prince need not necessarily possess virtue—indeed, it is often detrimental for the prince to be virtuous— but the prince must certainly be seen to possess virtue. "Thus," Machiavelli writes, "it is not necessary for a prince to have all the above-mentioned qualities in fact, but it is indeed necessary to appear to have them. Nay, I dare say this, that by having them and always observing them, they are harmful; and by appearing to have them, they are useful." Machiavelli, *The Prince*, 70.

26 Machiavelli, *Discourses on Livy*, in *Selected Political Writings*, ed. and trans. David Wootton (Indianapolis: Hackett, 1994), 108.

27 Machiavelli, *Discourses on Livy*, 108.

28 Machiavelli, *Discourses on Livy*.

29 Machiavelli, *Discourses on Livy*, 125.

30 Machiavelli, *Discourses on Livy*, 156.

31 Machiavelli, *Discourses on Livy*, 168.

32 Machiavelli, *Discourses on Livy*.

33 Machiavelli, *Discourses on Livy*, 209.

34 Examples abound here, beginning, perhaps, with Plato's examination of justice in *The Republic*. Seneca argues in his *On Mercy* that mercy is an appropriate virtue for rulers because mercy regulates the ruler's asymmetrical power. Mercy, Seneca argues, is "self-control by the mind when it has the power to take vengeance" or "leniency on the part of a superior towards an inferior in imposing punishments." Commending Caesar Augustus, Seneca writes that mercy means "supreme power exercised with the truest self-control. . . . [I]t means blunting the edge of one's imperial power." Seneca, *Moral and Political Essays*, ed. John M. Cooper and J. F. Procopé (New York: Cambridge University Press, 2003), 142-43, 160.

35 Machiavelli famously argues that while rulers cannot completely determine fortune, they can exercise some control over it: "Nonetheless," Machiavelli writes, "so that our free will not be eliminated, I judge that it might be true that fortune is arbiter of half our actions, but also that she leaves the other half, or close to it, for us to govern." As the flooding of rivers can be at least partially managed by "dikes and dams," so too can princes "resist" fortune when their virtue "has been put in order." Machiavelli, *The Prince*, 98.

36 Weber, "Politics as a Vocation," in *From Max Weber*, 115.

37 Michael Walzer argues that, in the case of dirty hands, it is wise to enforce or "at least to imagine a punishment or a penance that fits the crime and so to examine closely the nature of the crime." Walzer, "Political Action," 179.

38 A resurgence of interest in Niebuhr's political realism in recent years takes up this dimension of his social philosophy. See, e.g., Richard Crouter, *Reinhold Niebuhr on Politics, Religion, and Christian Faith* (New York: Oxford University Press, 2010); John Patrick Diggins, *Why Niebuhr Now?* (Chicago: University of Chicago Press, 2011); and Daniel F. Rice, ed., *Reinhold Niebuhr Revisited: Engagements with an American Original* (Grand Rapids: Eerdmans, 2009).

39 E.g., Traci West in her *Disruptive Christian Ethics* argues that women activists of color working in Harlem, contemporaries of Niebuhr's and working not far from Niebuhr's Union Theological Seminary, created organizations that advanced the interests of the marginalized. These organizations, such as the YWCA, did not, contrary to Niebuhr's theory, merely advance the narrow self-interest of the persons involved in them. See West, *Disruptive Christian Ethics* (Louisville, Ky.: Westminster John Knox, 2006), 3–35.

40 Reinhold Niebuhr, *The Nature and Destiny of Man: A Christian Interpretation*, vol. 1, *Human Nature* (New York: Scribner's, 1964), 182.

41 Niebuhr, *Nature and Destiny of Man*, 1:179.

42 Niebuhr, *Nature and Destiny of Man*, 1:192.

43 Niebuhr, *Nature and Destiny of Man*, vol. 1.

44 Niebuhr, *Nature and Destiny of Man*, 1:211.

45 Pathos, Niebuhr writes, "is that element in an historic situation which elicits pity, but neither deserves admiration nor warrants contrition. . . . Suffering caused by purely natural evil is the clearest instance of the purely pathetic." Niebuhr, *The Irony of American History* (New York: Scribner's, 1962), vii.

46 Reinhold Niebuhr, *Beyond Tragedy* (New York: Scribner's, 1937), 160.

47 Niebuhr, *Irony of American History*, viii.

48 Niebuhr, *Irony of American History*, vii.

49 Niebuhr, *Irony of American History*, 158.

50 Niebuhr, *Irony of American History*.

51 Niebuhr, *Irony of American History*, 155.

52 Niebuhr, *Irony of American History*.

53 Niebuhr's understanding of irony is therefore distinguished from that of Richard Rorty, for whom irony is primarily an intellectual habit inducing in persons an awareness of the contingent, historically situated character of their most deeply held beliefs and commitments (their "final vocabulary," in Rorty's term). See Richard Rorty, *Contingency, Irony, and Solidarity* (New York: Cambridge University Press, 1989), 73–95.

54 Ignatieff, *Fire and Ashes*, 58.

55 William Galston argues that toughness is a political virtue. Drawing on the Aristotelian scheme, Galston claims, "The toughness required for political leadership stands between squeamishness, wishfulness, and innocence (on the one hand), and callousness, cynicism, and calculation, on the other. It is the disposition that enables leaders to recognize harsh necessities without blinding themselves to moral costs." Galston, "Toughness as a Political Virtue," *Social Theory and Practice* 17, no. 2 (1991): 176.

CHAPTER 8

1 See, e.g., Kristen Deede Johnson's Augustinian "theology of public conversation," in her *Theology, Political Theory, and Pluralism*, 174–249. For theological explorations of humility and civility, see, respectively, Marshall, *Christians in the Public Square*; and James Calvin Davis, *In Defense of Civility: How Religion Can Unite America on Seven Moral Issues That Divide Us* (Louisville, Ky.: Westminster John Knox, 2011).

2 See Charles Mathewes' discussion of play in public conversation, in his *Theology of Public Life*, 279–87.

3 This is the main thesis of Gutmann and Thompson, *Spirit of Compromise*.

4 Michael Walzer proposes that passion, in addition to reason, can serve as a basis of political recognition and respect. To acknowledge competitors is to acknowledge them "not only as individuals who are rational in exactly the same way as we are but also as members of groups with beliefs and interests that mean as much to them as our beliefs and interests mean to us." Walzer, *Politics and Passion*, 104.

5 For Chantal Mouffe, the adversary is "the central category of democratic politics." Mouffe, "For an Agonistic Public Sphere," 126.

6 For Carl Schmitt, the distinction between friend and enemy is what fundamentally defines the political. Schmitt argues that the "distinction of friend and enemy denotes the utmost degree of intensity of a union or separation, of an association or dissociation. . . . The political enemy need not be morally evil or aesthetically ugly; he need not appear as an economic competitor, and it may even be advantageous to engage with him in business transactions. But he is, nevertheless, the other, the stranger; and it is sufficient for his nature that he is, in a specially intense way, existentially something different and alien, so that in the extreme case conflicts with him are possible." Schmitt, *The Concept of the Political*, trans. George Schwab (Chicago: University of Chicago Press, 2007), 26–27. A theology of political vocation takes as its starting point a particular understanding of the common good (the "project" of political vocation) as that which constitutes the political and orients political work, rather than imagined differences between friend and enemy.

7 Weber, "Politics as a Vocation," in *From Max Weber*, 115.

8 Walzer, *Politics and Passion*, 111.

9 Inverting Ralph Waldo Emerson's dictum that "nothing great was ever achieved without enthusiasm," Walzer notes, "Nothing terrible was ever achieved without enthusiasm." Walzer, *Politics and Passion*, 118.

10 John de Gruchy, *Christianity and Democracy: A Theology for a Just World Order* (New York: Cambridge University Press, 1995), 239-243. See also idem, *Liberating Reformed Theology: A South African Contribution to an Ecumenical Debate* (Grand Rapids: Eerdmans, 1991), 135-37.

11 "Since I perform part of what needs to be done," Kathryn Tanner writes, "and you perform the rest, to the extent I act, you need not; and the more I act, the less you need

to." Tanner, *Jesus, Humanity, and the Trinity: A Brief Systematic Theology* (Minneapolis: Fortress, 2001), 4.

12 See the note on Traci West's critique of Niebuhr in chapter 7 above.

13 Dietrich Bonhoeffer writes, "To say that in humankind God creates the image of God on earth means that humankind is like the Creator in that it is free. . . . Being free means 'being-free-for-the-other,' because I am bound to the other. Only by being in relation with the other I am free." Bonhoeffer goes on to argue that "human beings exist in duality, and it is in this dependence on the other that their creatureliness exists." He goes on to say that "the likeness, the analogia, of humankind to God is not *analogia entis* but *analogia relationis*." Bonhoeffer, *Creation and Fall*, 63-65.

14 "Christological realism" is the name William Schweiker gives to Dietrich Bonhoeffer's ethics of formation, since the ontologically real is where Christ takes form in the world. See Schweiker, *Power, Value, and Conviction*, 148-54.

15 Schweiker, *Power, Value, and Conviction*.

16 Calvin, *Institutes*, 3.7.6, 696.

17 Mary McClintock Fulkerson rightly argues that a better conception of the *imago Dei* invites a transformative encounter with difference. A "theological logic of the *imago Dei*," Fulkerson argues, implies not a simple recognition of difference but a genuine engagement with others that transforms the self in the process. For Fulkerson, the *imago Dei* is therefore not simply a feature of the self; it is a "task" that challenges persons to honor and learn from difference. See Fulkerson, "The *Imago Dei* and a Reformed Logic for Feminist/Womanist Critique," in Pauw and Jones, *Feminist and Womanist Essays in Reformed Dogmatics*, 95-106.

18 In his classic work *A Letter Concerning Toleration* (1689), John Locke argues that religion and civil government have two different tasks, the former to promote the "salvation of souls" and the latter to secure "civil goods." Civil government should not encroach upon the work of ecclesiastical authorities, for it cannot force persons to faith. It should therefore tolerate any (Protestant) religious expression, and ecclesiastical authorities should tolerate diverse (Protestant) religious expression. He writes that "ecclesiastical men . . . ought industriously to exhort all men, whether private persons or magistrates, (if any such there be in his church) to charity, meekness, and toleration, and diligently endeavor to ally and temper all that heat and unreasonable averseness of mind which either any man's fiery zeal for his own sect or the craft of others has kindled against dissenters." Locke, *Political Writings*, ed. David Wooten (Indianapolis: Hackett, 2003), 404.

John Rawls in his *Political Liberalism* argues that political liberalism prescribes a set of civic virtues, though they do not belong to the "perfectionist state of a comprehensive doctrine." He writes, "Even though political liberalism seeks common ground and is neutral in aim, it is important to emphasize that it may still affirm the superiority of certain forms of moral character and encourage certain moral virtues—the virtues of fair social cooperation such as the virtues of civility and tolerance, of reasonableness and the sense of fairness." Rawls, *Political Liberalism*, 194.

19 For a theological critique of the limits of toleration in engaging difference, see Johnson, *Theology, Political Theory, and Pluralism*, 28-81.

20 Schweiker, *Power, Value, and Conviction*, 13.

21 Joseph L. Allen notes that a politician can pursue a vocation in politics by pursuing one of two "competing visions" of the political vocation. The first is a vision of the politician as a fighter against social injustice. The second is a vision of the politician as

a conciliator among conflicting interests. Each vision, Allen argues, has both character-istic advantages and dangers. I would argue that politicians who inhabit formal political offices, and thus are more directly responsible for wielding political powers attached to those offices, are more often bound to pursue the second vision, of the politician as a conciliator among competing interests, to govern effectively. But even political officers must sometimes move into a more prophetic stance, in which they take a stand on principle. So, Allen's two "visions" are more like two poles that constitute a spectrum. The politician must determine when and how it is appropriate to move back and forth between these two poles. See Allen, "Politics as a Calling."

22 James Wagner, "From the President: America as . . . Compromise," *Emory Magazine*, Winter 2013, http://www.emory.edu/EMORY_MAGAZINE/issues/2013/winter/register/president.html.

23 Wagner, "From the President."

24 Faculty letter to President Wagner, *Emory Wheel*, February 18, 2013, http://www.emorywheel.com/faculty-letter-to-president-wagner/.

25 Wagner, "From the President."

26 Gutmann and Thompson, *Spirit of Compromise*, 10. Gutmann and Thompson argue that compromises are pragmatic arrangements; they do not presume strict coherence with higher moral principles or law (37). To be able to compromise effectively, one must possess a "compromising mindset," consisting of two dispositions, "principled prudence" and "mutual respect" (65). Principled prudence is a disposition to adapt one's principles to mutually agreeable outcomes. It begins with the understanding that principles are more like "directional signals" than rigid and predetermined standards to which all moral judgments must cohere (84). Since principled prudence allows for adjustment, it opens particular situations to learning about the principles at play in them and about what progress toward these principles might look like. Mutual respect is a disposition that aims at "greater understanding" and "accommodation" among those who disagree (100).

27 Immanuel Kant, "Idea for a Universal History with a Cosmopolitan Purpose," in Reiss, *Kant: Political Writings*, 46.

28 Here I follow an insight from Isaiah Berlin. For Berlin, there are plural and in many ways incompatible human goods, purposes, and worldviews. But human experience per se creates the conditions of moral intelligibility. It is not easy to say just what human experience per se is, but it is at minimum the condition that separates moral intelli-gibility from moral gibberish. Berlin writes, "There is a world of objective values. By this I mean those ends that men pursue for their own sakes, to which other things are means. I am not blind to what the Greeks valued—their values may not be mine, but I can grasp what it would be like to live by their light, I can admire and respect them, and even imagine myself as pursuing them, although I do not—and do not wish to, and perhaps could not if I wished. Forms of life differ. Ends, moral principles, are many. But not infinitely many: they must be within the human horizon. If they are not, then they are outside the human sphere." Berlin, *Crooked Timber of Humanity*, 11. See John Gray's analysis of what he calls Berlin's "value pluralism," in Gray, *Isaiah Berlin* (Princeton: Princeton University Press, 1996); and idem, *Isaiah Berlin: An Interpretation of His Thought* (Princeton: Princeton University Press, 2013).

29 Avishai Margalit, *On Compromise and Rotten Compromises* (Princeton: Princeton University Press, 2010), 54.

30 Margalit, *On Compromise and Rotten Compromises*, 42–43.
31 Margalit, *On Compromise and Rotten Compromises*, 54.
32 Margalit, *On Compromise and Rotten Compromises*, 16.
33 For Margalit, empathy is "an attentive effort to understand the enemy's concerns from the enemy's point of view." Margalit, *On Compromise and Rotten Compromises*, 42.

CONCLUSION

1 See Johnson, *Theology, Political Theory, and Pluralism*.
2 See Mathewes, *Theology of Public Life*.
3 Taylor, *Secular Age*, 81–82.
4 Taylor, *Secular Age*, 84.
5 See Weber's discussion of worldly asceticism in his *Protestant Ethic and the Spirit of Capitalism*, trans. Talcott Parsons (New York: Routledge, 1992), 53–101.
6 Berlin, *Proper Study of Mankind*, 289.

BIBLIOGRAPHY

Adair, Douglas. "Fame and the Founding Fathers." In *Fame and the Founding Fathers: Essays by Douglas Adair*, edited by Trevor Colbourn, 3–26. New York: Norton, 1974.

Aiken, Scott F., and Robert B. Talisse. *Why We Argue (and How We Should)*. New York: Routledge, 2014.

Allen, Joseph L. "Politics as a Calling." Cary M. Maguire Center for Ethics and Public Responsibility, Southern Methodist University. http://www.smu.edu/~/media/Site/Provost/Ethics/pdfs/99214%20Allen TextFA.ashx?la=en.

Aristotle. *The Basic Works of Aristotle*. Edited by Richard McKeon. New York: Random House, 1941.

Audi, Robert. *Religious Commitment and Secular Reason*. New York: Cambridge University Press, 2000.

———. "The State, the Church, and the Citizen." In *Religion and Contemporary Liberalism*, edited by Paul J. Weithman, 38–75. Notre Dame, Ind.: University of Notre Dame Press, 1997.

Augustine. *The City of God against the Pagans*. Edited by R. W. Dyson. New York: Cambridge University Press, 1998.

———. *Political Writings*. Edited by E. M. Atkins. New York: Cambridge University Press, 2001.

Authorization for the Use of Military Force. S.J. Res. 23. 107th Congress. *GovTrack.us*, https://www.govtrack.us/congress/bills/107/sjres23/text.

Barrow, Bill. "Voting Rights Act Decision Leaves GOP with Tough Choices." *Huffington Post*. Last modified September 3, 2013. http://www

.huffingtonpost.com/2013/07/04/voting-rights-act-gop_n_3546796
.html.

Bartels, Larry. *Unequal Democracy: The Political Economy of the New Gilded Age.* Princeton: Princeton University Press, 2008.

Bell, Daniel. *The Economy of Desire: Christianity and Capitalism in a Postmodern World.* Grand Rapids: Baker, 2012.

Bellah, Robert N., Richard Madsen, William M. Sullivan, Ann Swidler, and Steven M. Tipton. *The Good Society.* New York: Vintage, 1992.

——. *Habits of the Heart: Individualism and Commitment in American Life.* Berkeley: University of California Press, 1985.

Benhabib, Seyla. "Toward a Deliberative Model of Democratic Legitimacy." In *Democracy and Difference: Contesting the Boundaries of the Political,* edited by Seyla Benhabib, 67–94. Princeton: Princeton University Press, 1996.

Bennett, John C. *The Christian as Citizen.* New York: Association Press, 1955.

——. *Christian Ethics and Social Policy.* New York: Scribner's, 1946.

Berlin, Isaiah. *The Crooked Timber of Humanity.* Edited by Henry Hardy. Princeton: Princeton University Press, 1998.

——. *The Proper Study of Mankind: An Anthology of Essays.* Edited by Henry Hardy and Roger Hausheer. New York: Farrar, Straus & Giroux, 2008.

Bohman, James. *Public Deliberation: Pluralism, Complexity, and Democracy.* Cambridge, Mass.: MIT Press, 1996.

Bonhoeffer, Dietrich. *Barcelona, Berlin, and New York: 1928–1931.* Edited by Clifford J. Green. Minneapolis: Fortress, 2009.

——. *Christ the Center.* Translated by Edwin H. Robertson. New York: HarperOne, 1978.

——. *Creation and Fall: A Theological Exposition of Genesis 1–3.* Edited by John de Gruchy. Minneapolis: Fortress, 1997.

——. *Ethics.* Edited by Clifford J. Green. Minneapolis: Fortress, 2005.

——. *Letters and Papers from Prison.* Edited by Eberhard Bethge. New York: Collier Books, 1971.

——. *Sanctorum Communio: A Theological Study of the Sociology of the Church.* Edited by Clifford J. Green. Minneapolis: Fortress, 1998.

Bouwsma, William James. *John Calvin: A Sixteenth-Century Portrait.* New York: Oxford University Press, 1988.

——. *A Usable Past: Essays in European Cultural History.* Berkeley: University of California Press, 1990.

Bretherton, Luke. *Christianity and Contemporary Politics.* Malden, Mass.: Wiley-Blackwell, 2010.

Brunner, Emil. *The Divine Imperative.* Philadelphia: Westminster, 1947.

Calvin, John. *Commentaries on the Epistle of Paul the Apostle to the Romans.* Translated by John Owen. Grand Rapids: Baker, 1984.

———. *Commentaries on the Epistles to Timothy, Titus, and Philemon.* Translated by William Pringle. Grand Rapids: Baker, 1948.

———. *Institutes of the Christian Religion,* Edited by John T. McNeill. 2 vols. Philadelphia: Westminster, 1960.

Calvin, John, and Jacopo Sadoleto. *A Reformation Debate: Sadoleto's Letter to the Genevans and Calvin's Reply.* Edited by John C. Olin. Grand Rapids: Baker, 1976.

Caro, Robert. "The Transition: Lyndon Johnson and the Events in Dallas." *New Yorker.* Last modified April 12, 2012. http://www.newyorker.com/magazine/2012/04/02/the-transition.

Cavanaugh, William T. "A Fire Strong Enough to Consume the House: The Wars of Religion and the Rise of the State." *Modern Theology* 11, no. 4 (1995): 397–420.

———. *Migrations of the Holy: God, State, and the Political Meaning of the Church.* Grand Rapids: Eerdmans, 2011.

———. *Theopolitical Imagination: Christian Practices of Space and Time.* Edinburgh: T&T Clark, 2003.

Chambers, Edward T. *Roots for Radicals: Organizing for Power, Action, and Justice.* New York: Bloomsbury Academic, 2003.

Cicero. *On Government.* Translated by Michael Grant. New York: Penguin, 1993.

Clark, Meghan J. *The Vision of Catholic Social Thought: The Virtue of Solidarity and the Praxis of Human Rights.* Minneapolis: Fortress, 2014.

Clausewitz, Carl von. *On War.* Edited by Anatol Rapoport. New York: Penguin, 1982.

Cohen, Tom, and Michael Pearson. "All Nations Collect Intelligence, Obama Says." *CNN.* Last modified July 2, 2013. http://www.cnn.com/2013/07/01/world/europe/eu-nsa/.

Coles, Romand. *Beyond Gated Politics: Reflections for the Possibility of Democracy.* Minneapolis: University of Minnesota Press, 2005.

Connolly, William E. *Pluralism.* Durham, N.C.: Duke University Press, 2005.

Cox, Harvey. "Mammon and the Culture of the Market: A Socio-Theological Critique." In *Meaning and Modernity: Religion, Polity, and Self,* edited by Richard Madsen, 124–35. Berkeley: University of California Press, 2001.

Craig, Susanne, William K. Rashbaum, and Thomas Kaplan. "Cuomo's Office Hobbled Ethics Inquiries by Moreland Commission." *New York Times.* Last modified July 23, 2014. http://www

.nytimes.com/2014/07/23/nyregion/governor-andrew-cuomo-and-the -short-life-of-the-moreland-commission.html.

Crouch, Colin. *Post-Democracy*. Malden, Mass.: Polity, 2004.

Crouter, Richard. *Reinhold Niebuhr on Politics, Religion, and Christian Faith.* New York: Oxford University Press, 2010.

Davis, James Calvin. *In Defense of Civility: How Religion Can Unite America on Seven Moral Issues That Divide Us*. Louisville, Ky.: Westminster John Knox, 2010.

de Gruchy, John. *Christianity and Democracy: A Theology for a Just World Order.* New York: Cambridge University Press, 1995.

———. *Liberating Reformed Theology: A South African Contribution to an Ecumenical Debate*. Grand Rapids: Eerdmans, 1991.

DeSilver, Drew. "Congress Ends Least-Productive Year in Recent History." *Pew Research Center*. Last modified December 13, 2013. http:// www.pewresearch.org/fact-tank/2013/12/23/congress-ends-least -productive-year-in-recent-history/.

Diggins, John P. *Max Weber: Politics and the Spirit of Tragedy*. New York: Basic Books, 1996.

———. *Why Niebuhr Now?* Chicago: University of Chicago Press, 2011.

DiMaggio, Paul J., and Walter W. Powell, eds. *The New Institutionalism in Organizational Analysis*. Chicago: University of Chicago Press, 1991.

Dodaro, Robert. *Christ and the Just Society in the Thought of Augustine*. New York: Cambridge University Press, 2008.

Dorrien, Gary. *Economy, Difference, Empire: Social Ethics for Social Justice*. New York: Columbia University Press, 2010.

Douglas, Mary. *How Institutions Think*. Syracuse, N.Y.: Syracuse University Press, 1986.

Douglas, Richard M. "Talent and Vocation in Humanist and Protestant Thought." In *Action and Conviction in Early Modern Europe: Essays in Memory of E. H. Harbison*, edited by Theodore K. Rabb and Jerrold E. Seigel, 261–98. Princeton: Princeton University Press, 1969.

Dunn, John. *The Cunning of Unreason: Making Sense of Politics*. New York: Basic Books, 2000.

Eberle, Christopher J. *Religious Convictions in Liberal Politics*. New York: Cambridge University Press, 2002.

Edmonds, David, and Nigel Warburton. "Quentin Skinner on Machiavelli's *The Prince*." *Philosophy Bites*. Podcast audio. Last modified July 27, 2008. http://philosophybites.com/2008/07/quentin-skinner.html.

Eichner, Maxine, Barbara Fedders, Holning Lau, and Rachel Blunk. "Potential Legal Impact of the Proposed Domestic Legal Union Amendment to the North Carolina Constitution." University of North Carolina School of Law. Last modified November 8, 2011. http://www.law.unc.edu/documents/faculty/marriageamendment/dlureportnov8.pdf.

Ellul, Jacques. "Work and Calling." *Katallagete* 4 (1972): 8–16.

Erasmus, Desiderius. *The Education of a Christian Prince.* Edited by Lisa Jardine. New York: Cambridge University Press, 1997.

Faculty Letter to President Wagner. *Emory Wheel.* Last modified February 18, 2013. http://www.emorywheel.com/faculty-letter-to-president-wagner/.

Freud, Sigmund. *The Penguin Freud Reader.* Edited by Adam Phillips. New York: Penguin, 2006.

Friedland, Roger, and Robert R. Alford. "Bringing Society Back In: Symbols, Practices, and Institutional Contradictions." In *The New Institutionalism in Organizational Analysis,* edited by Walter W. Powell and Paul J. DiMaggio, 232–63. Chicago: University of Chicago Press, 1991.

Fulkerson, Mary McClintock. "The *Imago Dei* and a Reformed Logic for Feminist/Womanist Critique." In *Feminist and Womanist Essays in Reformed Dogmatics,* edited by Amy Plantinga Pauw and Serene Jones, 95–106. Louisville, Ky.: Westminster John Knox, 2006.

Galloway, Jim. "Sadie Fields Retires from the Georgia Christian Alliance." *Political Insider* (blog). Atlanta Journal Constitution. Last modified May 22, 2010; no longer accessible. http://blogs.ajc.com/political-insider-jim-galloway/2010/05/22/sadie-fields-retires%20the-georgia-christian-alliance/.

Galston, William. "Toughness as a Political Virtue." *Social Theory and Practice* 17, no. 2 (1991): 175–97.

Gamwell, Franklin I. *Politics as a Christian Vocation: Faith and Democracy Today.* New York: Cambridge University Press, 2005.

Gaus, Gerald F. *Contemporary Theories of Liberalism: Public Reason as a Post-Enlightenment Project.* Thousand Oaks, Calif.: Sage, 2003.

Gilens, Martin. *Affluence and Influence: Economic Inequality and Political Power in America.* Princeton: Princeton University Press, 2012.

Glaude, Eddie S. *In a Shade of Blue: Pragmatism and the Politics of Black America.* Chicago: University of Chicago Press, 2007.

Gordon, Michael. "Federal Judge Overturns NC Same-Sex Marriage Ban." *Charlotte Observer.* Last modified October 10, 2014. http://www.charlotteobserver.com/2014/10/10/5232525/nc-gop-leaders-given-until-noon.html.

Graham, Elaine. *Between a Rock and a Hard Place: Public Theology in a Post-Secular Age.* London: SCM Press, 2013.

Gray, John. *Isaiah Berlin.* Princeton: Princeton University Press, 1996.

———. *Isaiah Berlin: An Interpretation of His Thought*. Princeton: Princeton University Press, 2013.

Gregory, Eric. *Politics and the Order of Love: An Augustinian Ethics of Democratic Citizenship*. Chicago: University of Chicago Press, 2010.

Greenwood, Royston, et al. *The Sage Handbook of Organizational Institutionalism*. London: Sage, 2008.

Grim, Ryan, and Sabrina Siddiqui. "Call Time for Congress Shows How Fundraising Dominates Bleak Work Life." *Huffington Post*. Last modified January 9, 2013. http://www.huffingtonpost.com/2013/01/08/call-time-congressional-fundraising_n_2427291.html.

Gronow, Antti. "Not By Rules or Choice Alone: A Pragmatist Critique of Institution Theories in Economics and Sociology." *Journal of Institutional Economics* 4, no. 3 (2008): 351–73.

Gross, Terry. "Jane Mayer: Obama in 'Impossible Bind' over Donors." *Fresh Air*. Last modified August 22, 2012. http://www.npr.org/2012/08/23/159768245/jane-mayer-obama-in-impossible-bind-over-donors.

Gustafson, James M. *Ethics from a Theocentric Perspective*. Vol. 1. Chicago: University of Chicago Press, 1981.

———. "Professions as 'Callings.'" In *Moral Discernment in the Christian Life: Essays in Theological Ethics*, edited by Theo A. Boer and Paul E. Capetz, 126–38. Louisville, Ky.: Westminster John Knox, 2007.

Gutmann, Amy, and Dennis F. Thompson. *Democracy and Disagreement*. Cambridge, Mass.: Belknap Press, 1996.

———. *The Spirit of Compromise: Why Governing Demands It and Campaigning Undermines It*. Princeton: Princeton University Press, 2012.

Habermas, Jürgen. *Between Facts and Norms: Contributions to a Discourse Theory of Law and Democracy*. Cambridge, Mass.: MIT Press, 1996.

———. "Reconciliation through the Public Use of Reason." In *The Inclusion of the Other*, edited by Ciaran Cronin and Pablo De Greiff, 75–103. Cambridge, Mass.: MIT Press, 1999.

———. "Religion in the Public Sphere." *European Journal of Philosophy* 14, no. 1 (2006): 1–25.

———. *The Structural Transformation of the Public Sphere: An Inquiry into a Category of Bourgeois Society*. Cambridge, Mass.: MIT Press, 1991.

Hamilton, Alexander, James Madison, and John Jay. *The Federalist Papers, with Letters of "Brutus."* Edited by Terence Ball. New York: Cambridge University Press, 2003.

Hampshire, Stuart. *Innocence and Experience*. Cambridge, Mass.: Harvard University Press, 1989.

Hardt, Michael, and Antonio Negri. *Empire*. Cambridge, Mass.: Harvard University Press, 2001.

———. *Multitude: War and Democracy in an Age of Empire*. New York: Penguin, 2004.

Hauerwas, Stanley. *After Christendom? How the Church Is to Behave If Freedom, Justice, and a Christian Nation Are Bad Ideas*. Nashville: Abingdon, 1991.

———. *A Community of Character: Toward a Constructive Christian Social Ethic*. Notre Dame, Ind.: University of Notre Dame Press, 1981.

Hauerwas, Stanley, and Romand Coles. *Christianity, Democracy, and the Radical Ordinary: Conversations between a Radical Democrat and a Christian*. Eugene, Ore.: Cascade Books, 2008.

Hicks, Douglas A. *Money Enough: Everyday Practices for Living Faithfully in the Global Economy*. San Francisco: Jossey-Bass, 2010.

Hiskey, Michelle. "The Convictions of Sadie Fields." *Nieman Storyboard*. Last modified October 24, 2006. http://www.archive-org-2013.com/org/n/2013-10-28_3102026_77/Andre-Malok-8211-Nieman-Storyboard-A-project-of-the-Nieman-Foundation-for-Journalism-at-Harvard/.

Hollenbach, David. *The Common Good and Christian Ethics*. New York: Cambridge University Press, 2002.

Huijgen, Arnold. *Divine Accommodation in John Calvin's Theology: Analysis and Assessment*. Göttingen: Vandenhoeck & Ruprecht, 2011.

Hunter, James Davison. *To Change the World: The Irony, Tragedy, and Possibility of Christianity*. New York: Oxford University Press, 2010.

Ignatieff, Michael. *Fire and Ashes: Success and Failure in Politics*. Cambridge, Mass.: Harvard University Press, 2013.

Jackson, Timothy P. *Love Disconsoled: Meditations on Christian Charity*. New York: Cambridge University Press, 1999.

John XXIII. *Mater et Magistra (Christianity and Social Progress)*. In *Catholic Social Thought: The Documentary Heritage*. Edited by David J. O'Brien and Thomas A. Shannon. Maryknoll, N.Y.: Orbis Books, 2003.

John Paul II. *Sollicitudo Rei Socialis (On Social Concern)*. In *Catholic Social Thought: The Documentary Heritage*. Edited by David J. O'Brien and Thomas A. Shannon. Maryknoll, N.Y.: Orbis Books, 2003.

Johnsen, Gregory D. "60 Words and a War without End: The Untold Story of the Most Dangerous Sentence in U.S. History." *BuzzFeed*. Last modified January 16, 2014. http://www.buzzfeed.com/gregoryjohnsen/60-words-and-a-war-without-end-the-untold-story-of-the-most.

Johnson, Kristen Deede. *Theology, Political Theory, and Pluralism: Beyond Tolerance and Difference*. New York: Cambridge University Press, 2007.

Kant, Immanuel. *Kant: Political Writings*. Edited by Hans Siegbert Reiss. New York: Cambridge University Press, 1991.

Kaplan, Thomas. "Cuomo Says He Makes History, Then Repeats It." *New York Times*. Last modified April 27, 2012. http://www.nytimes .com/2012/04/28/nyregion/cuomo-says-he-makes-history-then-repeats -it.html?pagewanted=all&_r=0.

Kessler, Michael Jon, ed. *Political Theology for a Plural Age*. New York: Oxford University Press, 2013.

Kim, David Kyuman. *Melancholic Freedom: Agency and the Spirit of Politics*. New York: Oxford University Press, 2007.

Kirk-Duggan, Cheryl. "A Rose by Any Other Name: Deconstructing the Essence of Common." In *In Search of the Common Good*, edited by Dennis P. McCann and Patrick D. Miller, 190–210. New York: Continuum, 2005.

LaVaque-Manty, Mika. *Arguments and Fists: Political Agency and Justification in Liberal Theory*. New York: Routledge, 2002.

Lessig, Lawrence. *Republic, Lost: How Money Corrupts Congress–and a Plan to Stop It*. New York: Twelve, 2011.

Lindblom, Charles. *The Market System: What It Is, How It Works, and What to Make of It*. New Haven: Yale University Press, 2001.

Liptak, Adam, and Charlie Savage. "U.S. Asks Court to Limit Texas on Ballot Rules." *New York Times*. Last modified July 25, 2013. http:// www.nytimes.com/2013/07/26/us/holder-wants-texas-to-clear-voting -changes-with-the-us.html?emc=edit_na_20130725.

Locke, John. *Political Writings*. Edited by David Wooten. Indianapolis: Hackett, 2003.

Lovin, Robin W. *Christian Faith and Public Choices: The Social Ethics of Barth, Brunner, and Bonhoeffer*. Philadelphia: Fortress, 1984.

———. *Christian Realism and the New Realities*. New York: Cambridge University Press, 2008.

———. "The Future of Political Theology: From Crisis to Pluralism." In *Political Theology for a Plural Age*, edited by Michael Jon Kessler, 181–200. New York: Oxford University Press, 2013.

———. *Reinhold Niebuhr and Christian Realism*. New York: Cambridge University Press, 1995.

Luther, Martin. *Luther's Works*. Edited by Jaroslav Pelikan, Hilton C. Oswald, and Helmut T. Lehmann. St. Louis: Concordia, 1955.

———. *Martin Luther: Selections from His Writings*. Edited by John Dillenberger. St. Louis: Concordia, 1962.

———. *Works*. Edited by Jaroslav Pelikan. Philadelphia: Fortress, 1984.

Luther, Martin, and John Calvin. *Luther and Calvin on Secular Authority.* Edited by Harro Höpfl. New York: Cambridge University Press, 1991.

Machiavelli, Niccolò. *Discourses on Livy.* Edited and translated by Harvey C. Mansfield and Nathan Tarcov. Chicago: University of Chicago Press, 1996.

———. *The Prince.* 2nd ed. Edited and translated by Harvey C. Mansfield. Chicago: University of Chicago Press, 1998.

———. *Selected Political Writings.* Edited and translated by David Wootton. Indianapolis: Hackett Publishing Company, Inc., 1994.

MacIntyre, Alasdair. *After Virtue.* New York: Bloomsbury Academic, 2011.

Mansfield, Harvey. *Machiavelli's Virtue.* Chicago: University of Chicago Press, 1998.

Margalit, Avishai. *On Compromise and Rotten Compromises.* Princeton: Princeton University Press, 2010.

Marshall, Ellen Ott. *Christians in the Public Square: Faith That Transforms Politics.* Nashville: Abingdon, 2008.

Marshall, Paul. *A Kind of Life Imposed on Man: Vocation and Social Order from Tyndale to Locke.* Toronto: University of Toronto Press, 1996.

Martin, Joan M. "Between Vocation and Work: A Womanist Notion of a Work Ethic." In *Feminist and Womanist Essays in Reformed Dogmatics,* edited by Amy Plantinga Pauw and Serene Jones, 169–88. Louisville, Ky.: Westminster John Knox, 2006.

Martinez, Gaspar. *Confronting the Mystery of God: Political, Liberation, and Public Theologies.* New York: Continuum, 2001.

Mathewes, Charles T. "Faith, Hope, and Agony: Christian Political Participation Beyond Liberalism." *Annual of the Society of Christian Ethics* 21 (2001): 125–50.

———. *The Republic of Grace: Augustinian Thoughts for Dark Times.* Grand Rapids: Eerdmans, 2010.

———. *A Theology of Public Life.* New York: Cambridge University Press, 2007.

Mayer, Jane. "Schmooze or Lose." *New Yorker.* Last modified August 27, 2012. http://www.newyorker.com/magazine/2012/08/27/schmooze-or-lose.

———. "State for Sale." *New Yorker.* Last modified October 10, 2011. http://www.newyorker.com/magazine/2011/10/10/state-for-sale.

McBride, Jennifer M. *The Church for the World: A Theology of Public Witness.* New York: Oxford University Press, 2012.

McCann, Dennis P. "The Common Good in Catholic Social Teaching: A Case Study in Modernization." In *In Search of the Common Good,* edited by Patrick D. Miller and Dennis McCann, 121–46. New York: Continuum, 2005.

McGrath, Alister. "Calvin and the Christian Calling." *First Things* 94 (1999): 31–35.

Milbank, John. *Theology and Social Theory: Beyond Secular Reason.* Malden, Mass.: Blackwell, 1990.

Mommsen, Wolfgang J. *Max Weber and German Politics, 1890–1920.* Chicago: University of Chicago Press, 1985.

Montesquieu, Charles-Louis de Secondat, Baron de la Brède. *The Spirit of the Laws.* Edited by Anne M. Cohler, Basia C. Miller, and Harold S. Stone. New York: Cambridge University Press, 1989.

Mouffe, Chantal. "For an Agonistic Public Sphere." In *Radical Democracy: Politics Between Abundance and Lack,* edited by Lars Tonder and Lasse Thomassen, 123–32. New York: Palgrave, 2005.

Muller, Richard A. *The Unaccommodated Calvin: Studies in the Foundation of a Theological Tradition.* Oxford Studies in Historical Theology. New York: Oxford University Press, 2000.

Newport, Frank. "Congress Job Approval Drops to All-Time Low for 2013." *Gallup.* Last modified December 10, 2013. http://www.gallup.com/poll/166196/congress-job-approval-drops-time-low-2013.aspx.

———. "Congress Retains Low Honesty Rating." *Gallup.* Last modified December 3, 2012. http://www.gallup.com/poll/159035/congress-retains-low-honesty-rating.aspx.

New York Times. "The Decline of North Carolina." Last modified July 9, 2013. http://www.nytimes.com/2013/07/10/opinion/the-decline-of-north-carolina.html?_r=0.

———. "The Future of Voting Rights." Op-ed. Last modified June 29, 2013. http://www.nytimes.com/2013/06/30/opinion/sunday/the-future-of-voting-rights.html?_r=0.

Niebuhr, Reinhold. *Beyond Tragedy.* New York: Scribner's, 1937.

———. *Christianity and Power Politics.* Hamden, Conn.: Archon Books, 1969.

———. *Christian Realism and Political Problems.* New York: Scribner's, 1953.

———. *Essays in Applied Christianity.* Edited by D. B. Robertson. New York: Living Age Books, 1959.

———. *The Irony of American History.* New York: Scribner's, 1962.

———. *Love and Justice: Selections from the Shorter Writings of Reinhold Niebuhr.* Edited by D. B. Robertson. Gloucester, Mass.: P. Smith, 1976.

———. *Moral Man and Immoral Society: A Study in Ethics and Politics.* Louisville, Ky.: Westminster John Knox, 2001.

———. *The Nature and Destiny of Man: A Christian Interpretation.* 2 vols. New York: Scribner's, 1964.

———. *The Self and the Dramas of History.* London: Faber & Faber, 1956.

NPR. "The Multimillionaire Helping Republicans Win N.C." Last modified October 6, 2011. http://www.npr.org/2011/10/06/141078608/the -multimillionaire-helping-republicans-win-n-c.

O'Brien, David J., and Thomas A. Shannon. *Catholic Social Thought: The Documentary Heritage.* Maryknoll, N.Y.: Orbis Books, 2003.

O'Donovan, Oliver. *The Ways of Judgment.* Grand Rapids: Eerdmans, 2005.

Ottati, Douglas F. "What Reformed Theology in a Calvinist Key Brings to Conversations about Justice." *Political Theology* 10, no. 3 (2009): 447–69.

Pope Paul VI. *Gaudium et Spes.* In *Catholic Social Thought: The Documentary Herita.* Edited by David J. O'Brien and Thomas A. Shannon. Maryknoll, N.Y.: Orbis, 1992.

Peters, Rebecca Todd. *Solidarity Ethics: Transformation in a Globalized World.* Minneapolis: Fortress, 2014.

Philp, Mark. *Political Conduct.* Cambridge, Mass.: Harvard University Press, 2007.

Pius XI. *Quadragesimo Anno,* Section 79. In *Catholic Social Thought: The Documentary Heritage.* Edited by David J. O'Brien and Thomas A. Shannon. Maryknoll, N.Y.: Orbis Books, 2003.

Politico. "Edward Snowden Unsealed Complaint." Last modified June 21, 2013. http://www.politico.com/story/2013/06/edward-snowden-complaint -unsealed-93181.html.

Pope, Stephen J. "Natural Law in Catholic Social Teaching." In *Modern Catholic Social Teaching: Commentaries and Interpretations,* edited by Kenneth Himes, 41–71. Washington, D.C.: Georgetown University Press, 2005.

Porter, Jean. "The Common Good in Thomas Aquinas." In *In Search of the Common Good,* edited by Patrick D. Miller and Dennis McCann, 94–120. New York: Continuum, 2005.

Price, Russell. "The Theme of *Gloria* in Machiavelli." *Renaissance Quarterly* 30, no. 4 (1977): 588–631.

Rauschenbusch, Walter. *Christianizing the Social Order.* New York: Macmillan, 1913. Reprint, Waco, Tex.: Baylor University Press, 2010.

Rasmussen, Larry. "The Ethics of Responsible Action." In *The Cambridge Companion to Dietrich Bonhoeffer,* edited by John W. de Gruchy, 206–25. New York: Cambridge University Press, 1999.

Rawls, John. "The Idea of Public Reason Revisited." In *John Rawls: Collected Papers,* edited by Samuel Freeman, 573–615. Cambridge, Mass.: Harvard University Press, 1999.

———. *Political Liberalism.* New York: Columbia University Press, 1996.

———. *A Theory of Justice.* Cambridge, Mass.: Belknap Press Press, 1999.

Rice, Daniel F., ed. *Reinhold Niebuhr Revisited: Engagements with an American Original*. Grand Rapids: Eerdmans, 2009.

Ringer, Fritz. "Max Weber's Liberalism." *Central European History* 35, no. 3 (2002): 379–95.

Rorty, Richard. *Contingency, Irony, and Solidarity*. New York: Cambridge University Press, 1989.

——. *Philosophy and Social Hope*. New York: Penguin, 1999.

——. "Religion in the Public Square: A Reconsideration." *Journal of Religious Ethics* 31, no. 1 (2003): 141–49.

Rove, Karl. "More White Votes Alone Won't Save the GOP." *Wall Street Journal*. Last modified July 26, 2013. http://online.wsj.com/articles/ SB10001424127887323873904578569480696746650.

Sabl, Andrew. *Ruling Passions: Political Offices and Democratic Ethics*. Princeton: Princeton University Press, 2002.

Sandel, Michael. *What Money Can't Buy: The Moral Limits of Markets*. New York: Farrar, Straus & Giroux, 2012.

Schliesser, Christine. "Accepting Guilt for the Sake of Germany: An Analysis of Bonhoeffer's Concept of Accepting Guilt and Its Implications for Bonhoeffer's Political Resistance." *Union Seminary Quarterly Review* 60, nos. 1–2 (2006): 56–68.

——. *Everyone Who Acts Responsibly Becomes Guilty*. Louisville, Ky.: Westminster John Knox, 2008.

Schmitt, Carl. *The Concept of the Political*. Translated by George Schwab. Chicago: University of Chicago Press, 2007.

——. *Political Theology: Four Chapters on the Concept of Sovereignty*. Translated by George Schwab. Chicago: University of Chicago Press, 1985.

Schuurman, Douglas J. *Vocation: Discerning Our Callings in Life*. Grand Rapids: Eerdmans, 2004.

Schweiker, William. "Disputes and Trajectories in Responsibility Ethics." *Religious Studies Review* 27, no. 1 (2001): 18–24.

——. *Power, Value, and Conviction*. Cleveland, Ohio: Pilgrim Press, 1998.

——. *Responsibility and Christian Ethics*. New York: Cambridge University Press, 1995.

——. "Responsibility and Moral Realities." *Studies in Christian Ethics* 22, no. 4 (2009): 472–95.

Scott, Peter, and William T. Cavanaugh, eds. *The Blackwell Companion to Political Theology*. Malden, Mass.: Blackwell, 2004.

Scott, W. Richard. *Institutions and Organizations: Ideas, Interests, and Identities*. 4th ed. London: Sage, 2013.

Seneca. *Moral and Political Essays.* Edited by John M. Cooper and J. F. Procopé. New York: Cambridge University Press, 2003.

Senior, John. "Cruciform Pilgrims: Politics between the Penultimate and the Ultimate." *Journal of the Society of Christian Ethics* 32, no. 1 (2012): 115–32.

Shapiro, Ilya. "Supreme Court Recognizes Jim Crow's Demise, Restores Constitutional Order." *SCOTUSblog.* Last modified June 25, 2013. http://www.scotusblog.com/2013/06/supreme-court-recognizes-jim -crows-demise-restores-constitutional-order/.

Sifton, Elizabeth, and Fritz Stern. "The Tragedy of Dietrich Bonhoeffer and Hans von Dohnanyi." *New York Review of Books.* Last modified December 25, 2012. http://www.nybooks.com/articles/archives/2012/ oct/25/tragedy-dietrich-bonhoeffer-and-hans-von-dohnanyi/.

Skinner, Quentin. *Machiavelli: A Very Short Introduction.* New York: Oxford University Press, 2001.

Stout, Jeffrey. *Blessed Are the Organized: Grassroots Democracy in America.* Princeton: Princeton University Press, 2010.

———. *Democracy and Tradition.* Princeton: Princeton University Press, 2004.

Sullivan, Sean. "What Is a 501(c)(4), Anyway?" *Washington Post.* Last modified May 13, 2013. http://www.washingtonpost.com/blogs/the-fix/ wp/2013/05/13/what-is-a-501c4-anyway/.

Swift, Art. "Honesty and Ethics Rating of Clergy Slides to New Low." *Gallup.* Last modified December 16, 2013. http://www.gallup.com/ poll/166298/honesty-ethics-rating-clergy-slides-new-low.aspx.

Tanner, Kathryn. *Jesus, Humanity, and the Trinity: A Brief Systematic Theology.* Minneapolis: Fortress, 2001.

Taylor, Charles. *Philosophical Papers 1: Human Agency and Language.* New York: Cambridge University Press, 1985.

———. *A Secular Age.* Cambridge, Mass.: Belknap Press, 2007.

———. *Sources of the Self: The Making of the Modern Identity.* Cambridge, Mass.: Harvard University Press, 1989.

Teachout, Zephyr. *Corruption in America: From Benjamin Franklin's Snuff Box to Citizens United.* Cambridge, Mass.: Harvard University Press, 2014.

Thiemann, Ronald F. *Religion in Public Life: A Dilemma for Democracy.* Washington, D.C.: Georgetown University Press, 1996.

This American Life. "Take the Money and Run for Office" (episode 461). Last modified March 30, 2012. http://www.thisamericanlife.org/ radio-archives/episode/461/take-the-money-and-run-for-office.

Thomas, J. J. R. "Weber and Direct Democracy." *British Journal of Sociology* 35, no. 2 (1984): 216–40.

Thornton, Patricia H., et al. *The Institutional Logics Perspective: A New Approach to Culture, Structure, and Process.* Oxford: Oxford University Press, 2012.

Tipton, Steven M. "Social Differentiation and Moral Pluralism." In *Meaning and Modernity: Religion, Polity, and Self,* edited by Richard Madsen, William M. Sullivan, Ann Swidler, and Steven M. Tipton, 15–40. Berkeley: University of California Press, 2002.

Tocqueville, Alexis de. *Democracy in America.* Translated by Harvey Mansfield and Delba Winthrop. Chicago: University of Chicago Press, 2012.

Trawick, Robert C. "Ordering the Earthly Kingdom: Vocation, Providence, and Social Ethics." Ph.D. diss., Emory University, 1997.

Troeltsch, Ernst. *The Social Teaching of the Christian Churches.* 2 vols. Louisville, Ky.: Westminster John Knox, 1992.

Volf, Miroslav. *Work in the Spirit: Toward a Theology of Work.* Eugene, Ore.: Wipf & Stock, 2001.

Wagner, James. "From the President: America as . . . Compromise." *Emory Magazine,* Winter 2013. Last modified February 13, 2013. http://www.emory.edu/EMORY_MAGAZINE/issues/2013/winter/register/president.html.

Walzer, Michael. "Does the Free Market Corrode Moral Character? Of Course It Does." *John Templeton Foundation.* Last modified September 3, 2013. http://www.templeton.org/market/PDF/Walzer.pdf.

———. "Political Action: The Problem of Dirty Hands." *Philosophy and Public Affairs* 2, no. 2 (1973): 160–80.

———. *Politics and Passion: Toward a More Egalitarian Liberalism.* New Haven: Yale University Press, 2004.

———. *Spheres of Justice: A Defense of Pluralism and Equality.* New York: Basic Books, 1983.

———. *Thick and Thin: Moral Argument at Home and Abroad.* South Bend, Ind.: University of Notre Dame Press, 1994.

Warren, Mark. *Dry Bones Rattling: Community Building to Revitalize American Democracy.* Princeton: Princeton University Press, 2001.

Weber, Max. *From Max Weber: Essays in Sociology.* Edited by H. H. Gerth and C. Wright Mills. New York: Oxford University Press, 1998.

———. *The Protestant Ethic and the Spirit of Capitalism.* Translated by Talcott Parsons. New York: Routledge, 1992.

West, Traci. *Disruptive Christian Ethics.* Louisville, Ky.: Westminster John Knox, 2006.

Wetzel, James. *Augustine and the Limits of Virtue.* New York: Cambridge University Press, 2008.

———. "Splendid Vices and Secular Virtues: Variations on Milbank's Augustine." *Journal of Religious Ethics* 32, no. 2 (2004): 271–300.

Williams, Bernard. "Politics and Moral Character." In *Public and Private Morality*, edited by Stuart Hampshire, 55–73. New York: Cambridge University Press, 1978.

Williams, Rowan. "Politics and the Soul: A Reading of the *City of God*." *Milltown Studies* 55 (1987): 55–72.

Wogaman, J. Philip. *Christian Perspectives on Politics*. Rev. ed. Louisville, Ky.: Westminster John Knox, 2000.

Wolin, Sheldon S. *Democracy Incorporated: Managed Democracy and the Specter of Inverted Totalitarianism*. Princeton: Princeton University Press, 2010.

———. *The Presence of the Past: Essays on the State and the Constitution*. Baltimore: Johns Hopkins University Press, 1989.

Wolterstorff, Nicholas. "An Engagement with Rorty." *Journal of Religious Ethics* 31, no. 1 (2003): 129–39.

———. *The Mighty and the Almighty: An Essay in Political Theology*. New York: Cambridge University Press, 2012.

———. *Until Justice and Peace Embrace*. Grand Rapids: Eerdmans, 1983.

———. "Why We Should Reject What Liberalism Tells Us about Speaking and Acting in Public for Religious Reasons." In *Religion and Contemporary Liberalism*, edited by Paul J. Weithman, 162–81. Notre Dame, Ind.: University of Notre Dame Press, 1997.

Wolterstorff, Nicholas, and Robert Audi. *Religion in the Public Square: The Place of Religious Conviction in Public Debate*. Lanham, Md.: Rowman & Littlefield, 1997.

INDEX